FORD DRAG TEAM

A History of a Select Group of Individuals who Dominated
the Drag Strips of America for a Decade and Indelibly Etched
their Accomplishments in the Record Books

Charles R. Morris

Copyright © 2011 by Charles R. Morris

Published by:

Stance & Speed
3280 Edgerton St.
St. Paul, Mn 55127
www.stanceandspeed.com

All rights reserved. With the exception of quoting brief passages for the purposes of review, no part of this publication may be reproduced without prior written permission from the publisher.

The information in this book is true and complete to the best of our knowledge. All recommendations are made without any guarantee on the part of the author or publisher, who also disclaim any liability incurred in connection with the use of this data or specific details.

We recognize, further, that some words, model names, and designations mentioned herein are the property of the trademark holder. We use them for identification purposes only. This is not an official publication

Version 1.0 published October, 2011

Morris, Charles R.
Ford Drag Team

ISBN-10: 0-9830606-7-3
ISBN-13: 978-0-9830606-7-3

Layout and Design by Tom Heffron

Contents

ACKNOWLEDGMENTS / DEDICATION		4
INTRODUCTION		5
CHAPTER 1:	DICK BRANNAN	7
CHAPTER 2:	LES RITCHEY	25
CHAPTER 3:	GAS RONDA	33
CHAPTER 4:	LEN RICHTER (BOB FORD)	43
CHAPTER 5:	TASCA FORD, BILL LAWTON / JOHN HEALEY	54
CHAPTER 6:	AL "BATMAN" JONIEC	73
CHAPTER 7:	ED TERRY / DICK WOOD	88
CHAPTER 8:	HUBERT PLATT / RANDY PAYNE	104
CHAPTER 9:	PHIL BONNER	128
CHAPTER 10:	TOMMY GROVE	146
CHAPTER 11:	MICKEY THOMPSON / BUTCH LEAL	153
CHAPTER 12:	REGIONAL RACERS / DRIVERS	162
CHAPTER 13:	BILL HOLBROOK	190
EPILOGUE	DICK LOEHR / JOHN SKIBA AND THE END OF FACTORY SUPPORT	196

ACKNOWLEDGMENTS AND DEDICATION

Many fine and knowledgeable people deserve recognition for their efforts in helping to make this history of the Ford Drag Council and Drag Team as accurate as possible. I wish to thank:

Lloyd Wolfe, prolific collector of memorabilia relating to Ford drag racing

Joel F. Naprstek, noted artist and automotive historian

Fred Simmons, auto racing historian

Randy Ritchey, son of legendary Ford drag racer Les Ritchey

Dennis Kolodziej, authority on Ford race vehicles, collector and historian

Nick Smith, Ford dealer and collector of rare factory race vehicles

Jim Amos, videographer and drag racing historian

T. Allen Platt, son of legendary Ford drag racer Hubert Platt

"Butch" Engelbrecht, SOHC 427 engine builder and historian

Rick Kirk, Ford racing historian

Jerry Hammes, Ford dealer, friend and sponsor of Dick Brannan

This book is dedicated to the members of the Ford Drag Council and Drag Teams, with heartfelt thanks for giving Ford fans so much to cheer about.

INTRODUCTION

The intention of this book is to profile and celebrate the diverse and talented individuals who were involved in one of the most comprehensive efforts ever undertaken by an American auto manufacturer to dominate a particular aspect of motorsports. During this special place and time in automotive history, this group of remarkable individuals created a series of automobiles that would forever etch their names in the record books and place the products of Ford Motor Company in the winner's circle.

The Total Performance years at Ford spanned the decade between 1960 and 1970. Rather than rely entirely on the official corporate version of Ford's drag racing program (although company documents will be referenced throughout this book) and the often biased copy of the mainstream automotive press of the time, you will hear directly from many of the individuals who made the history. Contained herein is a compilation of interviews with those who participated in the construction and modification of Ford's drag cars, the members of the special fraternity known initially as the Drag Council and later the Ford Drag Team.

The major reason that this era will never be repeated is technology. The sophisticated means utilized to design automobiles and produce horsepower today were still decades away at the time these men were tasked with preparing Fords to cover a quarter-mile of asphalt quicker and faster then competing manufacturers. The people involved in Ford's drag racing program during the 1960's were truly men of their time—not necessarily engineers, but certainly innovators. They were men capable of modifying and adapting vehicles and parts designed by engineers and driving them to victory.

While researching this and my two previous books on similar topics, I have noted two common threads that exist among those men who were my heroes while growing up in the 1950s and 60s. First, the men who built, raced, and won with the products of Ford Motor Company as part of the Total Performance program were not aware that they were making history at the time. Second, these same individuals seem at first taken aback by the degree of interest in, and the recognition shown for their efforts some four decades hence.

I can vividly recall my first conversation with racing great Al Joniec, which took place more than twenty years after he had hung up his helmet. In response to my questions about his racing days Al, repeated several times "I can't believe this." And the comment made to me by the late Bill Lawton

Hubert Platt charges off the starting line in his 1970 Ford Drag Team Pro/Stock Mustang. (T. Allen Platt)

in 1994 as fans lined up to get his autograph: "Do these people know who I am?" Of course along the way I have encountered racers whose accounts follow a "the older I get the faster I went" pattern, but by and large most of the racers from that golden era have been honest, humble, and forthcoming. I have gained both insight and respect for those who gave young Ford fans such as myself so much to cheer about all those years ago.

While some of the greats who made up the Drag Council and subsequent Drag Team have since left us, their legacy is written in the records they set, races they won, memories they created, and lives they touched along the way.

CHAPTER 1

RICHARD H. "DICK" BRANNAN

DRAG RACING COORDINATOR, DRAG COUNCIL CAPTAIN

Growing up in South Bend, Indiana, Dick Brannan showed an interest and aptitude for aviation and automobiles from an early age. Dick worked after-school jobs such as a paper route and pin spotting at a local bowling alley in order to save money to buy his first car, a 1932 Ford coupe that he purchased from a local woman for the princely sum of $10. The coupe turned out to be a diamond in the rough as, according to Dick, the previous owner had applied a thick coat of house paint to the car with a brush which, when removed, revealed a well-preserved body beneath. Even before he was old enough to drive, Dick modified his $10 car into a hot rod, complete with a full-house flathead V-8.

The Deuce coupe was followed by a 1932 Ford roadster powered by a 312 ci, overhead valve, Y-Block Ford V-8 as young Brannan rose in the hot rod ranks around South Bend.

Dick was also able to pursue his passion for flying at a young age. He would eventually serve as a U.S. Navy aviator and later was a private pilot and airplane dealer.

In 1959, Dick was working at Romy-Hammes Ford in South Bend as a salesman. The dealership's manager and son of the owner, Jerry Hammes, learned that one of his salesmen had been racing his sales demonstrator at the local drag strip on weekends.

As Jerry puts it, "My first question was to ask how he was doing with it." After learning that Brannan, whom Jerry credits with being a gifted mechanic and possessed of a mind for engineering, was winning with the car, the racing relationship between Dick Brannan and Romy-Hammes Ford was formed, and would last until 1964. Dick Brannan's first Romy-Hammes drag car was a 1959 Ford, which was followed by a 1960 Starliner, powered by Ford's first dedicated performance engine of the decade, the 360-horsepower 352. With this car Dick continued to hone his mechanical and driving skills as his trophy collection grew. Another Starliner came next, this one a 1961 with the 401-horsepower 390 engine. While he was yet to become nationally known, and when asked today Dick humbly plays down his involvement in racing prior to 1962, Dick Brannan had already become a winning drag racer.

In 1962, Ford Motor Company would once again become actively involved in racing, and Dick Brannan would be instrumental in building a winning combination of cars and drivers at Ford. It could be argued that Romy-Hammes was a step ahead of Ford in understanding that cars that were

Dick Brannan's first "hot rod" was this 1932 Ford coupe that he purchased from a local woman for $10. Not yet old enough to drive, Brannan customized his pride and joy and powered it with a full-house flathead V-8 engine. (D. Brannan)

winning races at the local drag strip resulted in showroom sales.

It was to this end that Dick Brannan's first serious race car came about. With the introduction of Ford's latest high-performance engine, the 406, the dealership ordered a 1962 Ford Galaxie two door sedan, sans radio, heater, or any other horsepower-robbing weight. To prepare this car for drag racing in the Super Stock class, Dick Brannan was allocated a bay inside the dealership normally used for new-car preparation. With an NHRA rule book in hand, the car was meticulously prepared for competition.

At some point after all the new-car bugs had been sorted out and a number of class wins had been achieved on local drag strips, the Romy-Hammes team took its car to Detroit Dragway and entered it in a major Super Stock competition. It would seem that the young man with the dealer-sponsored Ford would have little chance against a field of the nation's hottest stockers, including two Ford factory entries. But as the rounds of competition progressed and the ranks thinned, the unknown racer from South Bend was still there. In the championship round the crowd saw Dick Brannan's Ford line up against the renowned Dave Strickler's 409 Chevy. While it would be safe to say that the Ford fans in attendance that night would have been in the minority, underdog Brannan had won over his share of supporters—in fact, when Brannan defeated Strickler and a protest was summarily lodged over the Ford's legality for the class (the attitude being that there was no way that any Ford could beat all the big names in S/S and be legal) the crowd stayed into the wee hours until a complete examination and teardown of the Romy-Hammes Ford entry proved it to be legal. Upon this announcement being broadcast, the crowd cheered. Dick Brannan had served notice that he and his Ford were a force to be reckoned with.

Soon representatives at Ford invited Brannan to Dearborn to talk about his winning combination. Heeding the advice of Romy-Hammes not to tell them everything he knew about setting up a car for drag racing, Dick played his cards close to his vest. Despite the knowledge that Brannan's car had been declared class-legal, the Ford brass still expressed some skepticism over how this young upstart could have defeated two Ford entries with the power of a major corporation and its engineers behind them. Dick was invited to bring his car to Ford's test track to face off against the factory cars, and to prove he was not just lucky. When he soundly trounced the factory team cars again, Dick Brannan found himself with a job offer to be Ford's Drag Race Coordinator.

Dick Brannan and Jerry Hammes continued to race the Romy-Hammes 1962 Ford through the season and provided Ford with regular updates on the car's performance and successes:

- May 5, 1962: At U.S. 30 Dragway in Gary, IN, Brannan won the Super Stock class and Top Stock Eliminator with a best E.T. of 12.74 @ 112.5 MPH. It was noted that fourteen 409 Chevys were in competition at this event.
- May 17, 1962: Brannan won Super Stock and Top Stock Eliminator at Bunker Hill, IN.
- May 24, 1962: The Romy-Hammes Ford took home Super Stock and Top Stock Eliminator honors at Onondaga, MI along with a trophy for Best-Appearing Crew. Performance at that date was 12.55 @ 112.62 MPH.

By 1960 Dick Brannan was working at Romy Hammes Ford at 226 N. Lafayette Blvd in South Bend, IN. As can be seen in this photo, he was having quite a bit of success drag racing his sales demonstrator. (J. Hammes)

- July 13, 1962: *National Dragster's* coverage of a Super Stock meet at York, PA began, "They said it couldn't be done. No Ford could possibly win out of a field of hot Super Stockers especially assembled for a big money meet. But in the midst of all the bad 409 Chevys, 405 Pontiacs, and 410 Plymouths and Dodges there popped up Mr. Dick Brannan of S. Bend, IN with his 405 H.P. Ford 'Lively One.'" Dick set low E.T. in Super Stock with a 12.94 and waded through the field to face the Max Wedge Dodge of Bill Neill in the final. During the course of the evening Brannan's Ford had lost a freeze plug and was overheating badly, but a hastily improvised repair in the form of a thermos cork kept his chances alive. When the overheating Ford lined up against the Dodge for all the money the anti-Ford bias shown by *National Dragster's* scribe seemed to carry over to certain officials of York U.S. 30 Dragway as Neill was allowed to jump the flag man (which would be considered a red light or foul start today) five times before finally being disqualified, handing a hard-fought win to Brannan.
- July 14, 1962: At Detroit Dragway Dick claimed yet another class and Top Stock Eliminator title, turning 12.84 @110 MPH.
- July 21, 1962: Brannan was apparently tired of the late nights spent tearing down his engine to satisfy protests from other competitors at every track he visited. It is reported that on this particular day the Romy-Hammes Ford arrived at the track with its engine already disassembled in order to prove its legality prior to the start of eliminations. Having been declared legal once again, Brannan reassembled the engine and blasted through the traps at 110.50 MPH but lost a clutch in the process, ending his day early.

Did Brannan invent the Line-Loc?

Drag racing has always been about getting an edge over the competition. Never was that more critical than back in the days when race cars were pretty much stock and sanctioning bodies allowed very little modification. Every little mechanical or driving trick really counted and part of Dick Brannan's success was found in his attention to detail. Brannan knew that an advantage off the starting line often meant the difference between winning and losing on the drag strip. In the early days, before Hurst developed its Line-Loc device, which applied the front brakes to hold a race car on the line, drivers of standard transmission-equipped cars had the disadvantage of having to hold the clutch pedal down to the floor, leaving no free feet to hold the brake and keep the car from rolling forward and creating a foul start while revving the engine. Brannan adapted a part from a Studebaker, which the manufacturer had designed to help drivers hold their cars steady when starting on a hill. By installing the system on his Ford, he gained an ever-so-slight edge off the starting line. Dick could then take up on the travel in the clutch pedal without concern that the car could creep forward.

As the 1962 season progressed, those in charge of the racing program at Ford were finally convinced that their racers were fighting an uphill battle trying to compete against cars that were hundreds of pounds lighter. A program to produce a limited number of "lightweight" Galaxies was launched. Eleven special factory lightweight Galaxies were built in 1962, ten of which were the last ten cars off the assembly line at the Wayne, MI plant; the remaining one would be built later in Chicago.

The cars were shipped from the assembly plant to Ford performance subcontractor Dearborn Steel Tubing Co. There, efforts were made to get the big Fords down to fighting weight. The cars ordered for this program were built on a chassis that was lightened through the removal of certain mounts and brackets. Then all sound deadener, the radio, heater, armrests and other creature comforts were deleted. The bodies were fitted with an aluminum front bumper and supporting brackets, aluminum inner fender panels, and fiberglass fenders, hoods, and deck lids. Lighter bucket-style seats were installed in place of the bench seat and carpet was replaced with a lightweight rubber mat.

Power for the special lightweight Galaxies would come from the 406 cubic inch FE engine, but the standard induction system consisting of three Holley two-barrel carburetors was replaced with a new dual four-barrel aluminum intake manifold recently developed by Ford, which mounted two 540 CFM Holley carburetors. The recipients of these special vehicles would be members of the newly formed Ford Drag Council. Drag Council members could buy a lightweight Galaxie for only one dollar. Dick Brannan received a light blue version that would bear the Romy-Hammes livery, as did his earlier dark blue 406 Galaxie.

Delivered late in the season, there was little time to test and prepare the lightweight Galaxies for competition. And, because the production number was well short of the NHRA's required 100 units, the new Fords were forced to run in the A/Factory Experimental class against cars that had even larger engines and lighter bodies.

It was too little, too late for the Ford Drag Council in 1962. At the 1962 Nationals Brannan's lightweight Galaxie was modified to compete in the B/FX class by installing a 380 cubic inch engine created by using a 406 crankshaft in a 352 block. The effort was for naught, however, as the combination lacked top-end horsepower. As the season waned Dick Brannan kept at it with his lightweight Galaxie, continually improving Ford's

On this day Brannan was at Mason-Dixon Dragway in Maryland for a match race against Don Nicholson's Chevy. After mechanical woes sidelined Nicholson's car, a local Chevy man stepped up and offered his 1963 409 Biscayne to "Dyno Don." The effort was for naught, as the Ford prevailed. (L. Wolfe collection)

drag racing program. By October it seemed that progress was being made as during a match race against George DeLorean's lightweight Pontiac, Brannan forced the lighter, larger-engined car to a fifth round in the best-of-five race before losing with an identical elapsed time.

Ford planned to introduce a version of the lightweight Galaxie for 1963 that would not only feature the new, more powerful 427 cubic inch engine but also be produced in sufficient numbers to be offered to independent racers through Ford dealers nationwide. Unfortunately the lightweight version was to be based on the new Sports Roof body style of the Galaxie that wouldn't be introduced until after the first of the year.

Determined not to start the 1963 season as far behind the curve as the previous year, Brannan obtained one of the new 1963 1/2 bodies from assembly and had the team at the Experimental Vehicles Garage (the skunk works where racing and other special projects were developed) install it on the chassis of his 1962 car. This car, Brannan's #823, was the first of a number of the original 1962 Drag Council lightweight Galaxies to be re-bodied in this manner.

However, as feared the production lines at the Norfolk, VA and Los Angeles assembly plants had not yet produced 100 of the new lightweight Fords by the opening day of the NHRA Winternationals, so once again the Ford team was forced into a class other than the intended Super Stock. For this event NHRA classified low-production factory lightweight cars into Limited/Production, where Dick Brannan posted the quickest time of the Fords entered and knocked off the highly regarded Z-11 Chevy of Frank Sanders in the early going. As it turned out the class-winning Chevrolet was found to be illegal and its win was nullified. Prior to the next event there would be a sufficient number of lightweight Ford Galaxies built and in the

Here Brannan defeats the Massey-Fischer Ford lightweight from Virginia with his #823 car in S/S class competition at Mason-Dixon. (L. Wolfe collection)

hands of racers to qualify for competition in the Super Stock class.

In the meantime Dick Brannan went on a tear with his #823 lightweight Galaxie. He became so sought-after for match races that a second car, #824, would eventually be prepared. Brannan's record during the 1963 season shows that he faced the top Super Stock drivers in the nation with enviable results.

- April 14, 1963: Brannan faced Jim Wangers' Royal Pontiac Swiss Cheese Catalina in a match race at Detroit Dragway.

When Fiberglass is Sheetmetal.

As if staying one step ahead of the competition wasn't challenging enough for Dick Brannan and his compatriots at the Experimental Vehicles Garage, the United Auto Workers Union did its best to complicate the situation. While the lightweight fenders and other fiberglass body parts were being installed on Brannan's lightweight Galaxie, a representative of the union happened to observe the work in progress. The official immediately objected to non-union workers performing a task which, under contract, was to be done only by those designated as "sheet metal workers." When it was explained that the parts in question were fiberglass facsimiles of production sheet metal, the union man refused to be deterred, taking the stand that, "If it looks like sheet metal it is sheet metal."

Brannan also relates another union problem that arose over changing spark plugs in one of the race cars. The contention in this case was that by contract a member of the electrical workers union was to perform the task.

So great was the demand for Brannan's Ford by track promoters that a second car was prepared and numbered #824, nearly identical to his primary car. Brannan crewman Ron Stealy would often drive #824 and at times they would double-team the competition with both Fords. (L. Wolfe collection)

After losing the first round on a missed shift, Brannan came back strong to win the second. Wangers then protested the cold air intake system on the Ford and it was removed. The removal of the air ducts did little for the Pontiac cause, as Brannan went on to win the match with a 12.29 @ 119.04 MPH.

- April 21, 1963: At Oswego Brannan won the Super Stock class with a 12.34 @ 116.88 MPH but lost in the Top Stock Eliminator final to his former 1962 Galaxie.
- April 28, 1963: Brannan defeated Pete Seaton's Swiss Cheese Pontiac in four rounds at Onondaga, MI and set a track record of 11.92 @ 120.80 MPH
- May 12, 1963: Brannan came up short in a match against Arnie Beswick's A/FX Pontiac station wagon but set a track record of 120 MPH in his losing effort.
- May 16, 1963: Brannan had to forfeit a match race against Don Nicholson's Chevy due to breakage but at the same event he drove the Bob Ford black '63 Ford to the Super Stock class win.
- May 25, 1963. A rematch between the Romy-Hammes Ford and Don Nicholson's Z-11 Chevy was held at Vineland, NJ.

Brannan's #823 and #824 cars appeared together for the first time in more than four decades at the All-Ford South event hosted by Dick in Cumming, GA in 2005.

Brannan participated in the development of the 1964 Fairlane Thunderbolt, and received the first one as captain of the Ford Drag Council. In this early photo his car sports the short-lived "cloverleaf"-style hood scoop and familiar Romy-Hammes livery. (L. Wolfe collection)

Brannan warmed up with an 11.98 @ 120.80 MPH and after Nicholson forfeited the match due to breakage, Dick challenged and defeated several local Mopar racers to the delight of the Ford fans in attendance.

• May 26, 1963: Brannan was at Mason-Dixon Dragway, where he defeated Bud Faubel's Honker Dodge and took home Super Stock class honors with a 12.23 @119 MPH.

• May 30, 1963: At York, PA, the big Ford ran in the A/FX class and won the trophy with a 12.03 @ 120.48 mph. On the following day it was reported that Brannan defeated an un-named aluminum Chevrolet in a match race at York with a 12.17 @ 120 MPH.

• June 2, 1963: Dick ran the car at Thompson in Ohio, where he won Super Stock and set the track record at 12.41 @ 118 MPH.

• June 15, 1963: At Martin, MI, the Packer Pontiac entry of Howard Marselles lost a best-of-five match race to Brannan's Ford in three straight runs. Brannan clocked a 12.21 @ 120 MPH.

• June 16, 1963: At Osceola, MI, the Super Stock and Top Stock Eliminator titles went to Brannan.

• June 23, 1963: Dick lost a match race to Dave Strickler's Z-11 Chevy at Vineland, NJ.

• July 5, 1963: Brannan took home honors in Super Stock at Manassass, VA.

Part-way into the 1964 season Brannan collaborated with Dearborn Steel Tubing to build an ultra-light A/FX Falcon powered by a 427 High Riser engine. Here the car is shown on a trailer behind the Romy Hammes Ford transporter carrying Brannan's S/S Thunderbolt. (L Wolfe collection)

Dick proudly poses with his 1964 A/FX Falcon on race day. (D. Brannan)

- July 6, 1963: Malcolm Durham's Z-11 Chevy lost to Brannan at York, PA, in three straight runs. Brannan recorded a 12.08 @ 120.48 MPH.
- July 7, 1963: Brannan dropped Vernon Rowley's Plymouth in three straight runs with a best of 12.15 @ 117.95 MPH.
- July 13, 1963: Dick Brannan set the NHRA class record for Super Stock at York, PA, and claimed the distinction of being the first Ford driver to do so.
- July 29, 1963 Brannan followed up at Martin, MI, by defeating Huston Platt's Z-11 Chevy with a 12.33 @ 118 MPH.

In September 1963 Brannan brought both the #823 and #824 Galaxies to Capitol Raceway, where the track promoter put a $25 dollar bounty on his head for any Super Stock car who could beat the Ford. Vowing to run the slightly slower #824 car until it tasted defeat before unleashing the #823, Brannan made a total of 15 runs, turning a best of 12.01 @ 118.75 MPH. It was noted that the only car to beat the #824 on that day was Smoker Smith's Plymouth, which then bowed to the #823.

- September 20, 1963: Brannan downed Ed Schartman's Z-11 Chevy in a match race with an 11.81 @ 119.52. At this same event the S/S class-legal lightweight Galaxie of Doug Nash and Ernie Mac Ewan defeated a 426 Plymouth, with Doug tripping the lights at 12.46 @ 117.60. Ernie was one of the men behind the scenes at Ford's Experimental Vehicles Garage and was considered a top engine builder. Doug Nash was a hot young driver who would go on to win much fame at the wheel of various Ford products over the coming years.

Drag News reported that when setting a track record of 11.93 @ 120 MPH in Onondaga, MI, Brannan's "lightweight" Ford tipped the scales at 3,460 pounds.

For a season where automotive publications reported, and have continued to report, that Ford was not competitive in drag racing, it seemed that Dick Brannan fared pretty well, with an NHRA

The now-restored 1964 A/FX Falcon is part of a collection of Brannan's former race cars owned by Don Snyder, Jr.

National record, 22 track records, and more than 65 wins to his credit.

NHRA rules for the Super Stock class in 1964 allowed engines with a maximum of 427 cubic inches and cars with a minimum weight of 3,200 pounds. Well aware that the Galaxie could not be competitive for the upcoming year, Dick Brannan became involved in a project that would result in one of the most iconic of all Ford performance cars, the Thunderbolt. The new drag cars would be based on the mid-size Fairlane body and followed a concept developed during 1963, when a Fairlane two door hardtop was modified to accept the 427 engine by Ford subcontractor Dearborn Steel Tubing and ultimately turned over to the Tasca Ford team.

Brannan, Danny Jones, and Vern Tinsler from Special Vehicles commissioned Dearborn Steel to build an initial series of ten 1964 Fairlanes, using the newly released 427 High Riser engine for power, for members of the Drag Council. Brannan had the two door hardtop version of the Fairlane

in mind for the project but because of some miscommunication between he and Tinsler, the factory delivered 10 two-door sedans, starting with VIN 4F41K118367 on October 9, 1963.

Dick Brannan began drag race development of the new car and on his very first run clocked a 12.26 @ 122 MPH. Working closely with the late James "Hammer" Mason at Dearborn Steel, and with the assistance of Tinsler and Danny Jones,

The 1965 A/FX Mustang "mule" car was built by Dearborn Steel Tubing and developed by Dick Brannan. Initially painted red, the car was later blue for a short time before receiving a beautiful coat of gold metal flake and Stark-Hickey Ford livery. (D. Brannan)

At the 1964 NHRA Winternationals, Drag Council Captain Dick Brannan led the charge of the Thunderbolts in the Super Stock class. Brannan dropped Dave Strickler's Dodge in the first round, 11.80 @ 122.28 MPH to 12.03 @ 122 MPH. Dick advanced through the field until a clutch failure took him out of competition in the semifinal round. From that point forward, "The world's fastest Ford" would be virtually unstoppable that season:

- June 1, 1964: Brannan won the Super Stock Bonanza at U.S. 30 Dragway on Friday night, turning a best of 11.08 @ 128 MPH among a field of 30 cars. On Saturday Brannan and the Thunderbolt faced the Ramchargers Dodge in a match race in Martin, MI. In time trials the Dodge had managed an 11.55 to Brannan's 11.41. After mechanical woes caused the Dodge to forfeit the match, Brannan took on another Hemi-powered Dodge and won three straight. On Sunday Brannan was in Gary, IN, for another Super Stock Bonanza, where he was runner up to Tom Sturm's A/FX Comet.

Brannan continued to make suggestions on how to get the full potential out of the car. Brannan's test car was soon followed by a second, 4F41K118368, which was put into the capable hands of Ford test driver Bill Humphrey. By the time the first series of cars was delivered into the hands of the Drag Council members on November 4, 1963, it was apparent that Ford had built a winner.

The legal A/FX car was followed by Ford's first "match bash" car, the ultra-light, altered wheelbase *Bronco*. This car was built for Brannan at Holman-Moody to do battle with the altered wheelbase Chrysler "funny" cars. (R. Ladley collection)

- June 6, 1964: Brannan defeated the A/FX Tempest of Arnie Beswick in a match race in Cordova, IL, with a best of 11.40 @ 125.17 MPH.
- July 21, 1964: At Bunker Hill in Indiana Dick Brannan claimed the title "King of the Hill" by winning the Super Stock Class and Top Stock Eliminator with an 11.28 @ 125.12 MPH.
- September 26, 1964: Brannan took home yet another King of the Hill title at Bunker Hill, defeating the Ed Martin Ford Thunderbolt in the final, 11.15 to 11.25.

During the 1964 season, when it became apparent that the Ford model that would carry the company banner in drag racing competition during the 1965 season was going to be the Mustang, Dick Brannan had the foresight to get a jump on development of the platform for drag racing. Because the Mustang had yet to be introduced, Brannan chose the Falcon chassis, on which the Mustang would be based, to build his next race car.

Dearborn Steel Tubing was again tasked with the project. The already light Falcon two-door hardtop was put on a strict diet, with fiberglass front bumper, fenders, hood, and doors. The factory side glass, as well as the front and rear windshields, was replaced by Plexiglas, and the rear quarter windows were fixed in place. In order to get the car back up to the class-required weight minimum, a heavy steel reinforcement was placed just forward of the rear bumper and a huge battery was mounted in the trunk. Power for the Falcon came from the same 427 High Riser as the Thunderbolts and the two also shared transmissions, rear axles, and traction bar designs.

Brannan's Falcon could often be found doing double duty alongside the Thunderbolt during the 1964 season and it was not unusual for him to take home Super Stock and A/FX class honors at the same event by jumping from car to car.

By the second week of May 1964, Brannan apparently had the new car bugs thoroughly

Brannan, at the wheel of his *Bronco* altered-wheelbase Mustang, does battle with the *Melrose Missile* Plymouth. By this point the Chrysler team had added fuel injectors to keep pace with the fleet-footed SOHC 427 powered Fords. (R. Ladley collection)

By 1966 Brannan's mount had become even more radical, sporting injectors, exotic fuels, a modified C-6 automatic transmission, and sponsorship from Bob Ford. (D. Brannan)

worked out of his Falcon, as he won the A/FX class at the NHRA Divisional Championships in Cecil County, MD, with an 11.37 @124 MPH.

- June 14, 1964: Brannan took his Falcon to S/XS class honors at an AHRA regional meet in Gary, IN, with an 11.28 @ 126.5 MPH over Tom Coward's Comet.
- June 20, 1964 Brannan's Falcon met Arnie Beswick's GTO at Martin, MI and took the match in three straight runs, 11.30 @ 125.17 MPH.
- July 12, 1964: Brannan traveled to Oswego, IL, for a match race against Mr. Norm's Grand Spaulding Dodge, which Brannon won in three straight. The Falcon's 11.30 @ 128.57 MPH was the best time recorded by any S/S or F/X at the track to that date.
- July 21, 1964: While winning his King of the Hill title at Bunker Hill, IN, with his Fairlane, Brannan also took home A/FX class honors with the Falcon at 11.10 @ 128.72 MPH.
- July 31, 1964: A crowd of 6,000 fans saw Brannan defeat the Hemi Dodge of Dave Strickler at Manassas, VA.
- August 1 and 2, 1964: Brannan ran match races against Malcolm Durham's 427 Chevelle, Smoker Smith's Plymouth and George Weiler's Comet at York, PA, and Atco, NJ. At York Brannan took the match in five runs with an 11.15 @ 127.5 MPH. The following day, after losing the first round to Brannan 11.05 to 11.60, Durham refused to face the Ford again and forfeited the match.
- September 13, 1964: Brannan defeated the Westborn Plymouth entry three straight times in a match race at Grand Bend, Canada. Brannan set a new track record at 11.10.

By December 1964, the A/FX '65-model Mustang program was ready to be launched. Dearborn Steel Tubing was contracted to build the "mule" car with collaboration from Brannan and Vern Tinlser. The car would be powered by the new SOHC 427 engine that Ford had developed

This is Brannan's 1966 backup/test car. It was this car that he crashed, and not the Bob Ford car, as was often reported. The car was a total loss and Brannan suffered serious injuries in the crash. (D. Brannan)

for NASCAR competition but was disallowed. In order to accommodate the huge engine, the standard Mustang front suspension was replaced with an unusual arrangement referred to as a torsion leaf, or twisted-leaf set up. By January the car was ready for testing and it was featured, along with Vern Tinsler, on the cover of *Rodder and Super Stock* magazine showing a single four-barrel induction system atop the SOHC engine.

When Dearborn Steel declined the contract to build 10 more A/FX Mustangs for the 1965 season, the contract went to Holman-Moody. Although there was a shortage of the new SOHC engines, resulting in some of the cars being fitted with 427 High Risers, the Ford teams were ready for the NHRA Winternationals in Pomona, CA. At that event Brannan fell victim to mechanical woes but his Drag Council teammate Bill Lawton took the Tasca Ford A/FX Mustang to the winner's circle.

As the Drag Council Mustangs dominated the A/FX class during the 1965 season the Chrysler teams were not sitting idly by. Radically altered wheelbases, acid-dipped bodies, fuel injection, and exotic fuels soon became the norm for the Mopar set. Ford maintained that it did not care to compete with cars that bore no resemblance to their available products and banned Drag Council members from match racing against the "Funny Cars." Soon, the only competition for the Ford team came from its counterparts at Mercury, which made little sense from a corporate sales standpoint.

In early April 1965, Charlie Gray and Dick Brannan decided to have two altered-wheelbase Mustangs, one of which would be a test car, built secretly by Holman-Moody. By mid-April, as the cars neared completion, Brannan and Gray had no choice but to inform their boss, John Cowley, of the project. Much to their surprise management gave its approval. The car designated as Brannan's was brought to Dearborn for testing and preparation for the AHRA Summer World Championships, to be held at Lions Drag Strip in Long Beach, CA in August. Dick Brannan's new altered wheelbase "Funny" Mustang, dubbed *Bronco*," not only made its debut at this event but took home all the marbles, defeating teammate Gas Ronda's A/FX Mustang in an all-Ford final.

The next major event for *Bronco* would be the NHRA Nationals in Indianapolis, where the car was forced into the B/Altered class. Brannan set low elapsed time and virtually annihilated the competition, only to lose in the final because of a blown head gasket. From that point forward Brannan would go undefeated. In October he faced the top Funny Cars and drivers in the nation at the "Factory Showdown." Once again Brannan would emerge victorious; his final-round opponent was none other than Phil Bonner in his *Daddy Warbucks* Ford Falcon.

The success that Brannan had with the altered-wheelbase Mustang in 1965 convinced the management at Ford to give the go-ahead for Holman-Moody to build a series of similar cars to be delivered to Drag Council members in 1966. Brannan had continued testing with his mule car, which had been built by H-M. While it bore a resemblance to Bronco, the car was fitted with an automatic transmission, Hilborn fuel injection, and aerodynamic modifications. The test car was also used to determine how much power could be wrung from the SOHC 427 by using exotic fuels, beginning with alcohol and eventually including nitromethane. During testing the car was hitting 150 MPH terminal speeds and handling problems began to arise. This led to the conclusion that the wheelbase needed to be extended on the next series of Mustangs.

Ford's official biography of Dick Brannan for press release in the 1966 season reads as follows:

> Dick Brannan qualifies as one of the mighty mites in drag racing, being slight of stature but having some of the quickest reflexes in the country. The 29-year-old Madison Heights, MI driver ranked as one of the top match racers in the country in 1965, his eighth season as a drag racer. While starting the season in an A/FX Mustang Brannan joined the ranks of "funny car" drivers halfway through the year. Brannan and his lightweight, altered wheelbase Mustang enjoyed considerable success in both match competition and in big eliminator meets. Running on gas and carburetion Brannan reached speeds of 140 MPH with elapsed times in the low 10 second bracket. Despite his late start with the altered wheelbase Mustang Brannan reached the final round in B/Altered in the NHRA

This Bob Ford-sponsored "stretched Mustang" came next for Dick. He would later turn over the reigns to Hubert Platt, who continued the car's winning ways. (Alan Wood)

Nationals before mechanical difficulties forced him to forego the final run. In the AHRA Nationals Brannan put down a top field of Ultra Stock equipment to win the Top Stock Eliminator title. He defeated teammate Phil Bonner in the final run. The car also proved well nigh unbeatable in match competition. While Brannan is campaigning the same car in 1966 it has been revamped. Holman-Moody, who first built the car, have given a new treatment to the front end. More importantly, Brannan has converted his 427 cubic inch, single overhead cam engine to run fuel injection, greatly increasing horsepower. When Brannan left the ranks of the factory experimental cars in mid 1965 he sought a car that would be greatly reduced in weight but still feature all of the safety features built into the A/FX Mustangs. Fenders, hood, deck lid and bumpers were all made from fiberglass. To provide better weight distribution the front wheels were moved forward five inches and the rear wheels ten. The engine was also moved back. A small aluminum gas tank was located in front of the engine, while the battery was placed in the trunk. The car features a full cage roll bar and a breakaway steering wheel. Both harness belt and seat belt help keep the driver in place and added braking power is provided by a parachute. Brannan wears a fireproof suit at all times behind the wheel.

By 1970 Dick Brannan was back behind the wheel, fielding a Maverick powered by a Boss 429 in the Pro/Stock class. (D. Brannan)

By the time this photo was taken in April of 1971, Ford's support, even for Brannan, had pretty much dried up. Brannan would soldier on for another year of so with help from Paul Harvey Ford, but the best years were over. Note the Piper Aircraft logo on the hood scoop. (D. Brannan)

Brannan collaborated with H-M's project manager Howard DeHart on the construction of a series of Mustangs with an extended wheelbase that came to be referred to as long-nose Mustangs, while he continued testing his mule car. This car was painted gold with blue coves and bore Bob Ford livery. Showing typical journalistic bias against Fords, *Drag Strip* magazine reported on the debut of Brannan's new mount by reporting that he "stole" the Funny Car class win at a U.D.R.A. meet. Next stop for the Brannan was the AHRA Winter Championships at Irwindale, CA in January 1966. The two recently completed long-nose Mustangs were delivered to Drag Council members Gas Ronda and Bill Lawton and arrived untested for the event. Brannan served notice on the competition by downing the supercharged Pontiac of Arnie Beswick for the Unlimited/Fuel class title, recording a 9.21 @ 149.50 MPH in the process. Bill Lawton wheeled the Tasca Ford long-nose Mustang to victory in the Unlimited/Stock ranks with a 9.71 @ 141 MPH.

On March 20, 1966 Brannan faced the *Seaton's Shaker* Chevelle funny car in a match race at Detroit Dragway and took the win handily.

In April 1966 while testing his mule car at U.S. 131 Dragway, Brannan had a devastating crash that would destroy the car and leave Dick badly injured. There has been some confusion regarding this car, as it has been erroneously reported that it was rebuilt and back in action three weeks later. The truth is the car was destroyed; the car Brannan appeared in three weeks later was his primary long-nose car. Dick would have a crash with the primary car in yet another match race against Seaton's car, which further added to the confusion.

Brannan would go on to claim victory at the 1966 NASCAR Grand Finale held at Atco Dragway to become the series points champion.

By this time the demands of his duties at Ford, and the concerns of his bosses over the potential consequences of losing their most valuable drag racing asset to a future crash, led Brannan to hang

A Brannan Mustang Primer

As a result of repaints, backup/test cars, mid-year changes of vehicle and modifications that were happening at a rapid pace, there has been some confusion about the Mustangs raced by Dick Brannan during the 1965-67 seasons. His first A/FX Mustang (which bore the number 690) was the mule car built by Dearborn Steel Tubing Company and was originally painted red when featured in magazine coverage. This car was painted blue and raced at the Winternationals by Dick. The car was then painted a beautiful metal flake gold with white coves and bore Stark-Hickey Ford sponsorship along with the name *Goldfinger*. Brannan drove this car early in the 1965 season.

During this time he also drove a white 65 A/FX Mustang test car for Ford. This car was not raced but used exclusively for testing. The 690 car was an A/FX class-legal car weighing 3,200 pounds and its SOHC 427 engine was carbureted and ran on gasoline.

His next mount was the Holman-Moody-built, altered wheelbase "match bash" Mustang, which also bore the Stark-Hickey Ford logo but was named *Bronco* and raced through the end of the 1965 season. *Bronco* weighed 2800 pounds and also ran on gas with carburetors.

There was also a backup or test altered wheelbase car built at the same time as *Bronco*. This car was painted in a similar fashion but never lettered. It was used for testing fuel injection and exotic fuels. This is the car that Dick crashed and destroyed in April 1966.

In 1966 Dick received his "long-nose" Mustang funny car from Holman-Moody. This car had an automatic transmission, fuel injection, and ran on exotic fuels. The car was gold with blue coves and bore Bob Ford livery. This car was passed into the hands of Hubert Platt. It is reported to have later been owned by Larry Coleman and driven by Sidney Foster, eventually finding its way into the hands of Clester Andrews, who re-bodied it as a '69 Mustang.

up his helmet. For the 1967 season Brannan chose Hubert Platt to wheel the Bob Ford long-nose Mustang. Brannan concentrated on the development of the Super Stock 427 Fairlane and later the 428 Cobra Jet Mustang, both of which paid enormous dividends to Ford's racing program.

Dick was called back to driving in 1970 behind the wheel of the Paul Harvey Ford-sponsored, Boss 429-powered Pro Stock Maverick. Returning with the same car in 1971, Brannan had by this time left Ford—they had ceased support of racing—and was working for Piper Aircraft. On January 4, 1971 Brannan took the Maverick to the winner's circle at South East Dragway outside of Dallas, defeating Bill Tanner's Dodge in the Pro Stock final. Later in the season Dick clocked a 10.10 @ 142.00 MPH to defeat Arlen Vanke's Plymouth in the Pro Stock class final at Oldsmar Dragway in Tampa, FL. Brannan's final ride came in 1972 at the wheel of the Paul Harvey Ford Pinto Pro Stock entry.

After leaving Ford, Dick Brannan had a successful career in aviation and owned several businesses. Today he lives in Georgia and remains active attending auto events around the country with his son, Brian.

CHAPTER 2

LES RITCHEY

"IF LES TOLD ME TO PUT THE ENGINE IN THE CAR BACKWARDS I WOULD. THAT'S HOW MUCH TRUST I HAD IN HIM"
— GAS RONDA, 2010

Les Ritchey was a great innovator and driver, and was a moving force behind Ford's success in drag racing during the 1950s and 60s. Sadly Les died as a result of a racing accident on May 1, 1966. This chapter is written to pay homage to the man who did more to further the fortunes of Ford in drag racing than perhaps any other. With the gracious assistance of his son Randy, I hope to capture the essence of a man who gave us so much to cheer about during drag racing's golden years.

Tenacious. A man who stood by his word. Not a man you would want to anger, but one who loved a practical joke. These are some of Les Ritchey's traits, as conveyed by a son who so adored his dad that, as he describes it, he "got into his back pocket" to be a part of his father's racing ventures at a very early age.

Les Ritchey was a man who was held in high esteem by the most respected racers of his time and who forged such a reputation for getting the utmost performance out of the products of Ford Motor Company that he was consulted by the company's top management on matters relating to racing.

"I knew Les by reputation, of course," said Dick Brannan, "And when we put together the Drag Council at Ford in 1962, he was one of the first to get a call. I called him Lester the Tester. He was always trying something new, and most of it worked. He was an innovator."

Bill Holbrook, supervisor at Ford's Experimental Vehicles Garage, told me that Ford test driver and successful drag racer Len Richter was disappointed in the performance of the SOHC 427 engine provided by Ford in 1965 until Les Ritchey worked on it.

Len also tells a story about the incredible dog that Les kept at his West Covina, CA, shop. "That dog would chew up two-by-fours, and one day while we were working there the dog kept bugging me to throw this big piece of wood for him. After a while I got tired of the game so I stood on the board. Don't you know that dog grabbed hold of it and yanked me off my feet! Les told me he didn't have to worry about getting rid of old cars. He would just put them outside for the dog to chew up."

Born in Childers, TX, on April 25, 1923, Leslie Ritchey moved with his family to Pasadena, CA, in 1929. During WWII Les served in the Army Air Corps and received training at the Pratt-Whitney Company as an aircraft mechanic. After the war Les continued his mechanical engineering studies at Pasadena City College and subsequently found work as a mechanic in Pasadena.

At the 1962 NHRA Nationals Les Ritchey prepared and drove the Ed Martin Ford Sales lightweight Galaxie. The car had been retrofitted with steel parts in order to run in the SS/S class, where it was felt it would be more competitive. Never best through the 1/8th mile at the event, even Ritchey's tuning and driving skills could not make up for lack of preparation time nor provide the brute top end horsepower needed to defeat the competition. Future events would bode much better for Ritchey and the fledgling Ford Drag Council. (D. Kolodziej)

Around 1948 he began racing on the dry lakes of southern California, a place that would breed some of the biggest names in drag racing. He eventually took a job at San Marino Motors, a Ford dealership in the San Gabriel Valley, where he advanced from tune-up mechanic to service manager. In 1955, Ritchey resigned his position at the Ford dealership in order to open his own business, which he called Performance Associates. His reputation for preparing the best-performing cars in southern California was soon established. A Valvoline Oil promotional piece described Ritchey's shop as "unique, not in equipment, but in the results he obtains that have seldom been equaled."

Les's shop was equipped with a chassis dynamometer and he employed Wally Cartwright, a man with roots in the Indianapolis 500, as his engine builder. In 1956, Les Ritchey's 1956 Ford Victoria, powered by a 260-horsepower, 312-ci engine, virtually owned the drag strips of Southern California, winning 31 straight Eliminator titles. Between December 1956 and May 1957, *Rod and Custom* magazine ran a multi-part series of articles by Les Ritchey explaining how to achieve maximum performance from the Ford Y-Block V-8 engine. Les followed the Victoria with a Latham supercharger-equipped '57 Ranchero with which he collected 46 additional wins over the next three years.

One of Performance Associates' customers at the time was future Indy 500 winner Parnelli Jones, for whom Les built engines, prepared cars, and acted as race-day mechanic. Jones was sponsored by Ford dealer Vel Miletich of Torrence, CA, and would take his cars to victory lane 21 consecutive times and win three NASCAR Pacific Coast Championships with Les Ritchey's help.

Les also prepared the '57 Ford of Marvin Porter and Wes Rourke, winners of the National Short Track Championship. In 1959, Les and Wally Cartwright were named co-mechanics of the year by NASCAR. Les would also serve as mechanic on Jones' car at the 1960 Daytona 500. A testament to Ritchey's abilities was shown in the fact that after starting in the 40th spot in the race, Jones had battled his way to 4th in just 40 laps, averaging 152 MPH before dropping out on lap 54 due to rocker arm failure.

Les Ritchey's ability to prepare Ford's products for top performance gained the attention of those who became the architects' of the company's Total Performance efforts during the 1960s.

Les' son Randy says his earliest memory of his dad's cars was a '40 Ford coupe that he street raced. On one occasion Les had removed the '40's hood. After painting it Les laid the hood in their home's driveway to dry when young Randy came along and walked across the still-wet paint.

From Randy's recollections Les apparently had quite the reputation in his home town as a street racer. On one occasion Les, his wife, and kids rolled into the local In-N-Out Burger with the family station wagon, a '57 Ford. One local hot shot must have felt the time was right to engage in some trash talk about Ritchey's street racing prowess. Much to the local hot rodder's chagrin, and Mrs. Ritchey's dismay, Les was more than up for the challenge; he proceeded to blow the loudmouth's doors off with the family wagon. A classic case of, "I'll run you with my tow car and if you can beat that I'll go home for the race car."

At the 1961 NHRA Winternationals, Les prepared and entered his 1961 Ford Starliner, powered by the newly introduced, 401 horsepower, 390 cubic inch FE engine. Despite being handicapped by a three-speed, column-shifted transmission in a heavier car with fewer cubic inches than the competition, he acquitted himself admirably, going to the semifinal rounds in both class and Top Stock. Ritchey had posted quicker elapsed times than eventual class- and eliminator-winner Don Nicholson's 409 Chevy. Had lady luck smiled on him that day, Les might well have found himself in the winner's circle. The May 1961 issue of *Rod and Custom* magazine contained a feature article in which Les Ritchey shared tips on how to prepare the latest Ford engine, the FE series, for competition.

At the 1962 NHRA Winternationals a Les Ritchey Performance Associates-prepared Galaxie, sponsored by Ben Alexander Ford of Los Angeles and driven by their high-performance salesman Dick Heyler, competed in the SS/SA class. While not victorious, the car's performance after preparation by Performance Associates was impressive enough to be noted in *Hot Rod*. The Performance Associates-prepared '62 Ford Galaxie of Joe Oliphant was runner-up to Terry Prince's Chevy in the B/Stock class at the Winternationals. Ben Alexander, owner of the dealership that sponsored the aforementioned car, was a Hollywood actor best known for his role in the television series "Dragnet," with Jack Webb.

In August 1962, Ford Motor Company enlisted the services of Les Ritchey to develop lightweight Galaxies and find a drag racing setup that would allow the cars to be competitive. Ford engineers were able to lighten the production Galaxie by nearly 400 pounds through deletions and the replacement of steel parts with fiberglass and aluminum. Taking advantage of Les' years of experience in preparing winning drag cars, Ford was able to supply the recipients of lightweight Galaxies with information on how their cars should be set up for maximum performance prior to the NHRA Nationals.

At the Nationals Les was tasked with driving the Ed Martin Ford car in the SS/S class, as well as his own car in A/FX. Late delivery and a lack of preparation time meant the Ed Martin car did not have the recommended setup. It suffered from wheel hop and poor traction, managing a best time of 13.44 @ 108.95 MPH. Gas Ronda's SS/S car, which had been prepared by Ritchey, recorded the best elapsed time and trap speed among the Fords entered in that class, with a 13.07 @ 110.28 MPH. Les Ritchey's own A/FX car was the quickest of all the Ford entries with a best of 12.73 @ 110.97 MPH. Unfortunately Les missed the call to the lanes for the A/FX class runoff and was disqualified. The class-winning Pontiac Tempest was both considerably lighter than the Fords and, at 434 cubic inches, had a much larger engine, allowing it to post a run of 12.66 @ 115.58 MPH.

The 1962 NHRA Nationals was a classic case of too little, too late for the Ford team. A pessimistic report regarding Ford's future in drag racing was prepared by Dave Evans on September 6, 1962. It reads in part, "Although we made considerable improvement, and in the majority of the events get off the line in better shape than our competitors, we feel we were unsuccessful because Ford engines are not adaptable to this type of competition. This is also evidenced by the fact that practically every other car, whether it be modified, rail car etc., is powered by a Chevrolet, sometimes by other manufacturers, but almost never by a Ford."

We must consider the fact that Mr. Evans' report was filed close on the heels of what can only described as a dismal outing for vehicles into which Ford had invested considerable money, if not time. And of course Mr. Evans would have no way of knowing the glory and number of future racing victories the FE series engine would bring the company.

The following day Dan Jones supplied a more realistic summary of events at the '62 Nationals. "Due to late delivery resulting in lack of preparation time, plus little or no pre-race practice, eight of the ten cars were not set up to the standards established by the Les Ritchey and Gas Ronda A/FX and SS/S machines. These two cars were never beaten off the line or through the initial phase of the quarter mile. The chassis and engine setups used by these two cars were made available to the entire group. This included part numbers, illustrated drawings of the suspension, curved distributors, carburetor parts and jets, plus any replacement items needed. Along with comparable weight, gear ratios, tire sizes, and superior traction, an increase in power in the upper ranges (5000 RPM to 7000 RPM) is needed to become competitive with the Dodges, Plymouths, Pontiacs, and Chevrolets."

Randy Ritchey remembers missing an important practice that might well have kept him from getting a starting position on his school football team in order to accompany his dad to the 1962 NHRA Nationals. Happily Randy's coach saw the young man's dedication to his father's racing efforts as a quality that would pay dividends on the gridiron, and Randy got to start with the team.

Dick Heyler did well in the SS/A class at the 1962 NHRA Winternationals with his Les Ritchey Total Performance-prepared, Ben Alexander Ford-sponsored '62 Galaxie. (Jim Demmitt, Jr.)

Ritchey's Drag Council Thunderbolt, *Amorous Agatha*, gets cooled in the pits between rounds. Ritchey spent more effort on friend and teammate Gas Ronda's Thunderbolt in 1964, and it paid off in an NHRA World Championship for Ronda. (Fermier Bros. collection)

In an effort to be ready for the competition in 1963 a number of the Drag Council members' 1962 cars, Ritchey's among them, were re-bodied as 1963 1/2 Galaxies and fitted with lightweight components. While the body swap took place at Bill Stroppe Engineering, the drag race preparation of both the Ronda and Ritchey cars was done at Performance Associates. Showing slightly more interest than normal in the performance offerings from Ford, *Hot Rod* magazine did a feature article on the 1963 1/2 lightweight Galaxies under the headline "Less Weight Means More Ford," in their July 1963 issue. *Hot Rod's* Ray Brock reported checking out a pair of lightweights in action on the drag strip at Pomona, CA, in his article. "One was driven by Ford tune-up expert Les Ritchey and the other by well-known Ford drag strip artist Gas Ronda." The article indicated that Ritchey's car was not equipped with fiberglass doors, and with steel-tube headers weighed in at 3510 pounds, while Ronda's came in at 3425. With temperatures soaring into the high 80's, Ritchey's car stopped the clocks at 12.29 @ 117.30, while Ronda's lighter version posted a 12.07 @ 118.04.

Brock indicated that there were not yet enough of these new Fords in the pipeline to qualify for Super/Stock class competition; as a result Ronda and Ritchey had to run in A/FX (they were declared S/S class-legal one week later). Brock estimated that had the Fords been allowed in Super

Les took his A/FX Mustang to victory at the 1965 NHRA Nationals. His final-round opponent was friend and teammate Gas Ronda, driving a Les Ritchey-prepared Mustang of his own.

This Mel Burns Ford ad boasts sponsorship of two AHRA national record-holding vehicles, an E/Sports Mustang and Ron Root's G/SA Fairlane. Both vehicles were Performance Associates-prepared by Les Ritchey.

Stock on that particular day they more than likely would have faced one another for both class and Top Stock Eliminator honors, based on the fact that they out-performed all other entries.

Performance Associates also prepared other brands. In 1963 Ron Root's Les Ritchey-prepared six-cylinder Dodge Dart took the C/FX class win at the NHRA Nationals alongside the Performance Associates Falcon Sprint, dubbed *Little Sam*, which claimed the J/Stock title.

The August 1963 issue of *Hot Rod* contained a feature article by Don Francisco on Les Ritchey's tune-up tips for the 427 Ford engine. It describes the head man at Performance Associates as "truly one of the best-informed Ford men in the country. What he tells you to do to get the most from your Ford isn't just hearsay. He knows it will work because he has done it."

As a member of the Drag Council, Les Ritchey was on hand in Dearborn, for the official unveiling of the Fairlane Thunderbolts. Prior to turning the #5 (VIN 4F41K118359) car over to Les, test driver Dan Jones had made four runs in the car, recording a disappointing 12.34 and a 12.53 @ 118.73 MPH on the first two runs. The tachometer was replaced due to a short and the carburetor jets were changed, resulting in passes of 12.11 @ 120.48 mph and 12.16 @ 120.15 MPH. The Thunderbolt that would come to be known as *Amorous Agatha* was then turned over to

Les Ritchey to receive the Performance Associates touch.

During the 1964 season Les Ritchey devoted most of his time to running his business and maintaining the Thunderbolt of friend and teammate Gas Ronda, rather than competing in weekly racing events and match races with his Thunderbolt. I did, however, find several references in official Drag Council weekly race results reports that indicate that when he did bring his Thunderbolt out, Les was in it to win it.

On August 23, 1964 at Long Beach, CA, Les found himself the only entry in the Super/Stock class. Rather than take the easy win, Les opted to run his car in A/FX, where he bested a Hemi Plymouth with an 11.76 @ 124.75 MPH to an 11.76 @ 124.95 MPH (an example of Ritchey's ability to leave the line first) before losing to a second Plymouth by 5/100ths of a second.

At Fontana, CA, on October 3, 1964, Les Ritchey took home Super/Stock class honors with an 11.40 elapsed time.

On October 4, 1964 after winning the Super/Stock class at Long Beach Ritchey once again stepped up to the A/FX class, losing in the final to Hayden Proffitt's factory-team Comet.

At the climax of the 1964 drag racing season, Gas Ronda was crowned NHRA World Champion with his Les Ritchey Performance Associates-prepared Thunderbolt.

Prior to the 1965 season Les was chosen to receive one of the A/FX Mustangs being built at Holman-Moody In keeping with his reputation as an innovator, Ritchey decided that in place of the standard two Holley four barrel carburetors used to feed the new SOHC 427 engine he would experiment with four 58IDA Weber two-barrels on a one-of-a-kind intake manifold. Ritchey believed that the design of these carburetors would lend themselves to more accurate tuning of the engine. Prior to the NHRA Winternationals, the Drag Council Mustangs scheduled to compete received final preparation at Performance Associates, which contributed greatly to their success at Pomona. In a stroke of irony, Ritchey's car was the last to be prepared; it was then discovered that the one-off intake manifold designed to accept the Weber carburetors had been cast incorrectly and ultimately could not be used.

Performance Associates had the distinction of receiving one of just two 1965 Fairlane Thunderbolts built by Dearborn Steel Tubing Company in the manner in which the '64 Thunderbolts had been constructed. Les Ritchey took a novel approach to preparing this car. He noted that when equipped with the 271 horsepower, high-performance 289 engine, the Fairlane was very well suited for the NHRA D/Stock class. With the newly available C-4 automatic transmission behind the high-performance small block, a one-of-a-kind Fairlane was created. With Mel Burns Ford sponsorship on the flanks and long-time Ritchey associate Ron Root at the wheel, it proved to be a successful combination.

Randy Ritchey recalls the pressure that Les was under at the 1965 NHRA Nationals when his Mustang, with its Weber carburetors, was running well off the pace of the Holleys being used by his teammates. While Les wanted to soldier on and work out his current setup, Charlie Gray wanted him to change back to Holley carburetors. Randy tells of his dad working late into the night at the Bob Ford agency in Indianapolis, performing the induction change prior to the next day's competition. Ritchey's decision turned out to be a good one, however as he drove to victory in the A/FX class. Les defeated his last four opponents through sheer driving skill, running slower elapsed times than each of them. Ironically, in the final round Ritchey faced a car he worked hard to prepare for the event, driven by his close friend Gas Ronda. Ronda simply explained how proud he was to be the first to congratulate Les on his win.

On October 3, 1965, Les Ritchey set the *Drag News* A/FX class record with a 10.36 second pass @ 135.64 MPH at Half Moon Bay drag strip.

As the 1965 racing season wound down, Les Ritchey showed the world just how well he had his SOHC 427 Mustang dialed in. He defeated Charlie Allen's fuel-injected, altered-wheelbase Dodge in a match race at Irwindale, CA, on November 7 and topped the *Drag News* West Coast Stock Eliminator list with a win over the *Flying Dutchman* Dodge on November 21.

At the AHRA Winter National Championship at Irwindale, Les drove his 1966 Mustang (which was in fact his 1965 car updated with '66 trim) to victory in the A/FX class, recording a 10.59 elapsed time @ 135 MPH. Les also set the *Drag News* A/FX class record at 10.39 @ 135.65 MPH.

For the 1966 season, when other Drag Council members received lighter, altered wheel base Mustangs for competition, Les Ritchey opted to remain with the A/FX class-legal car. His '65 mount was repainted a beautiful shade of red with Mel Burns Ford livery.

The description of Les Ritchey in the official Ford Motor Company press packet reads as follows:

> Les Ritchey's reputation as a driver is exceeded only by his reputation as a preparer of fast cars. A 42-year-old veteran of 12 years of competition, Ritchey owns Performance Associates, a sophisticated high-performance shop in Covina, CA, where some of the best-known drag cars in the country are meticulously prepared for the strip. Not as active as some racers because of his work in the shop, Ritchey manages to win more than his share of drag titles. This season, as last, he is campaigning an A/FX Mustang powered by a 427 cubic inch, single overhead cam engine. The highlight of Ritchey's competitive career came in September last year during the NHRA Nationals, when he defeated a top field to win the A/FX class championship. In the final run he put down Gas Ronda in a Mustang that he helped to prepare. Ritchey won almost 50 trophies last year as he also took class honors in the AHRA Nationals and was divisional points runner-up to earn a trip to the NHRA World Championships at Tulsa. He also was *Drag News'* Top Stock Eliminator on the West Coast. Ritchey has had a long association with Ford products, both as a driver and as a preparer of cars. In 1956 and 1957 he was virtually unbeatable driving a Ford powered by a 312 cubic inch V-8. His Galaxie with a 406 cubic inch engine was the country's fastest A/FX car in 1962. In 1963 and 1964 he was a top Super Stock competitor. In addition to his activity on the drag strip Ritchey has driven drag boats and engaged in some marathon boat racing in the past. Among his achievements is a Golden Gloves boxing title won in 1940 when he was attending junior college. Les and his wife Patricia live in Covina with their four children.

Les Ritchey died on May 1, 1966 as a result of injuries received in a racing accident. On that day the world lost one of the true innovators and icons of the sport of drag racing. His son Randy has continued Les's legacy through the continued operation of Performance Associates in San Dimas, CA, where some of the nation's best-performing Ford products are still built.

CHAPTER 3

GAS RONDA

THE MAN WHO BROUGHT CLASS TO DRAG RACING

"I had all these nice expensive clothes and I thought, 'Why should I go out and buy Levi's?' I never even had a pair of Levi's on."
— Gas Ronda, 2010.

Question: How did it all begin for you?

Gas: "I came from a very poor background and after coming out of the service after World War Two I found that I had an aptitude for dancing and thought I could make a living at it. There was a couple offering dance instruction. You had to master five steps and I completed the course in no time, so they hired me to be an instructor. Ladies would pay to dance with me and I danced with them all, fat ones, skinny ones, it didn't matter. After a while I went out on my own and eventually owned a series of dance studios."

Question: What got you interested in racing?

Gas: "I got interested in racing as a hobby and my first race car was a Hudson Hornet. I was disappointed with how the Hudson ran so I called Marshal Teague, who was a Hudson team driver, and complained to him that I wasn't doing well. He told me what parts I needed to get from the dealer and from then on I started winning."

Question: What came after the Hudson?

Gas: "In 1953 I opened a dance studio in Hayward, CA, next to a Buick dealership. The owners of the dealership, Bob Swiekert and Chet Richards, talked me into trying a Buick, so I bought a '54 Century. I was doing pretty good with my Buicks when one day in 1957 this Ford flies by me making this strange whistling sound. I went over and asked the guy what kind of engine he had and he told me it was a supercharged 312. That guy was Les Ritchey. I asked him if he could build one of those engines for my ski boat and he said ok. I entered my boat in a race at Lake Tahoe and won it going away. That's how I met Les."

In 1960 Gas turned to Ford for his next drag car, a 1960 Starliner equipped with Ford's first dedicated high-performance engine since 1957, the 360-horsepower 352. With the Starliner Ronda dominated the Super/Stock class at his home track in Half Moon Bay, CA.

"I remember on one occasion there were twenty Chevys and me entered in the class," Gas said. "At the end of the day there was just me."

Gas Ronda would rather be different and face long odds on the track than go along with the crowd. As he told one interviewer, he had tried a Corvette for a time in the late fifties but found no challenge beating Chevys with a Chevy.

At the same time Gas was racing his 1960 Starliner, a young salesman at Bill Waters Ford in Oakland, CA, named Ed Terry was racing one of his own. By his own admission Terry looked up to Gas as an older-brother figure.

"Ed could never beat me with his Starliner so one time I let him drive mine and I got in his," Gas said. "I still beat him."

In 1961 Bill Waters Ford added Gas Ronda to its sales team. A 1961 Starliner equipped with one of the new 401-horsepower 390 engines was next in a series of hot Ford race cars Ronda would field.

When speaking with Gas I asked him to elaborate on his racing activities in 1961. He informed me that he "really didn't do much" with the aforementioned 1961 Starliner. An account of Gas' success with the '61 car as related by his friend and fellow drag team member Ed Terry tells a different story.

As Ed recalls the promoter of Fremont Raceway in northern California had taken a cue from the southern tracks and began to pay towing and appearance money for Super Stock racers. The promoter's Northern California Nationals in 1961 attracted many of the hottest Super Stock drivers in the nation. In attendance were Dick Landy, Jess Tyree, Butch Leal, and none other than Dyno Don Nicholson with his Winternationals-winning 409 Chevy. According to Ed the crowd numbered in the thousands and traffic backed up on the freeway leading to the track for some miles. Gas Ronda was entered that day as well, and when the final round for the Super Stock class championship was called all the "big names" had been eliminated, leaving Gas to face Don Nicholson.

When Ronda's Ford defeated him in the final, Nicholson was so incredulous that he approached the track promoter and offered to put up $100 of his own money (a princely sum in 1961) if a rematch against the upstart could be arranged. The rematch was promptly set and, much to the chagrin of the man who had bragged to a scribe from *Hot Rod* magazine how he had not been beaten by a Ford since getting his new 409 Chevy, "Dyno" saw the Starliner's taillights a second time. Gas collected the $100 and left no doubt as to his driving skills or the power of his 390 Ford.

I also found an amusing reference to Ronda's '61 in a copy of *Drag News* from February 1961 that reports not only did Gas win the Super Stock class on that particular date at Half Moon Bay, recording a 13.42 @ 109.47 MPH, but he also won

At the 1962 NHRA Nationals, Gas Ronda's Bill Waters Ford lightweight Galaxie was fitted with steel parts in order to compete in the SS/S, where it would be more competitive. While Gas ran well, lack of testing and preparation time doomed his efforts. (Rick Kirk)

Gas' '62 lightweight was re-bodied as a 1963 1/2 Galaxie. As usual Ronda had one of the best-appearing and -running cars wherever he raced. While the accounts of certain auto magazines tell us the '63 cars were not competitive, the record books tell a different story. Ronda had moved to Southern California and was working at Downtown Ford by this point. (Jim Demmitt, Jr.)

$50 as the result of a side wager in a special match race. Gas faced off against "The world's greatest bull thrower," who apparently bragged that he could take Ronda over the first 100 feet.

By mid 1962 Ford had introduced the 406 cubic inch, 405-horsepower version of the FE engine. The Bill Waters Ford racing team fielded a black Galaxie 500 with Gas Ronda at the wheel. While the big Ford gave up cubic inches, horsepower, and had a weight disadvantage to the competition in the Super/Stock class, Ronda's driving skill often allowed him to prevail. Gas advanced through several rounds of competition at the 1962 NHRA Winternationals before bowing out. He only narrowly lost the California State Super Stock Championship to Hayden Proffitt.

With the formation of the Ford Drag Council later in the season, Gas Ronda and his friend Les Ritchey were selected as two of its charter members. Gas moved his base of operations to Southern California where Ritchey's shop was located. Both drivers were to receive lightweight Galaxies toward the end of the season, which barely were prepared in time for the NHRA Nationals in Detroit. "I was impressed by the '62 lightweight's performance potential but by the time we got them it was time to start working on the '63 cars," Gas said.

I have long harbored strong feelings over the bias shown by certain West Coast-based automotive publications against Fords. In particular for the last four decades it has been parroted, even by Ford-dedicated magazines, that the 1963 1/2 lightweight Galaxies were no match for the Chevys, Pontiacs, and Chryslers of the time. This was a major motivation behind the writing of my first book, *Total Performers*, and has been the impetus for my ongoing research into Ford's drag racing efforts during the 1960s. While perusing just a handful of *Drag News* papers from 1963, I noted the following regarding Gas Ronda's success with his lightweight Galaxie:

• On March 3, 1963 Gas took home S/S class honors with a 12.47 @ 115.30 mph. at Long Beach, CA.
• On May 25, 1963 Gas claimed the class title at San Gabriel with a 12.25 @ 116.16 mph.
• On the following day, May 26, 1963, the S/S win at Long Beach went to Gas Ronda's Ford with a 12.32 @ 116.16 mph.
• On June 22, 1963, Ronda was back at San Gabriel to once again take the class with a 12.25 @ 116.27 mph.
• June 23, 1963, found Gas Ronda in the

These contemporary ads which appeared in *West Coast Drag News* and *National Dragster* show just how serious Ford Motor Company and certain of their dealers, in this case Downtown Ford, were about performance in 1963. Note that Gas Ronda is Director of High Performance Sales.

winner's circle at Pomona by virtue of a 12.48 @ 115.08 mph.

• In their reporting of the festivities at San Gabriel on July 6, 1963, *Drag News* reported "Gas Ronda did it again when he beat Dave's Chevron (Dodge) with a 12.28 @ 115.23."

The publication *Super Stock Annual* for 1963 captioned a photo of Ronda's 1963 1/2 Ford Galaxie, "Californian Gas Ronda made Ford believers out of a lot of Chevy fans on his trip to the East Coast with his '63 427 Downtown Ford."

East Coast *Drag News* reported on a four-way match race that took place at York U.S. 30 on September 21, 1963 during Ronda's East Coast tour. On this particular evening Gas' Ford faced off against the Z-11 '63 Chevy of Malcolm Durham and two hot 426 Max Wedge Mopars, with Ronda emerging victorious. Gas Ronda's light-

weight Ford could not only beat the best the other manufacturers had to offer in 1963, he could beat them in multiples.

If we are to believe the commonly reported "facts" that the 1963 1/2 lightweight Galaxies were no match for the competition in the Super Stock class, and the oft-repeated statement that "Fords didn't win any major events during the 1963 season," wouldn't we also have to believe that on the above dates there were no Chevys, Pontiacs, or Chrysler products in attendance at the drag strips listed? Perhaps Mr. Ronda was far luckier than he was good and faced only other inferior Fords in class runoffs, or soloed for the win in each case? I think not.

For those not familiar with the NHRA schedule for the 1963 season I would like to point out that there were exactly two National events for the year. The first was the Winternationals at Pomona, CA, where the lightweight Fords were too few in required production numbers to be considered legal for Super/Stock class competition and thus were forced into the short-lived predecessor to the A/Factory Experimental class, L/P, standing for Limited/Production. At this event the L/P class was won by a Chevy that was later declared illegal upon post-race teardown, thus nullifying the class. The second NHRA National event for 1963 was the Nationals, where the lightweight Fords were found in S/S class competition. The class final found the Ed Martin Ford lightweight Galaxie facing a 426 Plymouth, with the latter taking the win. However, once again a post-race teardown showed the winning car to have an illegal camshaft. Again, instead of awarding the win to the Ford, NHRA nullified the class entirely, as was its practice.

Gas Ronda received one of the first 11 Thunderbolts built by Dearborn Steel Tubing Company in 1964. Originally painted Vintage Burgundy and carrying Downtown Ford sponsorship, Gas' Thunderbolt is seen in action early in the year. (R. Ladley collection)

On October 22, 1963, Gas Ronda was in attendance at the Ford Proving Grounds as the members of the Drag Council received the first eight 1964 Fairlane Super Stock drag cars, which were soon to become known as Thunderbolts. Ronda's car (#6, bearing VIN 4F41K118358) recorded three runs with Ford test driver Dan Jones at the wheel, with a best elapsed time of 12.18 @ 120.46 MPH. After taking delivery of the car, Ronda had it prepared for competition at the Performance Associates facility of his friend and teammate Les Ritchey. According to a report submitted to Ford, Ronda defeated all comers to win the Super/Stock class at Long Beach, CA with an 11.74 @ 121.00 MPH.

Gas and his Thunderbolt appeared again at the NHRA Winternationals, where he took home all the marbles in the hotly contested Super/Stock class over some of the quickest cars in the nation, including many of his Ford Drag Council teammates. According to Charlie Gray's report on the Drag Council members and other Ford products, Ronda claimed the class win with a 12.05 @ 120.16 MPH. From this point forward there would be no stopping Gas Ronda. He blistered the competition from coast to coast on his way to the NHRA World Championship, helping deliver to Ford its first manufacturers championship in the series.

Ronda's Thunderbolt undergoes driveline maintenance between rounds on the way to the 1964 National Championship. (Mark Ascher)

On May 11, 1964, Ronda's race report indicates that while running on 7" tires at Pomona, CA he won everything with a best of 11.60 @ 123.79 MPH.

On June 7, 1964 Ronda took home class and Top Stock Eliminator honors at Pomona, CA with an 11.91 @ 122.00 MPH.

Over the weekend of June 13-14, 1964, the NHRA National Championship drag races were held at Riverside, CA, where Gas Ronda took home Top Stock Eliminator honors with a best of 11.95 @ 122.48 MPH. At this event Ronda defeated teammate Butch Leal in the semifinal round and dropped the Lawman Plymouth of Al Eckstrand in the final.

On June 21, 1964, Gas Ronda took home Super/Stock and Top Stock Eliminator honors at Kingman, AZ. He took the lead in series points and laid down a best of 11.92 @ 121.78 MPH.

On August 23, 1964, Ronda increased his points lead while taking home class and Top Stock Eliminator honors at Julesburg, CO. Ronda also set a new track record with a 123 MPH pass.

By October 1964, Gas Ronda had wrapped up both the NHRA Division 7 and NHRA Top Stock World Championships.

During the season he changed the sponsorship and livery of his Thunderbolt from Downtown Ford and Vintage Burgundy to Russ Davis Ford and Poppy Red. Aside from his great-looking cars, Gas also brought his sharp dressing style to drag racing.

Question: Gas, you were always impeccably dressed at the track and your cars always looked great. Was this something you set out to do from the beginning?

Gas: "When I had the dance studios I had to be well-dressed, so when I started drag racing I had all these expensive clothes and I thought, 'Why should I go out and buy Levi's?' I never had a pair of Levi's on in my life. I learned a lot about marketing through my dance studio business and

The always dapper Ronda leans against his 1965 A/FX Mustang in the staging lanes. Ronda actually had two A/FX Mustangs in '65, having wrecked his first one when an axle broke during testing. (Martino family)

For 1966 Ronda received a Holman-Moody-built, "stretched" Mustang. He began the year with carburetion of the SOHC 427 engine but had to eventually convert to fuel injection to keep pace with the Chrysler team's Funny Cars. Gas would be the first fuel injected Funny Car into the 8-second range. (L. Wolfe)

that appealed to the sponsors. I always took great care in how the cars were lettered and how myself and my crew looked. Ford liked it because I represented their product well."

Gas took delivery of one of the Holman-Moody-built 1965 A/FX Mustangs and, along with other team members' cars, it was prepared for competition at Les Ritchey's shop. After wrecking his first Mustang because a broken axle during testing at Lions, Ronda received the car that had been slated to be the "show car" by Ford. At the NHRA Winternationals Ronda fell victim to the same driveline failures that plagued other Drag Council members during the event, as the SOHC 427 engines proved too powerful for axles and rears. Once his driveline woes had been remedied, Ronda went on to set an A/FX class record at Carlsbad, CA, at 10.88 and later lowered his own record with a 10.87 pass.

At the 1965 AHRA Nationals, Gas faced off against a field containing some of the best A/FX cars in the nation. The rounds of competition were recorded as follows: First round, Gas defeated the Sites Brothers Plymouth 10.45 @ 134.12 to 10.72 @ 133.73. Second round, bye. Third round, Gas faced friend and team mate Les Ritchey's similar Mustang, and Gas prevailed. Final, against Bill Reick's *Quarterbender* Dodge. Ronda claimed the Mr. Super Stock title with a 10.43 @ 134.73 to a losing 10.84 @ 130.62. Gas would go on to lose the overall eliminator title to team captain Dick Brannan's *Bronco* Mustang in a handicap race.

In 1966 Gas Ronda was one of the first Drag Council members to receive a new Holman-Moody-prepared, long-nose Mustang Funny Car. NHRA was so taken aback by these cars that they were first classified as C/Fuel Dragsters. At the NHRA Winternationals Gas Ronda's Mustang took home the class championship over all the conventional dragsters in attendance.

The April 1966 issue of *Hi-Performance CARS* magazine contains coverage of the AHRA Western Super Stock Nationals held at Bee Line Dragway in Scottsdale, AZ. A crowd of more than 9,000 was on hand to watch top ranking drivers from 17 states do battle. The Unlimited Gas class title went

Following a short stint in a Ford factory team Super Stock 428 Cobra Jet Mustang and a largely unsuccessful 1968 season in his Funny Car, Gas debuted his new flip-top Mustang Funny Car for 1969. By this time the SOHC Ford engine had a supercharger and was running on high concentrations of Nitromethane. An explosion and fire would put an end to Gas' driving career early in 1970. (Hank Richards)

to Gas Ronda's Mustang, with a 10.77 @ 132.15 MPH over Shirley Shahan's Plymouth at 10.91 and 128.93 MPH. Ronda would finish out his day with a runner-up finish for the Overall Super Stock title to Dick Landy's Dodge.

Ronda also claimed both the Top Stock and Factory Experimental Fuel class titles at the AHRA Nationals in Ft. Worth, TX, winning eight straight rounds of competition along the way.

At the Bakersfield Fuel Fest, Gas, now running fuel injection on his SOHC 427 engine, took home all the marbles, posting a best elapsed time of 8.96 @ 155.75 MPH. *Drag News* reported that Gas, "gave the supercharged cars such as Tom Mc Ewen's LA Plymouth Dealers' Hemi Cuda and Maynard Rupp's *Chevoom* Chevy a good beating."

This was the same Tom Mc Ewen who had boasted that if his supercharged Hemi was ever beaten by an injected car he would "turn over the keys to him." Randy Ritchey points out that his late father's sense of humor would not allow him to pass up such an opportunity, and Les demanded that McEwen surrender his keys to Ronda. As Gas recalls, he informed McEwen that he had already won two Barracudas with his Ford racers and didn't care to have another. One week later at Fremont, Ronda posted an even quicker 8.75 @ 169.89.

Gas proudly recalls his defeat of the highly regarded Ronnie Sox in the final round of the *Drag Racing Magazine* East vs. West meet and his win at the AHRA World Finals, where he set yet another class record.

The official Ford Motor Company press release describing Gas Ronda read as follows:

> There is no more popular or successful competitor in southern California, the nation's hot bed of drag racing, than Gas Ronda, a former dance instructor who has given up the light fantastic toe for the heavy foot. Ronda ripped off triumph after triumph last year in his ultra lightweight Mustang powered by Ford's 427 cubic inch single overhead cam engine. He plans to continue racing the

same machine in 1967. The colorful Ronda has been racing for 16 of his 39 years and has won some of the sport's biggest championships. For the past seven years he has been competing in Ford products in Super Stock and Experimental classes. Besides his frequent match race triumphs, Ronda walked off with some major triumphs in 1966. He had one of his best weekends at the AHRA Nationals in Fort Worth, Texas when he won eight straight races over two days to capture both Top Stock and Factory Experimental Fuel honors. In addition he won the Unlimited Stock class in the Bakersfield, CA meet and took class honors in the NHRA Winter Nationals at Pomona, CA. In a match race at Long Beach, CA he reached a speed of 174 MPH.

Ronda did not opt to run his stretched '66 Mustang for the 1967 season, however. Instead he turned to Exhibition Engineering to build a radical, tilt-nose funny car based on the 1967 Mustang body style. With the loss of his friend and mentor Les Ritchey in May of 1966, Gas Ronda enlisted the skills of engine builder Ed Pink for the 1967 season. He ran as quick as 7.67 with fuel injection before eventually realizing that he would need to bolt on a supercharger for 1968 in order to keep pace with the competition.

Gas found out in short order that the '67 funny car was not properly constructed to handle the amount of power his supercharged engine produced on fuel, and handling problems plagued him during the 1968 season. Also, prior to the NHRA Winternationals Ronda had been tapped by Ford to drive one of the team's Cobra Jet Mustangs, which he dutifully did. Gas' Russ Davis Ford Cobra Jet Mustang was one of several automatic transmission-equipped team cars built to run in the SS/EA class. At the Winternationals

Seen here at the 2010 Hot Rod Reunion in Bowling Green, KY, Gas Ronda still makes personal appearances to sign autographs and answer questions from his many fans.

Ronda narrowly lost in class competition to the factory Dodge Dart of Dick Landy.

Looking forward to the 1969 season, Gas had Logghe Chassis build him a 1969 Mustang funny car, his most beautiful yet, which was also powered by an Ed Pink-prepared, supercharged, nitro-burning SOHC 427 engine. Featured on the cover of the August 1969 issue of *Car Craft* magazine, this car would prove to be as fast as it was beautiful. Ronda clocked a 7.90 elapsed time @ 184.04 MPH on his way to winning the Manufacturer's Championship race at OCIR.

Tragedy would befall Gas Ronda at the 1970 AHRA Winter Nationals at Bee Line Dragway in Arizona. An explosion and fire in his Mustang funny car left him with burns over 40 percent of his body. After spending many months recuperating, Gas hired Dick Poll to drive for him. But the partnership was short lived and Ronda retired from drag racing. After operating a successful restaurant for a number of years Gas is now comfortably retired in Palm Dessert, CA. He still makes appearances at motor sports events and has in recent years been honored by numerous organizations for his contributions to drag racing.

CHAPTER 4

LEN RICHTER (BOB FORD)

"**I was born April 1932** in Detroit, MI and started working for Ford at the Rouge Plant when I was seventeen years old. My first job was drilling holes in connecting rods. After leaving to serve five years in the Air Force I returned to Ford in January of 1956 and got a job as a test driver. I drove cars for octane, economy, braking, horsepower, torque, and acceleration tests.

"In 1961 my boss, Dave Evans, had Bill Humphrey, John Conrad, and myself doing quarter-mile tests. We ran various cars out at Detroit Dragway and eventually Charlie Gray called upon me to test the '62 Fords out at the Kingman, AZ proving grounds. The tests consisted of trying various differential ratios, carburetors, transmission gears, valve lash, etc. I was chosen because I was a very consistent driver."

Len, along with fellow test driver Bill Humphrey, participated in various Detroit-area drag racing events in 1961-62, testing the products of Ford against those of the other manufacturers in a more or less unofficial capacity prior to Ford's announced return to factory-supported motor sports later in 1962.

Question: Did you have any hot rods of your own back in those days?

Len: "I had a '52 Ford with a 312 in it that was my daily driver. It ran real good and I eventually put a four speed in it. It had an 1100 pound pressure plate and the pedal was real stiff, which made it pretty hard for my wife to drive. Whenever she dropped me off at work with the car the guys would laugh because she always spun the tires leaving the plant.

"In 1963 I was called on to drive the black Bob Ford lightweight Galaxie (one of the re-bodied 1962 lightweight cars). In the beginning Bill Humphrey drove the car at Saturday events and I drove it on Sunday. Eventually I got the job as sole driver of the car and competed with it locally, at the NHRA Nationals, and in match races, and I did real well against the Mopars. Then in 1964 I got the Thunderbolt and we traveled all over the country with that. The Thunderbolt was my favorite car.

"I was on loan to the race group for three years, so five days a week I tested components and then raced on the weekends. I hated to lose. My biggest win came at the AHRA Championships where I beat the Ramchargers. We would have taken the overall win at that event but suffered a mechanical problem on Sunday. The only time I lost with the Thunderbolt was when something broke."

An agreement was signed between Paul Harvey of Bob Ford, Inc. and Ford Motor Company

Ford test driver Len Richter drove the Bob Ford-sponsored 1963 1/2 lightweight Galaxie known as *Big Sam* during the 1963 season. One of two lightweights that Bob Ford sponsored that year, this one was a re-bodied 1962 lightweight Galaxie.

to sell Harvey the 1964 Fairlane Thunderbolt, VIN: 4F41K118368, for the amount of $1. This standard "dollar car" agreement was signed by all Drag Council members upon receipt of Ford race cars being supported by the company. Having Ford test driver Len Richter available to drive the car certainly helped the Bob Ford team. As noted in the race reports, Len Richter's victories with the car during the 1964 season were many.

Test driver Dan Jones of the Performance and Economy Deptartment made three quarter-mile passes in Thunderbolt #2 and recorded the following times:

Run #1: 12.17 @120.48 mph
Run #2: 11.95 @120.96 mph
Run #3: 12.06 @ 120.80 mph

These runs were made to establish a performance baseline prior to the delivery of the car to the Drag Council team member, which in this case was Bob Ford.

On November 10,1963, Bill Humphrey made exhibition runs in the Bob Ford Thunderbolt at International Raceways, Detroit, recording a best time of 12.12 @ 118.8 mph.

On November 17, 1963, at International Raceway Park, New Baltimore, MI, the Bob Ford Thunderbolt defeated Al Eckstrand's Plymouth, both Golden Commandos Plymouths (automatic and four speed) and Roger Lindamood's Dodge with a best time of 12.07.

On April 13, 1964, Paul Harvey, Vice President of Bob Ford, sent a letter to Dave Evans, Manager of Ford's Performance and Economy, Special Vehicles Department regarding the performance of the Bob Ford Thunderbolt in a match race against Roger Lindamood's Dodge at International Raceway Park. Harvey's letter begins with the exclamation, "Happy days are here again !!

Just wanted to take time out this morning to give you a brief resume of yesterday's match race between the Dodge factory-sponsored *Color me Gone* driven by Roger Lindamood and the Bob Ford Thunderbolt driven beautifully by Len Richter. As you are aware the Dodge is an automatic transmission, whereas we were running the four speed.

"This was to be a three out of five match race, but I didn't know, until it was announced over the loud speaker, that it was to be witnessed by 20 Regional Service Managers from the Dodge Division of the Chrysler Corporation. Evidently they were in town for some sort of meeting and were guests of International Raceway Park.

They were there to witness the massacre, and that is just what they witnessed, only to their dismay it went the wrong way. We won the first, second, and fourth race and turned the fastest E.T. and speed of the day on the last run, 11.92 and 121.63 mph.

"The new suspension on the Fairlane worked beautifully, nearly doing wheel stands on a 7" Bruce Super Stock tire. On all three of the winning runs we were a car length ahead of the Dodge when we shifted into second gear and on the top end we could pull the Dodge. Also, another thing of great importance, the crowd went wild with enthusiasm in seeing a Ford beat a Dodge.

"I want to take my hat off to Charlie Gray, Ernie Mac Ewan, Bill Holbrook, and Len Richter for the improvements they have helped me make on this car since the Winternationals. I think each of

Big Sam was a test bed for performance innovations in 1963. Seen here are modifications to the rear floor pan made to accommodate experimental traction bar mounts.

these four men deserve a lot of credit and I sincerely hope their efforts are recognized by the Ford Motor Company.

"Again Dave, I say *Happy days are here again !!*"

The "new suspension" referred to in Mr. Harvey's letter was a pair of 68-inch long traction bars designed and installed on the Bob Ford Thunderbolt by Ernie Mac Ewan, who was one of the unsung heroes working behind the scenes at Ford's Experimental Vehicles garage. The new bars extended from the rear axle housing to the transmission cross member and eliminated the "hop" or lift off the starting line created by the original design. The Bob Ford Thunderbolt also benefited from pair of front spindles that were 3" taller vertically, which no doubt aided weight transfer greatly. Later research on the 11 original Drag Council Thunderbolts by historian Dennis Kolodziej indicates that not all may have been so equipped. We do know for sure that along with the Bob Ford car, the Ed Martin T-Bolt and the Mickey Thompson "Hemi" car had the extended spindles.

On May 9, 1964, Len Richter brought home Top Stock Eliminator honors at Detroit Dragway, recording a 12.09 @ 119.04 mph.

On May 10, 1964, Richter defeated Dick Housey's Plymouth in a match race, running 11.97 @ 120.97 in the process.

On May 17, 1964, before 5,000 fans at Thompson Dragway, Len Richter took home the Mr. Stock Eliminator title.

On May 23, 1964, Len Richter took the Super/Stock class title at Detroit Dragway, but lost the Top Stock Eliminator runoff due to mechanical difficulties. Best E.T. and speed were 11.91 and 119 mph.

On May 24, 1964 at International Raceway Park in Anchorville, MI, Len Richter won a "highly promoted" Super Stock meet over a field of 12 Plymouths and Dodges. Richter's best pass was 11.72 @ 122.9 mph.

On May 30, 1964, Richter took home Top Stock Eliminator honors at Detroit Dragway, defeating seven Chrysler products, including Roger Lindamood and Dick Housey, in the process. Best time recorded was 11.81 @ 124.30 mph.

On May 31, 1964, at Milan, MI, Richter downed Bill Shirey's *Mr. Professor* Plymouth three straight rounds with a best time of 11.37 @ 125.87 mph.

On June 6, 1964, Richter took home class and Street Eliminator at Detroit Dragway with a best of 11.61 @ 123 mph.

On June 13, 1964, Ford's weekly summary of performance events reported:

> Ford wins in AHRA National Championship drag racing. A 427 Fairlane, driven by Len Richter and sponsored by Bob Ford, Inc., won the coveted Mr. Stock

Len Richter was on hand in Dearborn, MI, when Ford turned over the newly released 1964 Fairlane Thunderbolts to the members of the Drag Council. Most of the top names in Ford drag racing are present in this photo. (D. Kolodziej)

Len Richter charges off the starting line at Detroit Dragway in the Bob Ford Thunderbolt. By this time the car had been repainted from Vintage Burgundy to black over gold. (D. Kolodziej)

Eliminator title at the American Hot Rod Association National Championship meet in Gary, IN, before a cheering crowd of 16,000 spectators. Richter won the title in a series of round robin eliminations in which all stock cars capable of covering the quarter mile in 12.5 seconds or less competed against each other regardless of class, without handicap. The eliminations were hotly contested with a field of 35 Chrysler Corporation products, including 10 super-lightweight hemi-head Dodges, making their best efforts. In the final run for the title Richter's Ford Fairlane defeated a Dodge, sponsored by the famous Ramchargers club, with a record-setting time of 11.37 seconds at 126.76 mph."

Always humble, Len is quick to point out that others deserve a great deal of credit for his racing successes. He particularly wished that Jim Vockler, Vern Tinsler, Bob Corn, and Danny Jones be recognized as instrumental behind-the-scenes members of the Ford Drag Council. And Bob LaFalla, a talented mechanic who also had his own small machine shop, was of great assistance in making one-off parts as needed. Len also points out that Don "Sully" Sullivan, who had worked on the original design for the flathead Ford V-8 engine introduced in 1932, was one of the most intelligent men he ever met—a sentiment echoed by Dick Brannan. It is likely that a fully-designed camshaft helped Len put the Bob Ford T-Bolt in the winner's circle, as it also had done for Brannan.

With the advent of "run what ya brung" match races, Len Richter and the Bob Ford team were ready for the best of them, no matter what "tricks" they brought to the track. The Bob Ford T-Bolt had two distinct personas in 1964. At NHRA or IHRA sanctioned events, where it competed in the Super/Stock or A/Factory Experimental class, the car was set up to strictly adhere to the rules. When

This shot shows Richter during performance testing with the Bob Ford Thunderbolt. Note the fifth wheel behind the car. (D. Kolodziej)

Len drops the hammer on the *Golden Commando* Plymouth. During the factory wars of 1964, Richter and the Bob Ford team gave the Chrysler guys fits from coast to coast. (D. Kolodziej)

Richter launches the Bob Ford T-Bolt at an AHRA event. Len would go on to win the 1964 AHRA Super Stock title over the Ramchargers Dodge. Richter had the car running low 11-second elapsed times at close to 130 MPH in 1964. (D. Kolodziej)

it came to match races it was all about who got to the other end of the track first, and at this point the gloves came off. Walter "Doc" Gould, a mechanic at the Bob Ford dealership, was kept quite busy exchanging components on the car according to the challenge at hand on each particular weekend.

The following is an example of how the car would be prepared for a match race with an agreed-upon minimum weight of 3,200 pounds. The car would be fitted with special lightweight front fenders and hood (described in a FoMoCo memo as "lightweight front sheet metal," but actually lighter versions of the Plaza fiberglass parts the car was fitted with by Dearborn Steel Tubing Co.). Weight would also be removed from other areas forward of the rear wheels. Accessories such as the wiper motor and linkage, horns, and so on, that were required for legal Super/Stock class competition would be removed. Weight was added back to the car and redistributed through the addition of a rear bumper filled with a heavy metal called Kirksite. Thus, with a rear bumper that weighed hundreds of pounds, the Thunderbolt would meet the minimum weight requirement for the match and at the same time gain some all-important traction off the starting line with a greater percentage of the car's weight at the rear. Another match race "trick" was the installation of a rudimentary propolyene oxide injection system that consisted of a small pump and reservoir positioned in the rear of the car. Flexible tubing carried this horsepower-adding chemical compound to the car's air intake ducts, where it could be introduced on demand into the engine's air/fuel mixture to increase power and performance.

"I studied flag men and I got pretty good at reading them," Len said. "When they came out with the Christmas tree starting system I remember Les Ritchey telling me to count, one, two three, four, and let the clutch out."

The Bob Ford Thunderbolt passed from the hands of Len Richter to Kenny Vogt for the 1965 season. A new yellow paint job and the name *Stinger I* distinguished the car. The class designation has also changed from Super Stock to A/Modified Production. (D. Kolodziej)

In July 1964 a white Mustang coupe, VIN 5F07F100028, was shipped from the Dearborn Assembly Plant to Ford sub-contractor Dearborn Steel Tubing Company. Modifications to the engine compartment similar to those performed on the Fairlane Thunderbolts were performed. Once the Mustang was converted to carry the FE series engine, it was transferred to the Experimental Vehicles Garage, where the metamorphosis from mundane to muscular continued. The car in question was to become Ford's first A/FX Mustang.

Power for the prototype Mustang came from a 427 High Riser engine equipped with the "7,000 RPM kit," which included lighter, sodium-filled exhaust valves. The engine was prepared by Kenny Salter of the Bob Ford racing team. The early, fragile aluminum-cased transmission was replaced by the stronger, albeit heavier, Ford T&C top-loader four speed. The nine-inch rear held 4.86 gears and a Detroit Automotive locker unit. The car featured custom-built headers and a non-functional single exhaust system that was required by NHRA class rules of the time. Traction was aided by 66-inch long, boxed-steel traction bars, clamped leaf springs, air lift air bags, and a trunk-mounted 45-pound battery.

To get the car down to just above the 3,200 pound A/FX class minimum weight, the front-end sheet metal and doors were replaced with fiberglass parts while Plexiglas replaced the windshield, backlight, and side windows. To accommodate driver Len Richter's gear banging requirements, parts from two Hurst shifters were first used, which were later replaced by a modified Ford shifter.

The *Hemi Haunter's* racing career proved to be a short one, however. After shakedown runs produced elapsed times in the mid-eleven second range, the car suffered various mechanical woes that ultimately sidelined it from competition at the NHRA Nationals. The availability of the Holman-Moody built, SOHC 427 powered A/FX Mustang fastbacks for members of the Drag Council saw the prototype car pass into the hands of Kenny Salter. The car ultimately met its demise in a racing accident.

Both Dick Brannan and Phil Bonner had gotten a pretty good jump on their fellow Drag Council members by each having built an A/FX Falcon in 1964 before the Mustang became available (Brannan's was built at Dearborn Steel Tubing company as an official Ford project and Bonner's was built independently by Phil with support from Ford). The Bob Ford *Hemi Haunter* and a second A/FX Mustang coupe built by Ron Pellegrini using parts from the Hawkinson Ford Thunderbolt get credit for being the first A/FX Mustangs. They would prove to be valuable test beds for things to come.

Prior to the NHRA Winternationals in 1965, the Bob Ford team took delivery of one of the Holman-Moody prepared, SOHC 427-powered, A/FX Mustangs (VIN 5F09K380237).

Question: Len what did you think of the new A/FX Mustang with the SOHC engine when you got it?

Len: "I was disappointed at first. We had a Mallory Roto-Faze ignition and the first time out with the car at Detroit Dragway the pick-up bulb (photo cell) in the distributor burned out. And the car just didn't seem to run like I thought it should. We had the car at Les Ritchey's shop and he re-did the cylinder heads. After that the car ran much better."

At the 1965 NHRA Winternationals Drag Council members Richter, Ronda, Brannan, Lawton, and Bonner fielded the SOHC 427-powered Mustangs in A/FX class competition against the best that Chrysler had to offer in the form of 426 Hemi-powered Dodges and Plymouths. All of the Ford team cars were plagued by rear axle and differential failures, which Richter attributed to the power of the SOHC 427 and the tire technology of the time. In spite of mechanical woes, Richter posted the best early elapsed time among the Mustangs with a 10.94, while Don Nicholson recorded a best of 10.90 for the factory Mercury Comets. On race day, however, favorites Nicholson, Brannan, and Ronda were eliminated because of parts breakage.

Richter and Bill Lawton marched through the field, however. The final run for the Mr. Factory Stock Eliminator title came down to the two Drag Council Mustangs, with Lawton taking the win

Len Richter at work in the Bob Ford 1965 A/FX Mustang. According to Len, after initial teething problems with the SOHC 427 engine were worked out by tuning ace Les Ritchey, the car came into its own. This car would be Len's last drag race ride; he went back to test-driver duties following the NHRA Spring Nationals. (L. Wolfe)

over a broken Richter on a solo pass. During class eliminations Len had taken the first-round win over the Ramchargers when driver Jim Thornton fouled away his chances. He nipped Gas Ronda in the second round 10.91 to 10.92. In the third round Richter's competition, George DeLorean in a factory Mercury Comet, red-lighted as Len limped through with the broken axle that would ultimately keep him out of the final against Lawton.

A sideplot at Pomona was the drama between the Chrysler teams and NHRA. The sanctioning body had been pretty specific in their rules regarding the legality of altered-wheelbase cars. As reported by *Super Stock and Drag Illustrated* magazine in their May 1965 issue, in an effort to comply with NHRA rules the Mopar teams appeared with Super/Stock cars that had been fitted with fiberglass body components. "They weren't the best Chrysler could have come up with to fit NHRA's A/FX class, but they still ran strong and helped round out a colorful factory experimental show," according to *SS and DI's* scribe. Do I detect a note of journalistic bias here?

Question: What can you tell us about the lettering on the front fender of the Mustang that read "Crew Chief Bill Halfbrook"?

Len: "Well, I wanted to put Bill Holbrook's name on the car and John Cowley didn't want it on there because of the connection to the factory. These were supposed to be dealer-sponsored cars. So we got around it by putting Bill Halfbrook on there instead of Bill Holbrook".

Question: Do you have any funny stories you'd like to share?

Len: "Yes, as the car kept getting faster we mounted a parachute on it to help slow it down on some of the shorter tracks, and I remember I only used the parachute twice. The first time I opened that thing the car slowed down so fast I almost broke my nose on the steering wheel."

Question: How did your participation in the racing program end?

The historic Mustang was driven by Len Richter, Jerry Harvey, Hubert Platt, and Don Nicholson before being turned into a street racer in New York. It has been restored to its former glory and is part of the Don Snyder, Jr. collection.

The Mustang's SOHC 427 engine has been restored to its configuration as raced by Len Richter in 1965 A/FX trim.

Len: "It was prior to the race at Bristol, TN and John Cowley had ordered that the car and engine be taken to Holman-Moody for some modifications. I didn't want anyone else to touch that engine, but these were Cowley's orders. Well whoever worked on the engine at H-M didn't tighten one of the camshafts down properly and didn't reinstall the baffled oil pan that we had worked so hard to perfect on the car. I got so disgusted that I quit and went back to being a special test driver. I was on loan to the race group for three years and all I did for five days a week was I tested components and then raced on the weekends. I retired from Ford in July 1994 after 45 years."

The Bob Ford A/FX Mustang next passed into the hands of Jerry Harvey, son of Mr. Paul Harvey, who had up to this point been driving the Bob Ford-sponsored *Quiet One* SOHC 427-powered '65 Galaxie with great success. In 1966 Paul Harvey left the Bob Ford agency and opened his own dealership, Paul Harvey Ford in Indianapolis. The former Bob Ford car would go on to have a long racing history in the hands of notable Ford drag racers Hubert Platt and Don Nicholson. Some years later the Mustang found its way into the hands of street racing drug dealers in the New York City area but was eventually purchased and restored to perfection. The car now resides in the collection of Don Snyder, Jr., and is one of the few original 1965 A/FX Mustangs in existence.

CHAPTER 5

TASCA FORD, BILL LAWTON / JOHN HEALEY

"Bob Tasca doesn't like to lose and I don't intend to lose" (Robert F. Tasca Sr.)

"I felt my Chevrolet was a winner. Then I got into a Ford and found out what a winner was" (Bill Lawton, December 1994)

"Someone once asked me, 'Do you have a college degree?' And I said, 'Certainly, I went to Tasca U'" (John Healey)

Sadly Bill Lawton left us in 1996 but I had the distinct pleasure of attending the grand re-opening of Tasca Ford at 777 Taunton Ave. East Providence, RI, in 1994. I sat in on an in-depth video interview of former Tasca team members by my friend Jim Amos. Jim has consented to share the words of the late Bill Lawton as recorded at that time in this work. In my transcript of excerpts from Jim's video interview with Bill Lawton you will see references by Bill to "The Bopper" or "The Big Bopper." This was a reverent nickname given to the late Robert F. Tasca, Sr., by the members of the Tasca Ford race team.

BILL LAWTON

Question: You were a Chevy guy right?

Bill: "I had a 409 Chevy, '62, four-speed, 4.56 Positraction. It had all the goodies that Chevrolet had. And one night I came up here for the Bopper and I discussed it with him and I told him, "Fix Or Repair Daily." And he aggravated me back. Oh yeah, he's good at that."

Question: Now this was a street racing kind of deal?

Bill: "Oh yeah. We had places here we called the Pink Elephant and Richard's Drive-In and the Kings of the Road, that kind of deal."

Question: You were the boss?

Bill: "Well, I used to win my share of the races. And Ford to that point, 1961, they didn't have anything. I started with a '57, then a '58 Impala. And then I had a '60 Impala with a 348 and three deuces, the 335 horsepower one. Then I had a '61 Corvette, 283 with 315 horse. I used to beat all the Fords. Well, I mean the 390 Fords, they didn't have anything in those days. And then they came out with the 406 in '62 and they finally had a decent engine with the tri-power on it. But up to that point they were no threat to the Chevrolets, unfortunately. Of course I was a Chevrolet guy anyway, to that point."

Author's note: Perhaps Bill Lawton's perception of how competitive the offerings of Ford Motor Company were up to that point may have been based on his experiences locally and not necessarily on what had been happening elsewhere in the country.

Question: If you were so entrenched in the Chevys, how did Bob Tasca convince you to come over to Ford?

Bill Lawton looks out proudly from behind the wheel of the Tasca Ford 1962 Super/Stock 406 Galaxie at the 1962 NHRA Nationals. The Tasca team took three cars to the Nationals that year in its first foray into drag racing on a national level. (Rick Kirk)

Bill: "We were preparing my car and it wasn't quite ready and I happened to be down at Charleston Dragway. They had taken their new Tasca car, the Ford, the '62 down. They had three or four guys try to drive it and they didn't do too good with it. And then the Bopper said to me. 'Why don't you try to drive a good car?' And I said, 'No Fix Or Repair Daily cars for me.' And then Dean Gregson came over and said 'Try it. Mr. Tasca really wants you to drive it.' So he said just take it somewhere in the back there (meaning not out on the dragstrip) and try it. If you don't like it, don't drive it. But I know you're going to like it. So I said ok. Well, I took it in the back and I never felt anything with that kind of power."

Question: More than your 409?

Bill: "You gotta be kidding me. My 409 was a sled compared to that thing."

Bill then explained how he informed Bob Tasca that the clutch was slipping in the car and, over John Healey's objections, Tasca ordered the clutch replaced.

Bill: "They changed the clutch and we ran 13.36 and set low E.T. and high miles per hour for the meet. That's how it all started."

Question: Did people call you a traitor?

Bill: "They said, 'what the heck are you driving a Ford for?' And I said, 'because it's faster and it's a better car.' It was a race car, but that's what I liked about drag racing then. You could take the tires off, open the exhaust, take the hubcaps off and go racing. Come back, put the stuff on, and go home. That was great because anybody could be [a drag racer]."

Question: You had a team behind you. John Healey gets credit for the wrenching. What did you know about the mechanics of the car?

Bill: "Nothing."

Question: You were just a hired gun?

Bill: "I didn't want to know anything about the mechanics. I don't claim to be any great wrench or anything. I could change spark plugs and stuff. You know I knew how to feel the car. I had a lot of feeling for the car and I could tell John what I wanted, or what I needed, or whatever I thought had happened. We had a great team me and John. We really worked together. And I'll tell you it was a great racing team all the way up to the fuel."

Question: In 1962, in your first ride now and you start rubbing elbows. You go from being a street racer here in Providence and all of a sudden you find yourself in Detroit. You're at the pinnacle of Ford Motor Company in the Experimental Vehicles Garage. What was that like? How did it affect you?

Bill: "It was a dream. It was fantastic. It's something that anybody who has any feeling or love of racing, they would die to get. I just happened to be a lucky guy. I was in the right place at the right time and I had the ability naturally. Because if I didn't have the ability I wouldn't have been there. But to rub elbows with those kind of people, it was just unbelievable. I was a kid from Rhode Island. What did I know?"

Question: Most people will associate your speed in shifting. You made them change gears like they were automatics. But there was more to it back then because what you didn't have was the tire technology. You had a very primitive approach to traction packages on the car. It took other things like driving skill too didn't it?

Bill: Oh, you had to know how to feather the clutch with those tires and, you know, feather the carburetors and work the clutch with the carburetors without smoking the tires. Because it was very easy to break the tires loose with that kind of power. It was amazing. Don't forget we used to run 32 pounds of air in those tires. Thirty two pounds. You know why? We tried to get the profile of the tire to go straight across. As the tire grew the center would blow out and the ends would go up, so you had no traction. We were actually on a seven inch tire and we only got three inches of the pattern on the ground. Marvin from M&H finally figured this out. But I'll tell you what we did. We started dropping the air pressure. That got pretty hairy. That was dangerous."

Question: Who thought of that?

Bill: "I think it was Marvin told us to drop the air pressure down to like 22 and we found the tire bit good. Then all of a sudden I figure, well gee 22, let's try 15. We tried 15 and it bit good but what happened was the car didn't handle on the other end. It used to start dancing. But we had to put up with it because we started winning races. And then he came out with his 8-inch slick. You couldn't use it for Super Stock though because we were limited to a 7-inch tire."

Question: Did you use it in match racing?

Bill: " Oh sure in match racing, and we found that we had the power to compete with any Chrysler. Of course Chevrolet was right there too."

Question: Did you feel the pressure having to run against Stickler, Ronnie Sox, Malcolm Durham, and those guys?

Bill: "No, because we never raced them. We were local. We ran at Charleston, Connecticut Dragway, Sanford, and Orange. Then we put a team together for the '62 Nationals. We brought three or four cars. We had a car carrier and loaded it in the rain. One of the race cars fell off the trailer. We had an A/FX car on the bottom it was the '62 with the fiberglass nose. The top car leaked and it ate the fiberglass. What a mess. So we get to the Nationals and this is when I met all these big names in drag racing for the first time. And what happened is John had gone to this place called Simplex, it was a machine shop, and they milled the heads wrong. Every time I made a run I'd bend the valves. We didn't do too good that year."

Question: What did that do to you?

Bill: "Well, it was very depressing, but it gave us the goal. We wanted to do good now. You know what I do remember about that year? They let us

Tasca Ford raced this 1963 1/2 lightweight Galaxie in the Super/Stock class with John Healey building the engines and Bill Lawton driving. A sign in the window tells how to reach Dean Gregson, Tasca's High Performance manager. Perhaps no Ford dealer was more serious about performance than Tasca Ford. The small Rhode Island dealership had 18 lightweight Galaxies on its lot at one point. (Alan Wood, Don Keinath)

drive the race cars on the street if we wanted. They made an announcement if you wanted to drive the cars within the city limits it was ok with the cops. They figured it would create interest with the people. I drove the race car to the local drive in. Here I am, the car's all lettered up, the headers are wide open and I'm ordering a burger and a soda. I was making blasts down the street, the people loved it. I swear to God it was great."

Question: Now in '63 you got two cars?

Bill: "In '63 we had three cars. We had the '63 1/2 Super Stock, we had a '63 1/2 A/FX Galaxie, and Ford gave us a Fairlane prototype to run in A/FX."

Question: Did you drive all of them?

Bill: "No, I drove two of them and this other kid from Connecticut drove one of them. He drove the A/FX car I believe. That's the only other time anybody drove a Tasca car. And that was the end of that, he didn't do too good."

Author's note: Bill may have mixed up the '62 and '63 Tasca race car lineups here, as in '62 they had both the Super Stock and A/FX Galaxies and the A/FX car was driven by someone other than Bill.

Bill: "You know I had a chance in the A/FX car to win? And you know what happened? Believe it or not there was somebody at Ford that had this notion in his head that we should run a Ford linkage.

Question: In the shifter?

Bill: Yeah, they said this would not break, would not do nothing and believe it or not I had a shot to win A/FX. This car was running like a bear. The Super Stock, no, because again it was with those stupid cheater slicks."

Question: And the Super Stock car had the Low Riser while the A/FX car had the High Riser?

Bill: "We had all the best that Ford had to offer. We had a shot. I got to the first round, I can't remember who I was running, and I was beating him and I never missed a gear. I just banged it and when I went to third there was no linkage. It was gone. I don't know what happened. And I'll tell you, the Bopper, he was very upset. He said he didn't care who thought whatever, we were going to put the best equipment in our cars to win the races and that was it. He was upset. We were all upset because this was '63 and Tasca Ford, we had a shot to win something, right?"

Author's note: The event that Bill Lawton is referring to was the 1963 NHRA Nationals, where it was mistakenly reported by automotive publications of the time that Bill Humphries was the driver of the Tasca Ford A/FX Fairlane. This mistake was repeated in my previous books, *Total Performers* and *Factory Lightweights*. Bill Lawton would later go on to set the NHRA A/FX class miles per hour record with the Fairlane at 121 MPH.

Question: In '62 you were on the outside looking in and in 63 you were right there?

Bill: "We were right there with the A/FXer."

Question: 1964: T-Bolt time.

Bill: "You know I'm very hazy. I don't remember that. I don't even remember what we did. I remember picking the car out of a hat."

Question: Out of a hat?

Bill: "We picked the cars out of a hat."

Question: The eleven Drag Council cars?

Bill: "There were eight cars. Each car had a number on it and they were lined up in order."

Question: This was at Dearborn?

Bill: "Yes, it was at the test track. Ford had all this hullabaloo stuff. They had these cars there and we were going to pick them. But you know I remember every other car after that, but I don't remember what happened."

Question: Well, you've got to remember one thing. You ran the *Lawman* car with it.

Bill: "Oh, I remember that stuff. I don't remember Indy. I don't remember what we did, nothing. It must have been terrible. Maybe my mind doesn't want to remember it. Let's see, we picked the car up, get it all ready, brought it back, we ran it. The car never did anything great. Because you see what happened was the Ford engineers, John Healey and everybody, all the team members would discuss what we were doing. Of course they would never give us all their secrets, they always kept that little tenth behind. But we were supposed to. But the deal was that the Drag Council members were supposed to discuss what we were doing with the cars. Because if you found fifty horsepower you were supposed to give it to everybody else. Now you know racers. You might give the other guy thirty but you had to have that little edge. And so what happened was we put so much power into this car that the seven-inch slick was useless. I couldn't even feather the clutch anymore. I mean I just couldn't come out you know? And I don't remember what happened, but in the middle of the year when we got our little kit."

Question: Kit? Is that what you called it?

Bill: "That's what I called it, the kit. We had gotten beat by Eckstrand and we were humiliated to tell you the truth. It was in New Jersey. And as you know the Bopper got on the microphone, which I thought was great, and he says, 'I'm going to be like Mac Arthur. We will return,' and we did. And we blew the doors off him. As a matter of fact his guys changed engines, they changed the headers, they did everything. I don't mean we beat him, we destroyed him."

Question: What was the kit?

Bill: "The kit was fender wells. It moved the wheelbase up. And we had to put the fender well in, the fiberglass nose and the fiberglass doors, and then we could put on the big tires. Because you see by altering the wheel well it made room for the big tire. It wasn't basically to get the wheels behind the engine. The big wheel well was for the big slick. The seven-inch tire we could just about get in there because it was a stock wheel well, you see?

The 427-powered 1963 Fairlane build by Dearborn Steel Tubing as the "mule" for the Thunderbolt project was delivered into the hands of Tasca Ford during the season. Driven by both Ford test driver Bill Humphrey and Billy Lawton, the car appeared on its way to an A/FX class win at the 1963 NHRA Nationals until a missed shift put it out of competition. Lawton would later set the NHRA A/FX class MPH record with the car. (Alan Wood)

And anyway we put the big tires on it and that's all it took. From that moment on we were winners.

Author's note: The "kit" that Bill refers to consisted merely of wheel well modifications that allowed for a bigger tire. But it seems that performance advances made by Ford, with considerable input from Tasca engine man John Healey, in the form of cylinder head modifications that included lightweight valves and an improved rotating assembly, may have escaped the driver's attention at the time. Period documents refer to upgrades made to the 427 High Riser engine at the time as 'the 7,000 RPM kit' and were no doubt a factor in providing an edge to the Ford teams. Robert F. Tasca, Sr. spoke of exerting his considerable influence upon Ford engineers to develop cylinder heads that would provide the additional horsepower needed to regain parity with the Chrysler teams during this time of escalation in the manufacturer's horsepower race. There was also what Ford referred to as a lightweight sheet metal package, which was in reality fiberglass doors and thinner fiberglass fenders and hood.

The Tasca team's early successes with the Thunderbolt are chronicled in the weekly race reports filed with Ford by each team. In the report filed regarding the testing and evaluation of the Drag Council Thunderbolts on October 31, 1963, the following is indicated for the Tasca Ford car: Vehicle #8 (Tasca) Run #1: 12.39 @ 118.73 MPH; Run #2: 12.37 @ 119.52 MPH. At this point it is noted that the carburetor jets were changed to #73 in the primaries and #75 in the secondary, after which three more runs were made with the car. Run #3: 12.29 @ 119.20 MPH; Run #4: 12.14 @ 119.68 MPH; and Run #5: 12.07 @ 119.84 MPH.

On November 20, 1963 the Tasca Ford team reported that they had made a total of 10 test runs with the car at Connecticut Dragway, posting a best elapsed time of 11.75 @ 124.48 MPH with an average over the ten runs of 11.79 @ 123.6 MPH.

While Bill did not mention the 1964 NHRA Winternationals, and the record books indicate the Tasca Ford team did not win at this event, Lawton was nonetheless rewarded for his efforts there. In a letter dated March 9, 1964, Frank Zimmerman congratulated both Lawton and Phil Bonner, informing them that by virtue of their individual performances at the Winternationals the drivers had won an inter-Ford Drag Council competition for its East Coast members. Bill Lawton received complimentary passes to the 1964 Indianapolis 500 as thanks.

On May 25, 1964, Dean Gregson reported that the Tasca team had run a best-of-five match race against Dave Strickler's A/FX Dodge at Connecticut Dragway on May 22. In his report Gregson questioned if the Dodge would even have met A/FX class rules, citing one hundred and eighty pounds of ballast mounted in the car's trunk and the alteration of its wheelbase. He went on to note that the Tasca car was run as a legal Super Stock entry. The best elapsed time for the Tasca team in a losing effort against the Dodge was 11.58 @ 124.64 MPH.

On June 1, 1964, Bill Lawton and his Tasca Ford Thunderbolt won the Super Stock Bonanza at Vineland, NJ, with a best elapsed time and speed of 11.78 @ 122.95 MPH. The following day Lawton took home Super/Stock class honors and Top Stock Eliminator with a best of 11.82 @ 121 MPH at the NHRA Divisional Championships held in Richmond, VA. At the same event the Tasca car won a match race against the Manchester Motors Mercury Comet in three straight runs.

On August 2, 1964 the Tasca team was back at Vineland where Bill Lawton was a runner-up

Tasca Ford received this 1964 Fairlane Thunderbolt along with other Drag Council members late in 1963. With John Healey's preparation and Bill Lawton's driving skills, the car had become nearly unbeatable later in the 1964 season. Lawton set both NHRA and NASCAR national records with the Thunderbolt. (Mark Ascher)

Bill Lawton in the Tasca Ford Thunderbolt goes off against Bill Gray in the Reynolds Ford T-Bolt for the N.Y. State Super Stock Championship. Lawton was able to overcome Gray's hole shot for the win. (Mike Gray)

to teammate Butch Leal's Thunderbolt by virtue of a red light in the final round of Super/Stock competition.

On September 13, 1964, at Connecticut Dragway, the Tasca team accepted a challenge from Harris Auto Hemi Head Dodge, which had just defeated Malcolm Durham's Chevy in a match race. Bill Lawton prevailed over the Dodge with an 11.03 @ 124.9 MPH to the Dodge's 11.22 @ 124 MPH.

On September 22, 1964, at Cecil County, MD. Bill Lawton won the Super/Stock class at the Divisional Championships and while doing so established a new NHRA record for the class at 11.69. He defeated Bud Faubel's Dodge in Stock Eliminator runoffs.

Ford's Drag Racing Achievements report for 1964, filed on October 21, reported that Bill Lawton was the NHRA Division 1 Champion in the Super Stock Class with the Tasca Ford Thunderbolt and that he claimed the New York State Super Stock Championship over Mike Gray's Reynolds Ford Thunderbolt.

At the 1965 NHRA Winternationals in Pomona, CA, Bill Lawton and the Tasca Ford team, in their new '65 Mustang, claimed their biggest win to date when they triumphed over a stellar field of factory-supported cars to claim the title of Factory Stock Eliminator. While other members of the Ford Drag Council had been plagued by broken axles due to the power the new SOHC 427 engines were capable to putting to the ground, the Tasca team rolled through the Eliminator unscathed.

In the first round of competition Lawton faced none other than "Dyno Don" Nicholson in his Mercury Comet. Bill prevailed over Nicholson, who broke, with an easy 11.59 E.T. Lawton's opponent in the second stanza was Dick Branstner of the Ramchargers, whom Bill dispatched with a 10.95. Tommy Grove in the feared *Melrose Missile* Plymouth fell next with a 10.95 to Lawton's winning 10.93. And when Drag Council teammate Len Richter was unable to answer the call for the final round due to mechanical woes, Bill singled into the Winner's Circle with a 10.92 @ 128.20 MPH.

Bill: "And that car, from that day forward won everything. We just couldn't lose. It was amazing. And then the greatest race, I say it to this day, I don't care which race you talk about."

Question: The *Super Stock* Nationals?

Bill: "That had to be the greatest race in drag racing's history. It was just unbelievable. *Super Stock* magazine at that time was the number one magazine and everybody wanted to get into *Super Stock* magazine. So what happened was *Super Stock* said they were having a magazine race. They wanted everybody to come and guess what? They all went. Everybody you could think of was there. Spaulding, The Ramchargers, all the Dodges, Harrop the Arab, Bud Faubel, the *Lawman*. Butch Leal was there, the *Melrose Missile* was there."

Author's note: At the 1965 *Super Stock* Nationals in York, PA, considered by most to be the greatest drag racing event of all time, Bill Lawton wheeled the Tasca Ford A/FX Mustang to a win in the Overall Handicap Eliminator class over a stellar field, beating Cecil Yother's Plymouth in the final.

Question: At this point we're talking about stock-looking, stock-acting cars. The '65 Mustang, the T-Bolt, the full-size cars and things like that. Pretty stock, four-speed manual and so on. You were telling me that around that time you had an opportunity to test your skills for Ford with shifting?

Bill: "Yes, they had put me on this machine. They put all these gadgets on a machine and they put it in the race car. And they told me to go out and drive it and shift as fast as I wanted and all this stuff. What it did was it checked the override between shifts, and it was almost zero. I think it was like one or two hundred RPM override. An automatic did that, by the way."

Question: But things started to change after 1965. You're still with the Mustang line but now we go to the stretched cars. You were putting injectors on it and things like that. But still running gasoline when you first started?

Bill: "Chrysler started that stuff because they couldn't beat us anymore. See once we put the big

The late Bill Lawton (L) and his former crew chief and engine builder John Healey with the T-Bolt in the showroom of Tasca Ford during the grand re-opening in 1994.

slicks on, and don't forget we went to the overhead-cam engine, and we were making all kinds of horsepower. And with those tires we destroyed them. Chevrolet, they were out by this time and as you know Dave Strickler, Dyno Don, and all them they switched from Chevrolet to whatever and they just couldn't compete with us anymore. So what do they do? Altered their cars. They brought the wheelbases up, they moved the engines, and that's where the word Funny Car came from. Then Ford said no, we want to stay with NHRA. We don't want you match racing with them, nothing. That's when the ban occurred."

Question: How did you feel about that?

Bill: "I hated it. Because we were match racers. That's where we made all our money. So now all of a sudden what are we going to do? Run a Ford against a Ford? The Chryslers were really the only competition we had, and that hurt. And

The late Robert F. Tasca Sr. poses with the restored Thunderbolt at VA Motorsports Park in 1995.

then the books went down and we had to run at all these national events. They wanted us to because they thought we were winners. Then that fell through after a while because we really didn't want to do it. So what do we do? The 1966 car was a cut Mustang that Holman-Moody built. In '66 we went down and picked up our new car at Holman-Moody and we couldn't test it, we couldn't do anything with it. We had to take it right to Detroit. Charlie Gray and Dick Brannan were the Ford people at that time. And we had a big race at Connecticut Dragway. I'll never forget this, Bill Flynn, the Yankee Peddler, and we were very tight because Frank Mirada had made all the arrangements, advertising and all. We got the car, took it to Dearborn, put the engine in it, and it scared the hell out of me."

Question: It did?

Bill: "Yeah, cause I [previously] had a Mustang with seats in it. You couldn't even see the roll bar, it had rugs in it and you couldn't even hear the engine except for the headers. Now I get stuck in this thing, it was nothing but a shell. The engine was way up, the wheels were moved, the front end was a mile long in it. I wasn't used to this stuff. You start the car and it sounds like guns going off, boom, boom, boom, because the tin in the car would be shaking. And I said, 'Listen to this thing, it's unbelievable.'

"I made the first pass and it scared me. I couldn't make a full pass. I don't know why, little nerves I guess. Then Dick Brannan got in the car and he drove it, and then I drove it again and I did alright. We had to get out of there because we had to get back here to race.

"We came back to Connecticut Dragway and I really hadn't gotten a good run in the car. I got up against Billy Flynn. The fastest I ever went was like 10.5 or 10.4 in the Mustang. First pass down [in the new car] was a 9.7.

I didn't care what the car sounded like when I had another competitor next to me. I wasn't a good tester. I didn't like testing. I had to race. The car didn't scare me, the noise, none of that stuff. I blew his doors off. It all went away. The same thing happened when I went from injection to a blower.

Getting back to that particular car, we started off with a four-speed with the overhead-cam engine. Every time I got ready to leave the line the left front tire would never turn. It just went right up and it wouldn't turn until half way down the track when the car would settle down. What a great car it was, and we were having a great time. And then Chrysler, we started beating them again and what do they do? They go to fuel. Ford says, ok, now we've got to go to alcohol.

We were the first ones to get an altered Mustang, that was the *Mystery 9* by the way. The first *Mystery* car. And when Les Ritchey got killed they said no more four-speeds in the fuel cars. They banned it on the fuel; when you changed gears with the fuel the engine revved high and it was just too violent when you changed gears. Chrysler started putting in alcohol, we put in alcohol and we beat them again. And of course we went to the automatic."

Question: So the car went from *Mystery 9* to *Mystery* 8 and the difference was you went to alcohol?

Bill: "And then we started putting nitro in it. We started off at 30 to 40 percent and by the end we were dumping the whole thing in it, 90 to 92. But we did very well with that car."

Author's note: A report was filed by Drag Council Captain Dick Brannan on April 14, 1966 outlining testing of the Tasca Ford Mustang at Connecticut Dragway following the installation of the automatic transmission. The first run on the car with 50 percent nitromethane resulted in an elapsed time of 9.27 @ 150.25 MPH. A second pass was made but cross winds caused Bill Lawton to slow the car early and end testing. It should also be noted in the legacy of Bill Lawton and the Tasca Ford Mustang that he was denied a second Super Stock Nationals class win when he was disqualified for taking too long to bring the car to the scales for a weigh-in.

Question: What kind of reception did you get with the Tasca cars on the West Coast?

Bill: "Oh, they loved us. Don't you remember we won the Winternationals at Pomona? They all knew us out there."

Question: what came next in the progression from *Mystery 9* to *Mystery 8*?

Bill: "Logghe Chassis built our new car. That was the beginning of the real Funny Car. The other Mustang was an altered-wheelbase car and that was the end of a chassis car. We went to a tube chassis. We picked that car up at Homan-Moody."

Question: What was the difference in driving that car to your chassis car?

Bill: "It was amazing. In the other car I sat where a driver would normally sit. The Logghe car had a roll cage and you sat in the middle, way in

Lawton is seen here backing out of his pit in the Tasca Ford A/FX Mustang. John Healey kept the SOHC 427 humming as Lawton mowed down the competition. (Martino family)

the back, where I was only used to being on this side looking out of the car. When you move somebody to the back and center the car becomes two and a half miles long. I said, 'Holy Christ, look at this thing!' We got the car, brought it home, got it painted and it was beautiful. Then we took it to Bristol for the Spring Nationals. First time out with the car and I remember we never even tested that car. We just took it right out there."

Author's note: The new Tasca Ford Funny Car was featured in the 1967 Crane Cams catalog and the full page Crane ad depicting Lawton, Healey, and the Mustang graced the back cover of the October 1967 issue of *Super Stock and Drag Illustrated* magazine. Also featured was an Atco Dragway time card showing an 8.28 second elapsed time at 173.63 MPH.

Question: And you ran an 8.32 the first time out as I recall?

Bill: "We were right there. That car was in all the magazines, that car was gorgeous. And then we went to the Summer Nationals and we were winning. But you've got to remember now all the blown cars were there. We got down near the end and I was running Doug Thorley and I got him out of the gate but he caught me and he won. So now we thought, 'What are we going to do?' I really didn't want to go to a blower because there were a lot of people having accidents. You've got to remember I cherish my life and I had my father's business. I wasn't looking to kill myself. I had a good life here. I wasn't one of those shoe guys they throw in the car and say "go kill yourself, don't worry about it." Some of those guys were nuts.

Author's note: In this segment of the interview Bill elaborates on how unsafe he thought the cars were becoming and points out the crash that Don Nicholson suffered at Cecil County, MD, as being a factor in Robert F. Tasca, Sr. no longer accompanying the team to races as he always had to that point. Bill also discusses the fuel additive Hydrazine and how some racers used it in an effort to gain performance in spite of the dangers associated with its use. The injected Tasca Ford Mustang Funny Car may not have won in each instance it faced off against supercharged opponents, but things weren't quite as bad as Bill made them sound. At the 1968 NASCAR Winter Championships Bill Lawton stopped the blown Corvette of Frank Federici on his way to face, and defeat, the blown GTO of Arnie Beswick. And *Drag News* printed an article, glowing with praise, over Lawton's match race defeat of the blown GTO funny car of Texan Don Gay at Connecticut Dragway while on the same day stopping the Red Baron Chevy of Mel Perry.

Bill: "Getting back to the injected car. That was right near the end and we came back to Epping, NH. They called that meet the King of Kings and they were all there. We had all come back from the Nationals. Epping had a big draw, they paid big bucks. After Indy all the West Coast guys would come through here and run this King of Kings meet. And we beat them all that day. We won the meet and were the only injected car there. All the big guns were there, but when we came back the blowers were already on the way. So we went blown.

We went to Connecticut Dragway and again I didn't like it. I didn't like the blower up there. I was used to the injectors sticking out of the hood and all of a sudden there's this big blower in front of me. And I saw all the stuff people were getting into with those blowers, a lot of people getting burnt and I said, 'Oh-oh here we go.' And I was going to quit. I said, "I don't think I want to do this anymore." I told the Bopper and [he] said, 'No, you've got to try it.'

I said, "Look I really don't want to do this you know? I've seen people get burned." I didn't do this for a living. I owned a moving company and we did very well. I went racing because I loved it. I said "I'll give it a shot." I just had a fear of this thing blowing up in my face.

Then I ran somebody and I wanted to put the can in it. I loved it! The first time out we went 187 MPH. The top end was just amazing! Then I realized how these guys had been catching me on the other end. Once you got it down track and the tires started really hooking up it was amazing. So we took it to Epping and set the track record at over 200 miles per hour. You've got to remember we had a three speed automatic transmission and we went 200 miles per hour!"

Question: Describe for me the day you lost the top.

Bill: "Describe it? I remember it very well. We were racing the *Seaton's Shaker*. This was one of the first tracks to have cement at the starting line and where the cement met the asphalt there was a little hump. Every time my back tires would hit that the car took a little jump and the engine spun. And we knew.

John said, 'This track is dangerous' because of what it was doing. You could hear the motor spin. And the one run it spun and when it came down it must have caught and threw too much fuel into it and ignited and 'Boom,' it just popped it. But the blower didn't come off the car. The concussion was unbelievable. When we came in the blower was cocked, it did break off. It was like somebody slapped me in the face. But then all of a sudden the sun came in. Because it was very dark in the back of that race car because you don't see much. Then I looked up and realized the roof was gone. They told me the roof went a mile up in the air."

Question: Was that the most serious incident that you ever had?

Bill: "No, we were racing at an AHRA National meet in Phoenix, and again we were winning, and we had trouble with our converter. So we had another converter. It was an old-style converter and what happened was there were recesses on the converter for the drain plug and on this old-style converter the head of the plug stuck out. So it caught and cocked the transmission and all the oil came out and it burned the car. Unbelievable, what a fire! Everybody thought I was dead."

Author's note: Bill described in great detail how the speed of the car caused the flames to blow toward the rear, giving the impression that the entire car was engulfed, while he was actually untouched by the fire.

Bill: "This was the *Mystery 9* car. And the Bopper was crying, he thought I was dead. And I couldn't stop the car because the fire caught the brakes too. I had no chutes, no brakes, and what happened was the car started spinning. And what kept the car from flipping was the oil coming out of the converter got on the tires and kept the thing from flipping. I got hurt trying to get out of the car and I was limping. I banged my knee on the roll bar. And they were trying to throw me in the ambulance and I'm saying, 'I'm not hurt, leave me alone.' The car was still running by the way, because the engine never got hurt. It was the transmission that went. The car was burnt bad though.

And that was Big Bertha, that was our engine. It was a little bigger than 427. It was like 440-something because we didn't have any limitations. And I remember fighting with the guys. The car's burning away and the engine's still running. I wanted to get to the car and pull the fuel shut off and they wouldn't let me go in the car.

I had my fire suit on. I said "Don't pour that stuff on the engine." What do they do? They're shooting this stuff all over and there goes the engine. Anyway we took the car from there, we were going to win the meet, by the way. We had it won. Drag racing's funny, you've got to have luck on your side because without luck you win nothing. We took the car to Holman-Moody in Long Beach and rebuilt the car and had it ready for Pomona. Then we won the deal at Irwindale."

Question: You go back in '68 to Super Stock racing with the Cobra Jet car?

Bill: "They forced me to. How the hell do you drive an eleven-second car and then get into a seven-second funny car? The thing of it was that was a bracket race, you've got to put your foot on the brake. I don't want to put my foot on the brake. I don't know how to do that. I ran out a couple of times. That's what happened to us at the Winternationals, I ran out, I ran too quick.

Question: So that wasn't for you?

Bill: "No, but they told me I had to drive the car."

Bill Lawton is captured in a rare still moment with the Tasca Ford 1966 altered wheelbase Mustang. Built from the '65 car the latest Tasca effort first ran in the nine-second range with carburetors, gasoline, and a four-speed transmission. Thus the name *Mystery 9*. (L.Wolfe)

Question: The factory?

Bill: "Somebody told me. I think it was the Bopper."

Question: Well he liked the Cobra Jet cars right?

Bill: "Well, he wanted to sell cars and in the meantime we had built up a pretty good name and he wanted the name on the car and that was it. But after a while I started enjoying it because we started match racing with them. We had rosin and it was just like the old days, and it was super. And then what happened? We were winning again and it kept breaking transmissions for some reason. I don't know what happened. Now the Bopper was aggravated so he puts an automatic in it. I don't want to drive that. Give me a break, will you? It's bad enough you just sit there and go. Now you gotta worry about how fast you go. It was like a sled.

Question: You didn't have an interest in Pro/Stock?

Bill: "We never got to Pro/Stock. I think that would have saved us."

Bill went on to explain how difficult it had become to maintain the supercharged, nitro-burning, SOHC 427 engine powering the Tasca Ford funny car, and how the Chrysler teams had the advantage of being able to do what amounted to a complete rebuild of their engine between rounds, while that could not be accomplished with the more sophisticated Ford engine. But the 1969 season wouldn't be all bad news for the Tasca Ford team, as they debuted their new car at Connecticut Dragway with a match race win over Mr. Norm's *Mini-Charger* Dodge Funny Car.

Bill: "We would go to meets, set low E.T. and high miles per hour and then put it on the trailer and go home. We were winners, but we were losers. That's when we decided we didn't want to do it anymore. As a matter of fact that's what happened to us at the '69 Super Stock Nationals in York. All

Lawton goes off against Phil Bonner's Falcon at Cecil County Dragway. By this point fuel injectors had been added and John Healey was experimenting with alcohol as a fuel. The car's violent reactions under power would soon lead to the replacement of the four speed transmission with an automatic. (Joel Naprstek)

the big guns were there. We went out and set low E.T. at 7.30 or whatever and I knew it. That was it for me. Every time we had a good run the engine would get hurt. We would burn a piston, put it on the trailer and go home. Bopper was disgusted, I was disgusted, we all got disgusted. They were just coming out with the 429 engine but it was too late. We were tired."

Question: You got tired?

Bill: "We couldn't win anymore. When you're a winner and then you become a loser it takes your heart out of it. If we had made it into Pro/Stock I know we would have made it.

Bill explains that he walked away from racing completely until someone talked him into attending a drag race in 1973. There he saw many of his old friends and competitors in action and once again he was bitten by the bug.

Bill: "In '73 I built my own Funny Car, with a Pinto body, and called it the *Mover* since I'm in the moving business. And John Healey and Steve Besch had a Pro/Stock car and they wanted me to drive it. But I had my own Funny Car and I would have to go to the national events with them and pay somebody to drive my fuel car. It was too much."

Question: Did you drive the Pro/Stock car?

Bill: "Yeah, it was a great ride. And then my Funny Car, I had all the best stuff."

Question: How long did you do that?

Bill: "Two years and that was it."

JOHN HEALEY

John Healey served as engine builder, crew chief, and integral part of the Tasca Ford Race Team from 1962-70.

Question: Tell us how you got involved in hot rods. Where you always a Ford guy?

John: "I had Chevrolets first. I built several cars with my father. I still have a lot of friends who were Chevy guys. They'll say "Hey Healey, remember when we called you a traitor?" I went to work for Mr. Tasca in the summer of 1959. I worked nights there and days at another Ford dealership.

Question: Were you a line mechanic at that time?

John: "Yes, it was a fifty/fifty deal. Flat rate."

Question: How did you get involved with Ford performance?

John: "I had one of those 360-horse Fords in 1960, but it was short-lived. It wasn't the right thing to do while trying to raise a family. And we don't talk about that. In '61-'62 I was doing performance work at the dealership full-time. At first I was involved with Gordon Carlson. He had a chestnut-colored '62 406 Ford."

Question: Did you prepare that car?

John: "Yes, I set the car up for him and Mr. Tasca sponsored him. But after a while they clashed over what to do with the car."

Question: Was Carlson's car a full-time racer or did he drive it on the street as well?

John: "He drove it during the week, then hooked a tow bar to it to go racing on the weekend. You know how we did it back then. Carlson raced the car on the street too. You know Billy Lawton had a 409 and Gordon used to beat him bad. Then Tasca got more involved and we ended up with three race cars in '62. We had the red '62 Fairlane with a 406 in it that was built at Dearborn Steel Tubing. It had an automatic in it and the worst set of headers. They were a nightmare. They came off the heads at a ninety degree angle."

Question: Were the headers that way because Dearborn Steel Tubing did not modify the upper control arms for additional clearance when they installed the 406 in the car?

John: "That's right. They put the engine in with everything in the stock location."

Question: Did you drive the Fairlane?

John: "Yes, whenever I could. Then we had the Super Stock car that Bill Lawton drove and one of the first lightweight Galaxies that Bob Price drove. We ran that car in B/FX as I recall."

Question: How did the Tasca team do in 1962?

John: "It was a learning curve in '62. We lost more than we won. In '63 we started winning

The performance progression of the Tasca Ford Mustang is seen in this photo. Fuel injection, exotic fuels, and an automatic transmission now had the car running in the eight-second range; A name change on the car's quarter panels was called for. Later, the seven-second range was reached with a fiberglass body on a purpose-built tube chassis. (Alan Wood)

A huge proponent of Ford performance until his death, Robert F. Tasca is seen here at a Ford Performance clinic with driver Hubert Platt in 1969. (T.Allen Platt)

more and by '64 we were beating everyone who beat us in '62 and '63. In '63 I pretty much had a free hand to do what I wanted. We were trying a lot of things on the '63 car. We used the lift-type traction bars (the style later used on the Thunderbolts) and about halfway through the year we got better at racing. We gave input to Ford and got input back.

Question: Tell us about the '63 Fairlane

John: "That car was built at Dearborn Steel Tubing for someone else and came to Tasca later. It was a green, two-door hardtop and was the mule car for the Thunderbolt. Ford gave it to Tasca in order to show a dealer connection and legitimize the cars for racing."

Author's note: In my research I have accessed a Ford intra-company communication regarding vehicle accountability, which lists a 1963 Fairlane, VIN 3F43K290758, as on loan to Roy Lunn. All indications are that this is the Thunderbolt "Mule" car later raced by the Tasca Ford team.

In their efforts to provide the air of legitimacy to the 427 Fairlane homologation, Ford assigned DSO number 33A to the car and even produced sales documents describing the option, including price and warranty. Relegated to the A/Factory Experimental class at the NHRA Nationals, the Fairlane lost in class eliminations because of a missed shift. Later in the fall of 1963, with Bill Lawton at the controls the *Zimmy 1* Fairlane set the NHRA A/FX class record at Charleston, RI.

John: "Then in '64 we got the T-Bolt and once we converted that car to A/FX specs it was unbeatable."

Question: Which of the Tasca cars was your favorite?

John: "They all were, really. Things were changing so fast back then and we were always looking forward to the next thing. The T-Bolt was one of my favorites and the '65 A/FX car after they stretched it."

Question: That brings us to 1965. What did you think of the "Cammer" engine?

John: "When I first saw it, I found it intriguing. I had seen the prototypes before. Since I was spending a lot of time in Dearborn with Sr. during those days, when he would be in meetings I would go over to Engine and Foundry and talk to them about what was going on."

Author's note: Ford Motor Company sold a 1965 Mustang "drag vehicle" VIN 5F09K380232 to Tasca Ford sales for the sum of one dollar. The car was delivered to the Tasca Ford team at Holman-Moody where it was constructed along with nine other Mustangs destined for members of the Drag Council.

Question: How about your insights on the A/FX Mustang and the 1965 Winternationals.

John: "Before the Winternationals we picked up the cars up and brought them to Les Ritchey's place, where they were prepared. Brannan was the go-to guy regarding what we could and could not do on the cars. The big thing at first was piston-to-valve clearance. We moved the cams around and fooled with lash caps, since you couldn't just turn an adjuster on a rocker arm on those engines. Everything else about them was pretty much the same as a High Riser.

"We tested the cars for about a week before the race and Billy was having trouble shifting the Top Loader, so we sent back home to have the aluminum T-10 transmissions and all the stuff to convert the car over shipped out. That didn't work because the Cammer had too much torque; we blew all of them up and had to go back to the Top Loader.

"It was a great feeling when we won the whole thing at Pomona. Strickler and Jenkins were next to us at teardown and they came over and congratulated us. Then I was left to do the teardown alone and the first time I leaned over the fender to lift the head off, my feet came right off the ground. The heads were cast iron. We didn't get the aluminum ones until later. The second time I reached in and started to lift the head I felt a hand on my belt holding my feet on the floor. It was Jenkins, and he asked, "How much does that head weigh?" Back then we only had one motor and some spare parts. When we got the aluminum heads that made a big difference. With the '65 car we raced both class and match races. For a match race we took as much weight out of the car as we could. We even took off the front brakes. Then for a points race we'd have to put it all back."

Author's note: Following their NHRA Winternationals victory the Tasca Ford team traveled to Dragways, Inc. in Newmedia, PA on April 25, 1965 for the East Coast *Drag News* Top Dog record runs. Bill Lawton wheeled the NHRA-legal Mustang to the A/FX class record with an elapsed time of 10.63 at 131.38 mph.

Question: Another big race for the Tasca team in 1965 was the Super Stock Nationals at York, PA. What do you remember about that?

John: "The who's who of drag racing was there. And I remember the crowd was so huge it overwhelmed the place. People were actually crowding around the cars on the starting line trying to look in the windows to see how high [RPM] they were being launched. One guy asked me how high Billy was launching the car and when I told him 7,800 RPM he said he had just lost $500. They were betting on everything. We won our class at that meet."

Question: And there was a big disappointment, along with some controversy at the 1965 World Finals isn't that right?

John: "We ran against Fenner and Tubbs in the final and when Billy left the line the green light came on, then the red light. NHRA said he red lighted but everyone had seen the green come on first. They (NHRA) wouldn't do anything about it, so that was it."

Question: That brings us to 1966. What happened then?

John: "The '65 car was stretched by Holman-Moody in '66. At first we ran the engine on gas with carburetors, then later with injectors. I think the first time we ran fuel was in Deland, FL, at the NASCAR Winternationals. We ran it on alcohol.

Question: Weren't there times when you and Mr. Tasca were at odds regarding what to do on the cars?

John: "Interesting story. I had come up with my own fuel system and I cut up the injector manifold. The old man was mad that I did this and said I couldn't use it. We had a match race against Charlie Allen at Connecticut Dragway and we were down two rounds to none. So I put my setup on the engine at the risk of being fired and when we came out for the next round the car went right into the eights and we won the next three rounds and the match. The old man said "You got one over on me this time."

Question: What came next for the Tasca team?

John: "In '67 we got our first flip-top, tube-chassis car. We ran the same chassis through 1969, just changed bodies. That Super Boss car was a pain. When we went to blowers I found out the cylinder blocks didn't like it. Tommy Grove was the only guy who really had that figured out. Things were getting too expensive and finally Mr. Tasca said he was going to park it. After that I was approached by the Drag Team and offered a job. Before I gave them an answer I discussed it with Mr. Tasca. He was a great man. He told me to go for it and even wrote my contract for me. I wouldn't have done as well as I did if it wasn't for him."

John went to work for the West Coast Ford Drag Team and Ed Terry readily credits John with

Having left Tasca Ford for a job on the West Coast Ford Drag Team, John Healey soon found himself on the outside looking in when Ford pulled its support. Falling back on his extensive talents, John went Pro/Stock racing with the Besch and Healey Pinto. The car was destroyed in a racing accident at Atco, NJ. (Fermier brothers)

turning their Pro-Stock program around. Unfortunately John's association with the Drag Team would be short-lived because of Ford's decision to drop their racing program.

Question: Didn't you do some racing on your own after the Drag Team?

John: " I formed John Healey and Associates and in '72 I teamed up with Steve Besch and we ran a Pinto in Pro-Stock as Besch and Healey."

Question: And I understand you had a career-ending crash at Atco Dragway?

John: "The panhard bar broke and the car crossed over into the other lane. I was fighting the car 'til I could see it was past the stands. Then I figured it would go into the woods, but I hit a cable. It took the nose off the car, pushed the engine back. I was covered in gas, battery acid, and one side of my helmet was ground down from scraping the ground. After that I went to Darwin Doll (NHRA Division One Technical Director) and talked to him about some changes that needed to be done, like the battery needed to be in it's own compartment. I think a lot of safety changes were made because of that."

Question: Did you have any other motorsports involvement after that?

John: "I helped John Downing with Harvey Cohen's '70 Mustang. I had helped John with his Fairlane before that and we remain great friends to this day."

John Healey is now retired and divides his time between Rhode Island and Florida.

CHAPTER 6

AL "BATMAN" JONIEC

If you happened to be a teenaged hot rodder growing up around Philadelphia, PA in the 1950's and early 60's Bob's Big Boy on Roosevelt Boulevard was the place to be. On any given night the owners of the hottest cars for miles around could be found there, cruising, checking out the girls, and looking for street races. Among the crowd at this popular hangout one would often find young Al Joniec.

During my first interview with Al Joniec in the early 1990's I asked him for his thoughts on being asked to recall the memories of his drag racing days. He said, "It's sort of like childbirth I guess. After a while you forget the pain and only remember the good parts.

"I was always a Ford guy. My first car was a '40 Ford with a Flathead. It had multiple carbs, a hot cam and could beat those '55-'56 265 Chevys. That really messed with their heads. But when the 283 came out in '57 I couldn't get by them and it wasn't long before I was helping a guy with a Chevy. This guy had won a big settlement from a railroad accident and his car was unbelievable for the time. The engine was bored and stroked to 327, it had a Paxton supercharger, and a four speed transmission. We had to cut the seat for shifter clearance; this car was wild.

"Then one night a guy, who was to become my best friend, rolled into the Big Boy in his 1958 Ford convertible. That guy was Louie Tomaselli and even though he had a brand new car, he wasn't old enough to drive and had to get one of his buddies to drive it for him. Louie had contracted rheumatic fever as a youngster, which left him in fragile health and his dad, who owned a hoagie shop, gave him whatever he wanted. Louie's Ford couldn't beat those hot Chevys, so one of his friends had helped him put a cam in it. That didn't help either and he couldn't figure out why. I listened to the car and through the exhaust note I could hear that it probably had a lobe wiped off the cam. I don't know how I knew that, I just did.

"Well, Louie's dad offered $100 to anyone who could help his son win a trophy with his car. That was a lot of money to a guy like me who was working just to buy food, so I offered to help. I can't believe to this day how I did it but I swapped out the cam with the car sitting on the street in front of the house with nothing more than caveman tools. I'm talking about adjustable wrenches and a big pry bar to get the damper off, but somehow I did it. I had found out that for the first few months of 1958 Ford had offered its new FE V-8 (332 cubic inches) with a solid lifter cam and

Al Joniec and Bud Rubino with the Swenson Ford 1962 406 Galaxie. This car provided a learning curve for Al and his regional success with it would lead to bigger and better things in the years to come. (A. Joniec)

adjustable rocker arms, so this is what I put in Louie's car and with that he won his first trophy."

Little did Al Joniec realize at the time that his early education into the intricacies of Ford's newly introduced FE series engines would eventually lead him down the road to drag racing fame.

"When we started racing the Ford it ran in A/Stock, but by 1960 the hot class was Super/Stock. Of course the '58 couldn't run there so we made some changes. Around that time on the East Coast, Gassers were the hot thing and for some reason C/Gas seemed to be the most popular class. Willys coupes with Chevy small blocks and '55-'56 Chevy's were what most guys ran, but we set the Ford up for C/Gas. I installed a roller cam, a six two-barrel induction system, Roto-Faze ignition, custom-built headers, and we poured a hundred pounds of concrete into the rear quarters to gain traction and make the class weight.

"We took the car out one night down to a spot called the meadows, where everyone went to street race. It was a beautiful night so we put the top down and here we are cruising along slow in first gear, open exhausts, and I told Louie to jump on it. The front of the car came up, the engine must have revved to eight grand, and the seat track broke. The difference in that car was unbelievable! But now with all that power and traction I started breaking every part in the drive train. I broke the pinion gear, twisted the driveshaft, and finally cracked the bell housing. The only way I could keep it together was to idle off the line and get into the throttle slow, lift off on each shift, and then stand on it in high gear.

"We towed the car out to the Nationals at Detroit Dragway and even having to drive it the way I did I was way out in front of this other guy going into high gear. All of a sudden the engine drops back to idle. A clip holding the throttle linkage had fallen off and here I was coasting with this guy catching up fast. Even so, at the end of the track it was so close that I didn't know who won. As it turned out he did, and this was the first, but not the last, time I should have won at the Nationals but didn't because of some stupid little thing."

In the early days of drag racing competitors often ran their cars on a section of straightaway at circle tracks, which created a unique set of challenges to those who just wanted to accelerate in a straight line. One such facility was Hatfield Speedway, a banked asphalt track that normally played host to stock cars, located fairly close to the

Philadelphia area. While wildly popular with local drag racers, Hatfield was hardly the optimum place to hold a drag race. First was the fact that the track was banked. Second, the straightaway was neither the standard distance 1/8 or 1/4 mile that drag racers normally set their vehicles up for. Nonetheless Al, Louie, and the '58 Ford were regular competitors at Hatfield, and Al describes one particularly memorable event there.

"The management at Hatfield would open the track for a special mid-winter race, the winner of which got a trip to Florida. We took the '58 out there and Louie's dad Gene came along with us. Since Gene owned a hoagie shop I never saw him dressed in anything other than white pants, a white shirt and an apron. And even though it was the middle of January and freezing cold, this day was no different: there was Gene in his apron. After we beat everyone in our class we ran in the Eliminator. It seems like we beat close to 100 cars that day 'till it came down to the final. All I had to do was beat one more guy and we were going to Florida.

"Just before we were to run, an Altered overheated and dropped some water on the track. Well, they just hit it with a mop and called us to the line. Nobody took into consideration that some of the water might have frozen before it got mopped up and that is just what happened. The car I was running against had an automatic transmission, which made things a little better for him, but when I let out the clutch the car went sideways on the banking and he was gone. I got the car straightened out and caught the guy right at the end of the track. Once again, so close I couldn't tell who won. The officials gave the win to the other car and Louie's dad went nuts! He said he didn't care and that we were going to Florida anyway. And that's just what we did.

"I swapped out the rear for a 2.91, put the deep-geared rear in the trunk, and off we went. We had no idea where we going. We were just two kids, I was about 18 and Louie was 16 and here we are, off on a trip to Florida. It was all so very innocent back them. At one point we ran out of gas and coasted to the side of the road. It was about three in the morning so we just slept in the car. When the sun came up there were people knocking on the windows and looking at us. We had coasted to a stop in front of Marine Land. So we said, 'What the heck?' and visited the park. We thought the dolphins were the best thing since popcorn. After that we got a can of gas and drove the rest of the way to Spruce Creek. (location of the NASCAR Winter National drag races)."

Question: How did you come to work at Swenson Ford?

Al: "As I said I had been helping my friend Pudgy with his '57 Chevy. It had a 283, bored and stroked out to 327, a four speed, and, get this, a McCulloch supercharger. At the time that car was unbeatable. We saw that Swenson Ford had an ad for night shift jobs, so we went up there and told the service manager that we had just been laid off from a nearby Chevy dealer that had closed down. We never had real jobs, but we knew he couldn't check with the Chevy dealer, so we got hired."

Question: You got hired as a line mechanic at Swenson Ford with no experience?

Al: "That's right. I started out with a little box of borrowed tools and here I am with all these other guys with big tool boxes all around me. I learned on the fly and before long I graduated to the day shift."

Question: "How did Swenson's involvement with racing come about?

Al: "They hired this new general manager who was from the South who loved racing. He had the NASCAR disease. A couple of guys at the dealership--one of them was the parts manager-- had 360 Fords that they ran on the street and then later the parts manager got a '61 Starliner. When the general manager heard how well they were doing racing on the street, he suggested getting a car, lettering with the dealer name and going racing. When the 406 came out in '62 he ordered one and we lettered it and prepared it to race."

Question: Where did you run the 62?

Al: "We ran at Atco, Vineland, local tracks."

Al Joniec in the Al Swenson Ford 1963 1/2 lightweight Galaxie leaves the starting line en route to another low 12-second run. (A.Joniec)

Question: How did you do?

Al: "One of the biggest problems was the Chrysler cars with the 413 and ram intake. Although we could beat them it seemed we could never beat Strickler and Jenkins. We didn't take that car to the Nationals because we just weren't competitive enough. I was impressed by Brannan and how fast he made his 406 go."

Question: What kind of tricks did you try on the 406?

Al: "I retarded the cam as much as eleven degrees, ran almost zero valve lash. I just kept chasing it. I believed what my time cards said and not what someone said to do to it to make it run."

Question: What happened to the '62 Galaxie at the end of the season?

Al: "It was sold off. I don't remember who bought it, but it was sold still lettered."

Question: That brings us to 1963 and Swenson Ford got a lightweight Galaxie for you?

Al: "Here comes the '63 lightweight. We had started to sell a lot of performance cars, Swenson became a Cobra dealer, and they ordered a '63 lightweight Galaxie. I remember that car being delivered on what looked like a fruit truck. It didn't come in on a regular transporter like the other cars. And when we got it, of course I had to drive it on the street. I told the general manager I needed to break the engine in. One weekend Bud Rubino and I loaded our fishing equipment in the trunk and drove it up to the Pocono mountains to do some fishing. I still remember how comfortable I thought those special lightweight bucket seats it had were. Then we were off to the races. We took everything we had learned with the '62 car and applied it to the '63 and won everything locally. Bud Faubel was a problem back then. He was tough because he had Bill Jenkins working for him at the time."

Al had a pretty busy month of August 1963 with his Swenson Ford Galaxie. *Eastern Drag News* reported Joniec met *The Newcomer* '63 Chevy at Vargo Dragway for a best of five match race on August 11. According to *EDN* this match was arranged for the Chevy to get revenge for losing to Joniec in four straight runs on July 21. Chevy man Bob Anderson fared no better in this match as the Swenson Ford showed him its big round taillamps in four of five rounds.

On August 18, *EDN* announced, "Al Swenson cleans house at Cecil County." On this particular day the Super Stock class, the *EDN* Top Dog title, and Top Stock Eliminator went to Joniec as he dropped Harold Ramsey's Pontiac, the *Bounty Hunter* and finally the similar fiberglass Ford of Bob Boyd.

Question: You took the '63 lightweight to the NHRA Nationals didn't you?

Al: "At the '63 Nationals I had the quickest car in Super Stock. The way I knew this was I sent this kid who was with me to listen to the public address system--they didn't have the big light-up score boards back then--and write down everyone's time. I should have won, but we saw guys putting ice on their intake manifolds between rounds to cool the engines. It was so hot at Indy, it must have been a hundred degrees and just as humid. I figured out that in that heat and humidity the engine was too rich, so I kept putting smaller jets in the carburetors and it kept going faster. I dropped the jet size ten steps. Another thing I had figured out was that the rocker arm shafts were flexing at the ends, so we made our own stabilizers. They replaced the wave washer and the flat washer at the end of the shaft and we drilled a small hole in the head bolt so we could bolt it down. We kept dumping more ice on the intake as it kept melting. We were just kids; we didn't know anything.

"I had this guy with a Dodge in the first round and I was very confident because we had been running way faster than him. He was toast. The lights come down, I let out the clutch, and the car bogs! We had gotten the intake so cold it caused the car to bog! I throw the clutch in, rev the motor, and go. Now I'm catching this guy and in third gear the water from the intake manifold is getting under the tires and the car is slipping and sliding all over the place. Still at the end it was so close I couldn't tell who won. But he did, and he went on the win the class."

The Dodge that Al is referring to was found to be running an illegal camshaft at the post-race teardown and was disqualified. However in keeping with the NHRA practice the class was nullified instead of awarding it to the rightful winner, the Ed Martin Ford entry driven by Don Turner.

Question: What do you attribute to Ford taking notice of how well you were doing in '63?

Al: "I went to a regional meet at York and I beat the Tasca car and Dick Brannan. I wasn't as fast as Brannan but I put a hole shot on him and won. Passino was there and asked to see me. I remember I was weak in the knees when I went over to talk to him. He asked me what I needed and I said I could use some help. They sent me a set of fiberglass doors. That was the first thing I ever got from Ford. Later on I got a cold air intake system and that picked the car up big time. Late in the year I took the car to a big Super Stock meet at Cecil County. I already had the car sold to Lon Raser by this time and he was going to take it after the race. We were eating everybody's face off that day. I remember I waved to "Grump" when I went by him in high gear. He was driving Bud Faubel's other car. The final came down to me and Faubel and I had him covered but broke

Al Joniec seems very happy in this photo taken of him in his 1964 Thunderbolt at the Al Swenson dealership. Originally delivered with an automatic transmission, the car's performances were dismal until it was converted to four speed. Joniec would once again claim *Eastern Drag News* Top Dog status in 1964 and post the quickest elapsed times in his class at the NHRA Nationals only to lose because of a clutch linkage failure. (A. Joniec)

the transmission and lost. Lon got the car with a broken transmission."

In ads for match races during the 1963 season the Al Swenson Ford entry of Al Joniec was referred to as, "The East Coast's Hottest Super Stock." He would finish the season with a coveted *East Coast Drag News* Top Dog title, which he successfully defended against the Hall Ford lightweight at Cecil County Dragway on October 27, 1963. The team of Goldy and Raser would also go on to win *Eastern Drag News* Top Dog status with the former Swenson Ford lightweight Galaxie, taking numerous AA/S class wins and Top Stock Eliminator titles during the 1964 season.

Question: Tell me about the Thunderbolt.

Al: "Here comes the Thunderbolt and it was an automatic. The thing wouldn't get out of its own way. Pussies drove automatics as far as I was concerned. I complained and got nothing until Al Swenson contacted a vice president at Ford who he had gone to college with. Then we got all the conversion stuff and made the car a four speed

Joniec got the call to become a member of the Ford Drag Council in 1965. He picked up this A/FX Mustang from Holman-Moody and continued his winning ways. Originally delivered with a 427 High Riser, the Mustang received a SOHC 427 as soon as enough became available. (A. Joniec)

halfway into the season. We had the fastest car at the Nationals that year and once again some stupid little thing kept me from winning. The clutch rod bent and when I brought the RPMs up on the line it engaged the clutch and pulled me through the lights."

Question: Who were you running against when that happened?

Al: "Len Richter."

Al Joniec had much regional success with the Al Swenson Ford Thunderbolt during the 1964 season, winning numerous events and match races.

The headline for an article that appeared in *Eastern Drag News* dated June 21, 1964m reads, "Ford Leads the Parade at Atco's $1000 S/S Meet." *EDN*'s scribe refers to Bob Harrop's Dodge Ramcharger as the betting favorite, but went on to indicate that Al Swenson's Ford driven by Al Joniec couldn't be counted out as his and the Harrop car were doing all the eliminating during the first round. Joniec faced Harrop in the final and the writer describes the Ford fans going wild as Al dumped the Dodge 11.73 @ 119.04 to an 11.85 @ 117.60.

Question: How did you get called up to the big league in 1965?

Al: "Well, as you know, Jenkins had the Plymouth deal and he wanted me to drive the *Black Arrow*. When he got the car he told me that since it was an automatic he didn't need me. He could drive it himself. I was helping him prepare the car when I got a call from Ford. I don't remember if it was Dick Brannan or Charlie Gray. They told me there was a Mustang being built for me at Holman-Moody and I would have to go there and pick it up. So I went down there and spent a day or two as Holman-Moody finished it up. I got it with a wedge in it because they didn't have enough Cammer engines to go around at that time and it ran real good with the wedge. When I got the Cammer I used the SK cams and I had been warned about checking the piston to valve clearance, so I made myself a fly cutter and cut the pistons with the engine in the car. Some guys didn't do that and they blew engines right away. The car ran so well with the wedge that I beat Tasca with their Cammer car at Cecil county.

"A funny story about when I got called up to the NFL as it were: I was invited to come out to Detroit for a big banquet that Ford was hosting. I had never flown on a jet airplane before that so there were all kinds of firsts. I get to the airport in Philadelphia and I'm waiting for my flight to board and I notice all these people are pointing and talking. I see this young woman asleep on her fur coat. So I ask what's going on and someone tells me that the woman was Dianna Ross of the Supremes singing group. About this time the plane starts to board so I go over and wake her up and I walk her down to the plane. Well these people must have thought I was with her because they sit me down with her in first class when I'm supposed to be in the back of the plane. I flew all the way to Detroit with Dianna Ross, eating shrimp and drinking champagne. She told me her whole life story. I couldn't believe all this was happening to me."

Question: You competed at the '65 Super Stock Nationals at York, PA. How did you do there?

Al: "I made it to the semi-final round and got third-place money. Not too bad since I was running a Wedge against Hemis and SOHCs. I remember saying, 'wait 'till I grow up and get a SOHC.'"

Question: How long was it before you got the Cammer engine for the car?

Al: "It wasn't long. And when we took the car to the Nationals at Indy I had the quickest times in the A/FX class. I ran 10.60's. But there was a problem with the metallurgy in the connecting rods that Ford had and we could only make a couple of runs before it beat the bearings out of the rods. If I recall I put 47 rod bearings in the engine that weekend at the Nationals. I remember we were in the parking lot of the motel and we were parked next to the Tasca team. It was so hot and we had been at it all day and now John Healey and I are under these cars, sweating, dirty, trying to get the cars ready for the next day. And I look up and there is Billy Lawton standing on the balcony in the motel drinking a beer!"

Question: How did you correct the problem with the rods?

Al: "I listened to Connie Kalitta and widened the crank journals to Chrysler size and went to aluminum rods. That cured the problem."

Question: Tell me about when you faced off against the Tasca Ford car at the Nationals that year.

Al: "Well I guess Bob Tasca figured I was some local turkey and would be easy because they hung back so they would get me in the first round. I put a big gate job on Bill Lawton and I won. Tasca was so mad I think he almost fired Billy that day.

Question: Which brings us to the car you are most identified with, the *Batcar*. That was marketing genius. How did you come up with the idea?

For the 1966 season Joniec hit upon one of the most successful promotional schemes of the era for his A/FX Mustang. Taking a cue from the T.V. series *Batman*, Joniec repainted the car in *Batcar* livery and took on a new sponsor, Rice and Holman Ford of Pennsauken, NJ. Al and Bud Rubino pose with the Batcar, which at this time was powered by a carbureted, gas-burning SOHC 427. (A. Joniec)

In order to keep up with the competition, Joniec soon added fuel injectors to his *Batcar*. The car was in great demand from drag strip promoters up and down the East Coast, and Joniec's match-race dance card was kept full. (A. Joniec)

Al: "We were sitting in a bar after a race having a beer and a sandwich when the Batman T.V. show comes on. I liked the black car with the red scallops and my friend Louie's car (the '58 Ford convertible) was black with red scallops, so it was a natural progression. And we really got into it with the bat spinners on the wheels and the bat-shaped taillights.

"Things were changing so rapidly, it was like the wild West out there. Ford wanted me to run the NASCAR series and I started with carburetors in the 2800 pound gas class. Then I went to the 2500 pound Unlimited class with injectors. The car got harder to shift with a four speed as it went faster, and on nitro it was twisting really bad so I went to an automatic.

Question: And along with the Batcar theme came a change in dealership names on the side of the car from Al Swenson Ford to Rice and Holman Ford. How did that come about?

Al: "In '65 I stopped working at Al Swenson. The performance sales had lost their luster. As a matter of fact he had a Cobra on the showroom floor and they couldn't sell it. So Gene Angelino got me the deal with Rice and Holman. They gave me a truck and some money to go racing with their name on the car."

Question: Tell the story about the first time you tried nitro.

Al: "I had a match race against Bob Harrop at Atco. We started with a real low percentage of nitro but when I let the clutch out the car went straight up! It scared the hell out of me and I let off, which caused it to come crashing down. It bent the oil pan and all kinds of stuff. It was my most memorable race. In the second round I was ready for it and rode it out. I blew right by Harrop."

Author's note: I witnessed the match race Al describes from the stands as a spectator. When I told Al that at the time I thought he meant for the car to go skyward, he had a good laugh. His teen-aged fans thought he was fearless.

Question: How did the *Batcar* come to be stretched? As I understand your car was not done at Holman-Moody as were some of the other cars.

Al: "I was at Center Moriches on Long Island (N.Y. National Speedway) for the *Super Stock* magazine race. By that time I was breaking a lot of parts, but the car was running good. I had Ed Schartman's flip top Comet and I was well ahead of him when I noticed that the clutch pedal didn't seem to be where it should be and I couldn't get the car into fourth gear. I didn't know it at the time but the clip that held the clutch and and brake pedal on the shaft under the dash had come off and the pedals were sliding off. I went to hit the brakes and the pedal fell to the floor. I pulled the parachute and it didn't open, it just sort of fell out. Now I'm going 144 MPH but I thought it was going to slow down. Jack Chrisman had crashed earlier and his car was still sitting down there smoldering. I got to the end, hit the fence, and instead of stopping me, it shoots me out. Now I'm flying through the air, straight armed. The car came down, the frame rails dug into the ground and it flipped fifty to sixty feet in the air. I went over some trees while I was in the air and later they had to cut down the trees to get the car out of there. The car did a complete flip in the air, landed on its wheels and finally stopped."

Question: Were you hurt?

Al: "I had seat belt welts and a big bruise where the steering shaft just touched my sternum. I had straight-armed the steering wheel so hard it had bent in the opposite direction. My friend Jim was there with his airplane and he flew me home. When we got the car home we got the long front end, built new front frame rails, and moved the rear wheels forward. The *Batcar* reinvented itself several times. In 1967 when we took it to Spruce Creek, FL, the car looked beautiful under the lights at night with the metal flake paint. Charlie Gray and Brannan both admired how good the car looked. And it was running good too. I had run quicker than Sox did with his Funny Car and I really wanted to beat him bad to make a good impression. When I lined up against him I really brought it up hard against the converter. What I would normally do is leave from just off idle but this time I really jacked it up. Well, the rear housing started to twist and it pulled me through the lights and I red lighted. That was it, and it was probably a good thing because the rear housing was twisted really bad and I hate to think what would have happened if I launched the car like that."

Author's note: Prior to his crash at the '66 Super Stock Nationals Al had defeated Doc Burgess' *Black Arrow* Plymouth and Doug Nash's *Bronco Buster* in the first two rounds of competition.

Question: And then you got offered the Cobra Jet team car for 1968?

Al: "In late '67 they gave me the Cobra Jet deal and it was back to stock type cars with rules and limitations. I liked this because the other had become chaos. Chuck Foulger called and told me about the program. We went out to Stroppe's shop in California where the car was and [we] worked on it and tested them for about a week. Ford had

Joniec carried the Batman theme throughout the car, including the injector stacks. The car's parachute featured a large bat design as well.

So popular was the *Batcar* theme, along with Joniec's success with the car, that Crane cams chose to feature them in its 1967 catalog. Crane was a top supplier of camshafts for the SOHC 427 Ford engine.

In support of a close friend's business venture, Joniec covered the Batcar with an experimental finish called flocking for 1968. The *Batcar* then became the *Hairy One*. (A. Joniec)

rented the track prior to the Winternationals to get the cars ready."

Question: How did you feel about the other members of the factory Cobra Jet team?

Al: "Well, some of them were running automatics so I didn't pay any attention to them, and some of the others really didn't seem to have their hearts in it. Remember, these guys were coming from Funny Cars and I think they looked at this as a step down. The guy I paid the most attention to was Hubert Platt, because I could see he was working as hard as I was to be successful."

Al's estimation of Hubert Platt was right on the money, as the SS/E class championship at the 1968 NHRA Winternationals came down to he and Hubert, with Al taking the win. Al would again face Hubert in the Super Stock Eliminator runoffsm with Hubert fouling out there. Al would go on to win his first NHRA Eliminator title on that day.

Question: Describe your experience at the Winternationals.

Al: "I was having fun. I was winning round after round and not really thinking too much about it. Just having fun. Then one of the Ford guys told me that I had better win this thing because his job was on the line. After that I got nervous."

One of the biggest concerns for the Ford brass at the Winternationals was that the Cobra Jet engine would be re-factored by NHRA if they ran too quick (indicating that perhaps the factory rating of 335 horsepower was slightly conservative). These fears were proven accurate as NHRA had factored the engines to 360 horsepower by the close of proceedings at Pomona. With the continued success of 428 Cobra Jet cars over the ensuing years, NHRA remained true to its history of stifling winning Fords by re-factoring the engine several times.

Question: What happened after the Winternationals?

Al: "Ford had this big get-together and Emil Loeffler showed me the new high-performance parts catalog and asked what I thought. Well, I was just a young kid, 24 years old, so I told him the truth. I said, 'Why don't you offer the good parts you have to the everyday racer and not this junk?' Well, that caused me a lot of trouble with

Al Joniec's 428 Cobra Jet-powered Mustang has been restored to exactly as it appeared at the time it won the SS/E class and Super Stock Eliminator titles at the 1968 NHRA Winternationals.

Ford. I didn't know about all the politics that was involved."

Question: Did you continue to run the Cobra Jet in SS/E competition for the rest of the '68 season?

Al: "I ran it once in a Divisional race at Englishtown and it swallowed a valve. After that I put a 427 Tunnel Port in it and went Super Stock match racing. Jenkins, Bash, Sox, and others had put together this series."

Question: By this time you had covered the exterior of the *Batcar* with blue flocking and in this incarnation it was known as the *Hairy One*, isn't that right?

Al: "I was still running the Funny Car with the flocking on it at the same time I was running the Cobra Jet, so sometimes if I had a conflict with schedules for a match race or whatever I would hire someone to dive for me. And later I put flocking on the Cobra Jet and called it *Hairy Too*."

The former *Batcar* Mustang was covered in a blue flocking that was applied through an electrostatic process, while the Cobra Jet car remained white with blue flocking stripes over the hood, roof, and deck lid. Al continued to run the Funny Car in the NASCAR drag racing series and match races during the 1968 season. *SS&DI* magazine reported that at the '68 NASCAR Winter Championships Al Joniec defeated Wayne Gapp's Cougar in the first round of competition in the 2400 pound gas class, only to lose to Pee Wee Wallace's Plymouth due to a red light in the second stanza.

Question: What became of the Mustang Funny car after 1968?

Al: "I sold it to a guy who was the service manager of Willow Grove Park (a now-defunct amusement park outside of Philadelphia) and I don't think he did much with it."

Question: What about the Cobra Jet?

Al: "I sold that to another guy, but I can't remember his name."

I am glad to report that Al's Mustang Funny Car was found and restored to it's 1967 *Batcar* style. After carrying noted Maryland drag racer

Dick Estevez to the winner's circle a number of times before being retired, the Winternationals-winning Cobra Jet Mustang has also been located and restored to its former glory.

Question: By 1969 you were no longer being supported by the factory, so what did you do?

Al: "I had opened a franchise speed shop in Pennsauken, NJ, called Mr. Speed, and I went over to Rice and Holman Ford and bought a new Boss 429 Mustang with my own money. Then I drove the car four miles to my shop and took the engine out so I could put the Cammer in it and build a race car."

Question: If you intended to use the Mustang as nothing more than the starting point for a race car, why did you buy the top-of-the-line Boss 429 and not a cheap model?

Al: "I had measured the engine compartment of the Boss 429 and saw how wide it was, so I knew it would be easy to put the Cammer in it. And that's what I did."

Question: So you went racing in what was to later become Pro/Stock with the Mustang?

Al: "That's right, and I remember my first match race with that car was against Jenkins and I beat him. That was a pretty proud moment."

Question: What became of the Boss 429 Mustang?

Al: "I eventually put the Boss 429 engine back in it and sold it."

Author's note: The Boss 429 Mustang has also been found and restored to as it looked when raced by Al Joniec in 1969.

Question: What came next?

Al: "I had the '71 Maverick with the Cammer in it. That was also a completely solo effort. It had a Lakewood chassis but was never properly tubbed or lowered. That car went through two

In 1969 Joniec campaigned this Boss 429 Mustang with sponsorship from Rice and Holman Ford and Joniec's own Mr. Speed Inc. With this car the veteran Ford racer ran in Heads Up Super Stock competition (the forerunner of Pro/Stock). The Boss 429 engine was shelved in favor of the proven SOHC 427. Al is seen here in competition against Jack Werst's Hemi Barracuda at Atco Dragway in NJ. (J.Spinelli)

paint schemes and then later it got tubbed and dropped and was painted black with flames. At the end I ran a Boss 429 in it with help from Gapp and Roush. To make the Boss run we went to a smaller intake port, the same size that the Cammer used."

Question: Isn't there an interesting story about the hood scoop on the Maverick?

Al: "I had this great scoop on the car and the painter had painted an eye on each side of the scoop. My wife hated it."

Author's note: Having seen one photo of the Maverick with the scoop bearing the painted eyes, I would have to agree with Mrs. Joniec on that one. The eyes painted on the scoop were kind of creepy.

Al: "That scoop was only on the car a short time and one night when I came back from the track with the car on the transporter the door to the garage wasn't all the way up and the scoop crashed right into it as I pulled the truck in. My wife got her way because that was the end of that scoop."

Question: Didn't you run a Pinto in Pro/Stock when you were affiliated with Sam Feinstein?

Al: "I did. My friend Sam Feinstein approached me and said he needed help with his Cobra. He called the car *Ollie the Dragon* because every time he started it, fire came out! I could see that he needed help. He bought me a dyno, a truck, and sponsored my Pinto Pro-Stock car for helping him. I took a look at the Cobra that he was road racing. The chassis twisted and the engine made no power. So within one year I had taken the car to Fred Faulkner to ladder the chassis for rigidity, did some aero modifications on the car, and built the 427 so it made 670 horsepower at 3,500 RPM for endurance racing. With that car we won the National Championship, the last Cobra do to so, and at Road Atlanta we beat a field of 106 Corvettes, and among the Corvettes we whipped was [John] Greenwood. One Cobra beat them all."

Question: What became of the Pinto?

Al: "I had the Pinto Pro/Stock for two years but I was burnt out by then and tired of using my

Chassis modifications, a new paint scheme, and lack of sponsorship can be seen in this last version of Al Joniec's Pro/Stock Maverick. The long-time racer soon tired of running the entire operation out of his own pocket. (A. Joniec)

Joniec replaced the Mustang with this beautifully painted Maverick in 1970. Sponsorship was again from Rice and Holman Ford and power came in the form of a carbureted SOHC 427. This was Al's first true Pro/Stock car. (A. Joniec)

own money to go racing, so I gave it up in '73. I sold the car to Drake Viscome from Carmel Ford."

Question: A lot of racers and engine builders named their engines. Did you ever name any of yours?

Al: "No, except the broomstick motor."

Question: The broomstick motor?

Al: "Yes, you know how mallory metal is put into a crankshaft during balancing? Well I had this plug of mallory come out of the crank with such centrifugal force that it went right through the block and lodged in the starter. We took the starter off, retrieved the plug, pounded it back into the hole in the crank, welded it up, and I cut a piece of broomstick to fill the nice round hole it had made in the 351 Cleveland block."

Question: What did you do after you quit racing full time?

Al: "I went to work for the enemy, as it were. I took a job as Application Development Manager for United Technologies, manufacturers of emissions testing equipment."

Question: Any reflections on those years?

Al: "As I reflect on it now somehow it reminds me of the wild West, with it all being so new and different combined with the adventure of discovery. And of course being young and impressionable helped. I guess it really was a special time and not likely to be repeated."

Al Joniec has remained active in the development of engine technologies and currently resides in Aiken, SC. In 2008, on the 40th anniversary of his historic win at the 1968 NHRA Winternationals a new Cobra Jet Mustang, owned by Hajek Motor Sports, driven by John Calvert and lettered to mimic the car Al drove to victory in '68, won the Super Stock Eliminator title at the NHRA Winternationals with Al Joniec looking on proudly.

CHAPTER 7

ED TERRY / DICK WOOD

THE WEST COAST DRAG TEAM

Ed: "**I started drag racing** in the late 1950's. My first sponsored car was a 1960 high-performance, 360-horsepower Starliner. I was a Ford salesman, raced on Sunday, sold on Monday! In the late '50s and '60s there were nine drag strips in Northern California within a 120 mile radius, Fremont being the largest. It was located just off the Nimitz Freeway between Oakland and San Jose, two of the largest cities in Northern California. When they would hold the Northern Nationals it would attract 25,000 to 35,00 fans and bring the freeway to a stop. We did not have match racing like the south; the track promoters got the big names like Dyno Don, Dick Landy, Don Garlits, Don Prudhomme, and so on, by paying their gas and motel expenses, and putting up a large purse to come and win. In Super/Stock the Chevys and Pontiacs were the kings and I watched Gas Ronda work his way to the winner's circle with his '60 Ford. The fans went crazy. Gas at the time owned two Arthur Murray dance studios in San Francisco. He and his equipment were always dressed to the nines."

Question: What was your relationship with Gas Ronda?

Ed: "Both of our '60 Starliners arrived at Broadway Motors on the same truck. One was black with red interior and the other black with gray interior. My boss insisted on taking my car for a test drive and don't you know he blew the rear. We put 4.11 gears in it. Gas's car had a 3.89 rear. Gas had a guy helping him who was really sharp on tuning. At Half Moon Bay one day Gas beat me and set the record at 107 MPH. I accused Gas of cheating, so Gas asked the track owner to let him stay and make a run in my car. Gas installed a screw in the carburetor secondary, set the timing and ran 106 MPH with my car. From that time on I always looked up to Gas. He was sort of like an older brother to me.

"In 1961 Bill Waters Ford opened a new dealership in Oakland. I talked them into a high-performance department. We persuaded Gas to join us. Our service manager was Joe Clement, one of the most respected Ford performance men in Northern California. We started Bill Waters Ford Race Team and we competed in five classes. The team took top honors at local and the Northern Nationals. The race promotion really paid off; between Gas and I we sold over 100 high-performance Fords that year."

Question: What did you run in 1961?

Ed: "Gas had the 401-horsepower 390 and I had a 390 Police Interceptor with an automatic. With Joe Clement's help I won for the first time.

Ed Terry, a high-performance salesman at Bill Waters Ford in Oakland, CA, took this 406 Galaxie to his first big win in the B/Stock class at the 1963 NHRA Winternationals. Gas Ronda had driven this car to the runner-up spot in the California Super/Stock championships the previous year. Note Gas' name next to Ed's on the door. Ed had replaced the tri-power carburetion with a single four barrel to fit into B/Stock. (Ed Terry)

That season we gave Ronnie Broadhead fits. And the Pontiac guys all had Mickey Thompson parts.

"In 1962 Ford Motor Company started really getting involved. They sent representatives out to our dealership and we helped create the Performance Corner on the showroom floor and the tune-up stalls in the shop. Nineteen sixty-two was the year that competition really got stiff with Chrysler, Chevy, Pontiac, and Ford. Everybody was working longer and harder at the sport than at their jobs. Everybody's dream was to make a living at it.

"Tommy Grove was the first in our area to do so with the *Melrose Missile*. I met Tommy in the late '50s. There were a lot of drive-in restaurants in the Bay Area and we would cruise them looking

Next up in what was to become a long line of winning cars for Ed Terry was this 1964 Falcon Sprint. With a Shelby Cobra 289 and preparation by Les Ritchey's Performance Associates, this little car became a national event winner as well. Note the rearward-facing traction bars that were a Les Ritchey trademark. (Ed Terry)

Disappointed that he didn't receive a Thunderbolt in 1964, Ed's pain was no doubt eased somewhat when Ford's Charlie Gray offered him a ride in one of the Shelby Dragon Snakes. A national tour followed, during which the hopes and dreams of many a Corvette owner were dashed. (Ed Terry)

for drag races. I would have to say that Tommy was the king of the street. He had a '48 Plymouth with an OHV Cadillac with six carbs. It would fly. He then graduated to a '55 Chevy called the *Weiner*. It became famous both on the street and strip. He then had a new 409 bubbletop Impala. He set both ends of the record with it. A guy by the name of Charlie DeBarie approached Tommy at Fremont, said he owned Melrose Chrysler-Plymouth, had a new performance program, and would Tommy be interested in working for them? So Tom had a full-time job working on the many *Melrose Missiles*."

"In late '62 Gas Ronda left for Southern California to be with Les Ritchey at Performance Associates. They went to Dearborn to help form the original Drag Council. Gas came back with a job and a lightweight 1962 Galaxie with two four barrels and a four speed. I bought Gas's old 1962 406 and I won B/Stock at the 1963 Winternationals. I was undefeated locally in 1963 with the 406."

Ed Terry replaced the multiple carburetor setup on the '62 Ford with a single four-barrel, dropping the car to the B/Stock class, which he won handily at the 1963 NHRA Winternationals with a 13.28 @ 108.04 MPH.

"Late in 1963 was all about the T-Bolts. I talked to Charlie Gray weekly and was told that I was going to get one to cover Northern California. That didn't happen and I was so devastated that I hung up the phone on him. About two weeks later he called on a Saturday morning and asked me if I was interested in running a 289 program.

"In 1964 Bill Waters Ford donated a 1964 Falcon Sprint and I went to Carroll Shelby's for an engine and drivetrain. We were too late for the NHRA Winternationals but on time for the AHRA Nationals in Phoenix. We set both ends of the records in class and won Middle Eliminator."

Question: Can you provide a little more information on how the Falcon was prepared?

Ed: "The engine was a Shelby-prepared 289 that had been destined for Dave MacDonald's Cobra. Shelby told his guys to put two four barrels

There were two team cars built at Broadway Motors for 1965: Tommy Grove's A/FX Mustang and Ed Terry's B/FX small block-powered version. To avoid having to compete against fellow Ford team members in B/FX, Terry converted the car to run in the C/Gas class with great success. (Ed Terry)

and a blow-proof bell housing on it. In testing the car wouldn't hook up so we took it to Les Ritchey's for traction bars. The first time out with the bars they broke, so we didn't make the Winternationals. After that the car stayed with Les and different bars were made. Then we went to the AHRA Winter Nationals and won class and the eliminator. It was a great car.

"The next big meet was the *Hot Rod* Magazine meet at Riverside, CA. We won C/MP and Street Eliminator. It was a good race for Ford. Gas Ronda beat a new Dodge Hemi for Super Stock in his T-Bolt and I beat a new Dodge Hemi for Street Eliminator.

"Ford had a banquet at the Riverside Hotel and all the big wheels were there, including Shelby. Charlie Gray asked me if I would meet with Shelby the next morning at his office. At the meeting Shelby asked me to introduce the *Dragon Snake* to drag racing nationwide. It was my first full-time job racing. Two weeks later we headed southeast with a truck, trailer, *Dragon Snake*, and a Shelby tech. [We visited] Texas, Alabama, Louisiana, Georgia, North Carolina, Virginia, Ohio, Detroit, Indy, and then back west through Kansas, Oklahoma, New Mexico, Colorado, and [then came] home to Long Beach.

While in the South, segregation was still in existence, with Black folks on one side of the track and Whites on the other. Buster Couch at Phenix City, AL, had lined up a bunch of Corvettes to race against the Cobra, which of course nobody had seen 'til now. A young Black guy came up to me before the race and asked if I could really beat the Vettes. I said, 'Of course I can.' He replied, 'Good, cause we all bet on each race and we will be betting on you.' So I gave him $20 to bet for me and of course I won, so I was a big hero in their eyes."

Ed won the A/SP class at the 1964 NHRA Nationals at the wheel of the *Dragon Snake*. As reported by *Hot Rod* Magazine, "Terry bested six other Cobras and a fleet of Corvettes to win the A/SP title." Ed's winning pass was recorded as a 12.06 @ 113.49 MPH.

Here Ed points out the four Weber carburetors that gave the 289 cubic inch small-block engine its fire. Ed credits Tommy Grove for his innovative development of the small-block Ford engine for drag racing. (Ed Terry)

"In 1965 Tommy Grove quit Chrysler and wanted to come to Ford. We called Charlie Gray from my office at Broadway Ford in Oakland. Charlie said the budget was spent for the year but he wanted Tommy, so he agreed to send Tommy all the parts to build a 1965 A/FX Mustang. So we started 1965 with a pair of black Mustangs painted and lettered alike. Mine was the *Quarter Horse* B/FX and Tommy's was the *Charlie Horse* A/FX.

"Early in 1965 Charlie Gray wanted us to get real serious about R&D on the 289s so he sent six assembly-line engines and purchase orders for anything we needed. Not many people know Tommy was a real engineer. He designed and ground camshafts, designed combustion chambers and pistons, and blueprinted engines. It seems that everybody who attempted to build a 289 approached it like a small-block Chevy, including Holman-Moody, and it didn't work. Tommy said the combustion chambers were too small for pop-up pistons and long-duration camshafts. We used a 1.150 deck height block, 4-5 thousandths piston-wall clearance, tight ring gaps, Mickey Thompson flat top pistons with .250 valve reliefs, aluminum rods, and a stock five-quart

Ed charges out with his *Quarter Horse* during C/Gas class competition at the AHRA Winter Nationals. Note the change of sponsorship on the car and the addition of Joe Clement's name alongside Ed's. Terry gives high praise to Joe's abilities and credits Clement's preparation and tuning with much of the car's success. (Ed Terry)

Ed poses with his one-of-a-kind factory ride for 1966. The big Galaxie was powered by a 289 cubic inch small-block and ran in the C/FX class. This car was also prepared and tuned by Joe Clement. (Ed Terry)

oil pan with a windage tray. We used stock Ford rod and main bearings (red), a Crane 298R roller cam, 298 degrees of duration, .546 lift, 1 5/8" one-piece Corvette exhaust valves (under 100 grams each), 48cc cylinder heads, four Weber carbs, and a dual-point distributor. RPM range was 7,000-8,500. The end result was bulletproof, 500-plus horsepower engines. The 1965 Mustang ran at 2,650 pounds, 11.00 @ 123 MPH and the 1966 Galaxie at 3750 pounds 12.30 @ 113 MPH.

"At the 1966 Winternationals we ran a '66 Galaxie in C/FX and won, and a '65 Mustang in C/Gas and won. I ran out in both cars in Street Eliminator. At the Bristol, TN Springnationals we won the C/FX class and ran out in the Street Eliminator. At the Indy Nationals we won the C/FX class and again ran out in Street Eliminator. At the Division 7 points race we finally won Street Eliminator.

"In 1967 I got the 1966 Fairlane prototype with the 427 for the SS/B class. At the Winterna-

Ed Terry leaves the starting line in his 1966 Galaxie at the NHRA Winternationals. Victory on most occasions for the huge car with the tiny engine was not much more than 12 seconds away. (Ed Terry)

Terry's big Ford is underway at the 1966 NHRA Winternationals. The small block-powered car ran quicker than some with 427's. (Ed Terry)

tionals, with seven inch tires, I lost. During 1967 I went to all the Division 7 points races and raced against Wiley Cossey's Hemi Plymouth, Bill Bagshaw's Hemi Dart, Dick Landy's Hemi Dart and Bob Lambeck's Dodge and was able to maintain second place in the points. At the 1967 Indy Nationals with new engine parts it was the biggest factory shootout ever, with the biggest names in drag racing. I won the shootout but was disqualified on a technicality and re-instated after the event."

The technicality that Ed refers to that caused his initial disqualification at the 1967 Nationals was caused by the fact that Ford had failed to provide the NHRA tech officials with a part number for the newly issued pistons. Once this matter was rectified, Terry's well-deserved win was re-instated.

"The next big race I had to get ready for was the Division 7 finals in Carlsbad, California. My mechanic and good friend Bob Spears and I had a parting of the ways. My car with the new parts was definitely better, but still not up to par with Hubert Platt and Jerry Harvey. Again Tommy Grove came to the rescue. He started checking everything out and found out that the carb jets had been drilled out and the engine was running too rich, had too hot of a plug, and not enough timing.

Another addition to Terry's trophy cabinet came from the 1965 NHRA Winternationals with his *Quarter Horse* Mustang. (Ed Terry)

This Division 7 meet was important enough that Chrysler had a lot of their top guys there. Ford asked Hubert Platt to show, so Tommy decided to park his car and spend the weekend with me. My best E.T. had been 11.22 at Indy. I came off the trailer with a 10.98 and when all the smoke cleared it was Hubert and I in the final. I prevailed with a 10.92 E.T. at 127.88 MPH.

"In 1968 there was a flock of Cobra Jets at the Winternationals, but I didn't have one so I drove Hubert Platt's SS/C 67 Fairlane and was the class runner-up to Bill Jenkins by inches. The Eliminator class was made up from the winner and runner up in each Super Stock class. I drew "Grumpy" in the first round to the delight of all the the Cobra

Next up for Ed was this SS/B 427 Fairlane and new sponsorship from Hayward Ford. Note the Tom Grove Racing Engines logo on front fender. Ed couldn't go wrong there. Terry became the spoiler for Bill Jenkins at the 1968 NHRA Winternationals, where his defeat of the Grump aided the Ford cause greatly. (Ed Terry)

Jets, as Grumpy could have beat any one of them. I beat Grumpy by inches and became the temporary hero for the Ford brass. Al Joniec went on the win Super Stock Eliminator.

"I left the Winternationals with a new, Bill Stroppe-prepared Cobra Jet Mustang. I returned home and signed up Hayward Ford [as a sponsor] for truck and trailer expense money. I opened a Texaco service center in Hayward.

"Division 7 track promoters got together Washington, Oregon, California, and Utah to form a Heads-Up Super Stock racing series and it was quite popular. My contract with Ford was to run the Division 7 points meets with the Cobra Jet. I called Chuck Foulger at Ford and talked him into sending me a 427 Tunnel Port for the Cobra Jet so I could switch from Stock to Heads-Up on the off weeks. I ran the Cobra Jet and the Fairlane in the Heads-Up against the Hemis and Camaros and was winner and runner-up to myself (both his CJ and Fairlane advanced to the final) at four of the events. We won class honors at the *Hot Rod* magazine meet but ran out in the Eliminator. We were holding our own in the Division 7 points chase.

Ed Terry's 427 Fairlane on the return road after a run at Carlsbad Raceway in California. (Mashie Mihalko)

Ed's performance at the 1968 Winternationals was rewarded with this Hayward Ford-sponsored Cobra Jet Mustang. Here he goes off against Ronnie Sox at Riverside, CA. Ed is quick to point out that the great Ronnie Sox did not put a hole shot on him—Sox actually had the handicap start. (Ed Terry)

In October, 1968 I got a call from Ford asking me to come to Dearborn and plan on being there a few days. Hubert Platt and I were given the two drag teams and we got to help design the colors and transporters and concepts. Larry Shinoda from Ford Styling did 90 percent of it. I was so excited I could hardly breathe.

"On December 27, 1968 I went to Stroppe's to get ready for the New Year's Day press show and car testing. At the Winternationals we won Best Appearing Cars and Team, qualified well with both cars, but did not win. We held clinics twice a week and raced on the weekends. We were supposed to be West Coast but ended up in Pennsylvania and New Jersey."

Question: Did you enjoy doing the clinics?

Ed: "They were great! I remember one we did at Drew Ford in San Diego. So many people showed up that traffic was backed up. The owner of the dealership wrote Ford a real nice letter after we did the clinic."

Along with drag clinics and car preparation, Ed Terry and Dick Wood were competing with their respective team cars. And, as evidenced by the headline in the March 28, 1969 issue of *National Dragster*, which read, "Terry rips West Coast Super Stocks at OCIR," they were winning as well.

"Around June 1969 we added a Heads-Up early Pro/Stock, which was my '68 Cobra Jet modified with a 427 Tunnel Port engine and some fiberglass parts. It ran 10.20's at 135 MPH for IHRA and Midwest tracks. In August of '69 we ran at Detroit Dragway with over 100 Heads-Up cars. I was runner-up on Saturday and Sunday behind the Kimball brothers' Camaro.

"November of 1969 at the World Finals in Tulsa, OK, NHRA decided to go Pro/Stock racing for 1970 and had Chrysler, GM, Ford, and AMC stay for a rules meeting. [They decided on] 7.5 pounds per cubic inch, stock wheel base, fiberglass parts, etc. I asked Emil Loeffler if we could get started right away. There was no budget for cars but they had engines and parts accounts for Holman-Moody Stroppe. So I called Chuck Foulger at Foulger Ford to send me a stripped-down Mustang so we could get started. Hubert Platt did likewise.

"At the end of November we were back at Stroppe's in Long Beach to start rebuilding everything. Our shows had become so popular at Ford stores that they became very political. When our season was supposed to be over in late November, a dealer in Lake Geneva, WI had enough political power to have us come back across the U.S. in bad weather to do a show that year. I got the flu and then pneumonia and had to be flown home.

"On New Years Day 1970, we went to Irwindale to test the '70 Pro/Stock Mustang. There were so many cars I only had time for two runs, 10.20 seconds at 135 MPH. At the '70 Winternationals the Mustangs were two to three tenths off the

Ed and Dick show off their respective Drag Team Super/Stock cars. Ed got the Cobra Jet Mustang and Dick the Cobra Jet Torino. (Ed Terry)

Ed Terry speaks at one of the many performance clinics he and Dick did at Ford dealers as part of their Drag Team duties. Many a young Ford man was inspired through this program. (Ed Terry)

The Super/Stock Mustang was converted to 1970 trim to avoid building another car, and the Drag Team's winning ways continued. Here the car is running in the SS/H class. (Ed Terry)

leaders. There was no time to worry as shows and races were already booked, so we tried to work it out on the road.

"The original plan was for Holman-Moody Stroppe to supply engines for research and development. Dick Wood and I would do the fine tuning. Considering the performance hole we were in

Ed wrinkles the slicks in the Drag Team Cobra Jet Mustang in 1969. The car ran in the SS/I class at this time. Minor modifications allowed the car to move from class to class according to the team's mission. (Ed Terry)

the plan got changed, so they tried to find a sixth team member to make the car competitive. There were no Tommy Groves or John Healeys available so they tried Roger Caster.

"Even in 1970 I realized that what we did would be making history. They moved our headquarters to Dallas to accommodate Caster. Roger had the biggest ego of anybody I had met. When he would build an engine there were ten to fifteen guys watching every move. It looked like a hospital operating room, everything sanitary with white coats and gloves. He spoke directly to Ford daily and referred to me as 'his driver.'

"In May 1970 at Shreveport, LA, at a big Heads-Up Pro/Stock meet with lots of big names, we were the main advertising attraction. Roger had installed a Joe Hunt magneto and threw the carb jets away, [figuring] the more fuel, the more power. He always timed the engine with a small light bulb and then checked it with a timing light. He pulled the number one plug wire so he wouldn't get shocked. Roger could not attend this race due to personal reasons. Our public relations guy got arrival plans wrong so we showed up four hours late. The races had already started, so

After the Mustang body proved too heavy for the new Pro/Stock class, Ed had this Maverick built. With John Healey SOHC 427 power, the *Silver Bullet* showed great potential. Unfortunately Ford dropped the program before the car's full capabilities could be reached. (Ed Terry)

we went straight to the line. The second I dropped the clutch the car laid over. The magneto was dead. So we had towed 700 miles round trip for nothing except egg on our face. Roger blamed everything on Joe Hunt magnetos.

In this 1970 Pro/Stock matchup, Ed Terry in the Maverick goes off against the author's friend Sam Auxier, Jr. in his wheel-standing, Cammer-powered Maverick. (Ed Terry)

"The next week there was a Heads-Up Pro/Stock meet in the Dallas area. [It was] the same scenario as the week before. Roger could not attend and the car nosed over. But this time Joe Hunt was there. Joe checked Roger's procedure. When Roger had previously pulled the number one plug wire to check timing, it blew out the secondary coils in the magneto. So at two big meets in a row we shot ourselves in the foot.

"In the meantime Roger had been talking to Ford about a Don Hardy-built Maverick. I didn't know anything about it but was excited when I heard. Roger didn't include NHRA or anybody else on the specs of this car. When we showed up at the Spring Nationals the car was 20 years ahead of its time, adjustable four link, coil over shocks, etc. The car was declared illegal. I got a call from Jacques Passino himself wanting to know what the heck was going on. This was the kind of attention I did not need. We took the car to Dearborn Steel Tubing to see if they could salvage it and they changed the suspension front and rear. We left for Indy and didn't even have a set of headers. They announced [our request for headers] on the public address system and a fan had a set of Hooker headers for a Mustang. John Healey from Tasca Ford was now a team member and we has able to fabricate them to fit. John was able to make big improvements.

The *Silver Bullet* shows off some of that John Healey horsepower in these two starting line photos. (Ed Terry)

"Ford rented the track before the World Finals in Tulsa and all the Ford racers in the area were there: Dyno Don, Hubert Platt, Paul Harvey, etc. We were the fastest Ford at the testing. We had made a complete circle; I was never so proud. At Tulsa in qualifying I ran a friend, Arlen Vanke from Chrysler. We were glued together from one end to the other and he jumped out at the end of the race and congratulated me on getting competitive.

"When we returned to Long Beach I could hardly wait for 1971. The shows were super popular and we finally had a car we could work with. In 1971 Ford decided to go lightweight [with] the Boss 351. We were too late for the Winternationals but on target for the Gatornationals. Running two shifts on the dyno and the entire team working seven days a week, there was no time for testing, just get there. My first qualifying run with the 351, I revved the engine and let the clutch out and didn't move. They had machined the axles too

Ed's former Drag Team Mustang was found in as-last-raced condition several years ago. It was one of several on display when the Ford Drag Team was honored at the 2010 Hot Rod Reunion in Bowling Green, KY. The H-M Stroppe logo is still in place on the car.

short and they sheared off. Dick Loehr's engine was weak, so we took the engine and transmission out of my car so he could qualify. Needless to say it was a terrible outing."

Question: Was that the Maverick that you called *Silver Bullet*?

Ed: "That was the *Silver Bullet*. What a beautiful car that was. Foulger Ford sent a new Maverick over to Stroppe's and they took it totally apart and acid dipped the body. Then they put it all back together again and it was beautiful. I sold that car to Hubert Platt and he ran it with a Boss 429 for a while. After that I don't know what happened to it."

Question: What was your relationship with Dick Loehr?

Ed: "He came on about eight months before the whole thing ended and while we were around each other at Stroppe's and [shared] lunches and

things like that I never really got to know him that well.

"After the Gatornationals Ford had everyone to a meeting and announced that they were getting out of racing. They put the entire motorsports division into smog research. We went back

The Drag Team program gave birth to many Ford dealer drag teams and performance parts programs. Foulger Ford was one of the most active. Here their Muscle Parts van is on display in the pits at Pomona, CA. (Bob Bowman)

to Holman-Moody Stroppe in Long Beach with uncertainty."

Apparently the Ford corporate decision to end factory participation in racing had been made well in advance of the time when drag team members became aware. A document titled, "Drag Program withdrawal proposal," was submitted by Emil Loeffler on February 13, 1970. This proposal called for the Super Stock drag clinic cars being fielded by Terry, Wood, Platt, and Payne to be turned over to Car Merchandising.

"At HMS we were able to get my car back together and take it out to test. The engine had a couple of issues. The valves were too heavy and floated around 7,000 RPM, and oil was staying up topside so we lost two engines in eight passes. Dyno Don and Hubert were having the same problems. Ford put an engineer on it and came up with blocking the lifter bores on the passenger side, which cured it."

"In April Ford had every racer and team to Dearborn for the final parting of ways. They thanked everyone for their participation and sold us all our equipment and cars for a dollar. I couldn't imagine working for a better company than Ford. I had some tough decisions to make. I went to Southern California and spent a week with Earl Wade, Dyno Don's number one man, on the Maverick."

Question: What did Earl Wade do for you?

Ed: "The first thing Earl wanted us to do was scale all four wheels on the car. Then he wanted the car to roll unimpeded before he even looked at the engine. Earl said, 'You've got to address the horsepower you're losing before you make more horsepower.'

"I was having a tough time at home. My wife wanted to quit living like a gypsy and buy a home and settle down. I wanted to call John Healey and go east for Heads-Up racing, but after a lot of thought I decided against it, as we still had to work out a lot of details on the car and John had a big family to support. Even though this decision was 38 years ago I still wish I had continued racing. When I look at Don Prudhomme, Connie Kalitta, the late Ronnie Sox, and Dyno Don, we probably could have made it."

DICK WOOD

Richard "Dick" Wood made up the other half of the Ford Drag team on the West Coast. Sadly, Dick has passed on so I will quote from his official Ford press release biography from 1969:

> A consistent winner on the drag strip for more than ten years, Richard Wood of Fremont, CA, teams with Ed Terry to form Ford's Western Drag Team. Wood has managed to pursue his career as a drag racer without sacrificing his home life. Married, and the father of five (four girls and a boy) Wood often has made the family car double as a drag racer, and with a great deal of success.
>
> His first effort in drag racing came at the wheel of a 1935 Ford coupe. He followed up with a 1934 Ford before switching to a 1958 Chevrolet, which also served as the family's basic means of transportation.
>
> In 1960 Wood met Terry for the first time and formed the friendship that has resulted in their present association. Starting in 1961, Wood was back campaigning a Ford, this time a 1961 Galaxie with a 390 cubic inch engine.
>
> With the start of the 1962 season, Wood returned to a Chevrolet. Alternating power plants, Wood continued to win regularly. Competing in the popular D/Modified Production class, Wood posted class victories in both the 1967 and 1968 NHRA Nationals.
>
> In 1969 Wood and Terry will be campaigning a 1969 Mustang Mach 1 and a 1969 Fairlane Cobra, both powered by the 335 horsepower Cobra Jet 428 cubic inch engine. In addition to his driving Wood will help conduct performance clinics and form drag clubs at Ford dealerships.

The July 1969 issue of the Ford Drag Club newsletter contained the following on the activities of Dick Wood:

> "Dick Wood has driven his Torino past competition from coast to coast. On his home ground in California, Dick topped the field at Division 7 Super Stock circuit meets at Santa Maria and Fremont. He made it into the semi-finals of the Sears Point Open, where he ran into a fellow by the name of Ed Terry. In Las Vegas he was runner-up to a Mustang in the Stardust Open. At the Grand Nationals in Detroit, Wood won his class and was runner-up for Stock Eliminator, losing because he ran out of his bracket (too quick). Two weeks later Dick showed he still had the AHRA groove by winning E/SA at the Bristol Spring Nationals."

CHAPTER 8

HUBERT PLATT / RANDY PAYNE

While Hubert Platt may not be able to take credit for bringing show business to drag racing, a good argument could be made for the fact that he brought it to a whole new level. In my humble opinion Hubert epitomizes the all-out, balls-to-the-wall. Southern match racer. Hubert is a larger-than-life character, a man whose life reads better than fiction, and a man alongside whom the so-called characters in today's motorsports pale by comparison. If there was ever someone who could be called a man of his time, it's Hubert Platt.

Question: What sparked your interest in cars and when did you start racing them?

Hubert: "I started racing in the late fifties. I had a '51 Ford that I put an Oldsmobile engine in. That's what everybody did back then. I was hauling liquor and Oldsmobile motors ran better than anything else. And that's what got me interested in drag racing."

Question: What came after the '51 Ford?

Hubert: "After that I went to DeSotos. Them damn DeSotos would fly. Everybody had them Oldsmobiles and the Mercurys. We'd go out there and race a mile or two miles. We couldn't run from a standing start. We would just take off and then everybody would nail it. Nothing would outrun them DeSotos though. They had the Hemi in 'em and by the end of that two miles Hu Baby was first. I hauled liquor back then, and wasn't nobody could outrun me. I must have hauled a million gallons back in my time. I had a hell of a time. But the Oldsmobiles run real good and the Mercurys too. The '54 Mercury was a bad ass. But them DeSoto's had that Powerflite transmission. That's where I got started and I enjoyed every minute of it."

Question: What was the first drag strip you ever went down? Legal drag strip, that is.

Hubert: "It was Manassas, VA. I was in the Army and I had a brand new '57 Chevrolet with two fours on it. I raced there and then after that I raced at Myrtle Beach, SC. That's where I was born and raised. And we raced on dirt too. Then when I got out of the Army in late '57, early '58 I got caught with a load of liquor in the car and the law took it, my '57 Chevrolet. Then I moved to Atlanta, but before I left I bought a '58. It was a '58 Police Interceptor with two fours on it. It was one the police had ordered but it was the wrong color so they wouldn't take it. It was a chocolate brown and my buddy there called me and said, 'Hey Hubert, I heard the law got you the other night with a load of liquor.' And I said, 'Yup,' and he says 'Now you ain't got no car, and I said, 'That's right.' He said, 'I got one over here for you," and he said, 'I'm

After successfully racing Chevrolets for a number of years, Hubert Platt took delivery of this Fairlane Thunderbolt on December 13, 1963 and became a member of the Ford Drag Council. The car was wrecked by its second owner and restored 29 years later.

In 1965 Hubert built this match-race Falcon powered by a 427 High Riser engine. According to Hubert he made more money with this car than any other. One particularly satisfying victory for Hubert came against the Hemi Barracuda of NASCAR racing legend Richard Petty. (T. Allen Platt)

going to finance the whole nine yards.' And he did. That's what I went down to Atlanta in.

"After that I had a service station and I built a '38 Chevrolet and that was the baddest S.O.B. there was. My brother worked for Chevrolet when I had the service station and he called me up and said 'Hubert, they got one of them bad 409's over here.' He said 'It's a Biscayne, no back seat in it. A man bought it new but didn't like it so he traded it back in.' I had a '61 Chevrolet with a 348 in it.

I went over and traded it in for the 409. Then I called Dyno Don and he told me what to do to it and that was one bad ass. A while after that, Nalley Chevrolet had hired Nicholson and when he got there I was over there, so we talked and they hired me and then they hired my brother. We worked in the Nalley-Nicholson dyno shop. I built the heads and my brother would balance the motors and Don put them together."

Question: I remember seeing a photograph of your '62 Chevy and you had the names of all these other drivers painted on the trunk lid. Was that your wanted list?

Hubert: "Yeah, that was *The Bounty Hunter*, and after that I got the '63 and I named that *The Georgia Shaker*. And then Nicholson got me the better heads and intake, the Z-11 stuff, and we had that for two or three months. Then Chevrolet quit, pulled the plug. And then we went with Ford after that."

Question: How did you get your first Ford? You had a 1963 Galaxie for a while right?

Hubert: "Well, that's a long story. Fran Hernandez (Lincoln-Mercury's racing director) was going to build some Comets and I was supposed to get the first one. I told Nicholson about it and he shot me down. And this is the truth. So they gave him the car. And then him, and Sox and them got the Comets and I'm sittin' home. I didn't get shit. Then Ford called and they gave me a 63 1/2 Galaxie."

Question: You didn't have the Galaxie too long, isn't that right?

Hubert: "I run the Galaxie about two months and then I sold it to a guy in Tampa, Florida."

Question: And then you got the famous Thunderbolt?

Hubert: "Yep, I got the Thunderbolt. I went to Detroit to pick it up on December 13. When I got there I got the 13th car and it snowed for three

Platt's Falcon went through a number of modifications, including the alteration of its wheelbase and the addition of fuel injection to the 427 engine. The car was recently found in as-last-raced condition and is the center of attraction wherever it appears.

Hubert campaigned this Dick Walters Ford-sponsored, long-nose Mustang until he received the call to take over driving duties for Ford Drag Council Captain Dick Brannan. The combination of Brannan, Platt, and the Paul Harvey Ford, Larry Coleman-injected, SOHC 427 stretched Mustang proved nearly unbeatable. (Sol Stewart)

days. We drove all the way back to Panama City, Florida to race for Sol Stewart. First run I missed a shift and bent all the valves. After that it was a pretty good car. That S.O.B. was so squirrelly, oh shit. You had to hold the steering wheel real tight because if you didn't and did a wheelstand you didn't know where it was going."

Question: So, the Thunderbolt was scary to drive?

Hubert: "Oh man, you had to have more nerve than Dick Tracy to drive that damn thing. I drove that car almost a year and then I sold it to Lee Malkemes and he wrecked it on the way home."

Hubert's beautiful stretched Mustang Funny Car waits to make another 8-second pass. (Hank Richards)

This official Ford Motor Company promo shot shows Hubert under power in the stretched Mustang funny car.

After buying the Thunderbolt, some spare parts, and a homemade trailer from Hubert, Lee Malkemes was stopping at various tracks on his way back to Pennsylvania to pick up travel money by match racing the car. Hubert had arranged for Lee to face Ronnie Sox in Piedmont, NC, and it was there that Lee crashed the car and was hospitalized with a broken neck. The Thunderbolt rolled over numerous times before coming to rest.

Question: After the Thunderbolt you built your first Falcon?

Hubert: "That's when I built the Falcon. I built that car in my basement."

Question: You had a lot of fun with that car didn't you?

Hubert: " The Falcon made me more money than any other car I had."

Question: I've been told by other racers that running a match race against you back in those days was a lose-lose situation. If they won the crowd hated them for beating you and if you won the crowd still loved you.

Hubert: "If I couldn't win I'd stand the car up and the crowd would give me a standing ovation. I was in California and Pappy Hart (Lions

Hubert strikes a very confident pose alongside his Paul Harvey Ford-sponsored '67 Fairlane, and with good reason. Platt terrorized the formerly dominant Chrysler team cars in SS/B competition in 1967. (Joel Naprstek)

One of the cars Platt dominated in 1967 was the Hemi Plymouth of Mopar great Jere Stahl. Stahl's car is seen here sitting behind Platt's Fairlane in the staging lanes. (Fermier Brothers)

Drag strip promoter) said 'Hubert, you have to be the craziest S.O.B. I've ever seen.' Let me tell you, that Falcon won me millions of dollars. People wouldn't believe me but that Falcon is what put me on easy street."

When asking Hubert's Ford Drag Council teammate and friend Phil Bonner about Platt's antics on the track, Bonner quipped, "Ol' Hubert was a clown. If his car wasn't runnin' right he would put a tool box in the trunk and go out there and do wheelstands. The crowd loved him.'

While moderating a question and answer session for former T-Bolt drivers at the 40th Anniversary of the Thunderbolt, in Carlisle, PA in June 2004, I passed along a question from a fan asking why in so many photos of the period Hubert was seen doing his burnout and dry hops while holding the door of the car open. Hubert, in typical fashion, replied, "That was in case I had to jump out real quick."

Hubert's famous '65 Falcon actually bore two names during its racing career. The first being *The Littlest Georgia Shaker* and later, *Georgia Shaker III* after the alteration of its wheelbase. One of Hubert's proudest moments in his Falcon came when he defeated NASCAR legend Richard Petty's *43Jr.* Barracuda drag car in a match race in South Carolina. Petty had decided to go drag racing when Chrysler boycotted NASCAR

Suddenly it was 1968 and at the NHRA Winternationals that year Hubert Platt was in the thick of things, driving two factory-sponsored 428 Cobra Jet Mustangs. (T. Allen Platt)

Hubert drove the Tasca Ford-sponsored Cobra Jet Mustang in C/SA class competition at Pomona in 1968. (T. Allen Platt)

in 1965, and he proved as formidable a foe on the quarter mile as he was on the high-banked oval tracks. Another victory came at LaPlace, LA, on August 15, 1965 when Hubert's wheel-standing Falcon defeated the West Coast-based Chevelle match racer of Tom Sturm. *National Dragster* reported that Platt ran a best of 10.52 at 136 mph to the Chevy's 10.62 at 134, which was according to their scribe "Almost, but not quite good enough to surpass Platt, who really had himself a day with his 426 [sic] Falcon." The reporting of this match closed with a comment on how the crowd of 3,000 loved every minute of it. No doubt Hubert's showmanship had much to do with this.

Question: Tommy McNeely had a car that looked just like yours. Tell us about that.

Hubert: "I had three of those cars ('65 Falcons). The one I built, the one Dick Walters (Iowa Ford dealer) gave me and then I built the other one for Tommy Mc Neely. The car I built called *The Iowa Shaker* (pronounced 'Eye-Oh-Way' by Hubert). A guy in Arizona still owns it."

Question: After the Falcon you went to a Mustang funny car?

Hubert: "I started driving the Dick Brannan gold Mustang. He had a couple of wrecks and they (Ford) didn't want him to drive anymore. So they put me in it. I never got outrun. I raced that whole year and never got outrun."

Late in 1965 Hubert built yet another *Iowa Shaker*, this one being a radically altered Mustang powered by an injected 427 Wedge engine.

Hubert leaves the starting line in the Paul Harvey Ford SS/E Cobra Jet Mustang--the other car he drove at the 1968 NHRA Winternationals. Platt was runner-up to teammate Al Joniec in class competition, and red-lighted against him during the Super Stock Eliminator runoffs. (T. Allen Platt)

The consummate racer/showman, Hubert Platt. Hubert was made captain of one of two Ford Drag Teams in 1969. Along with partner Randy Payne he competed in class competition from coast to coast and gave performance seminars at Ford dealerships east of the Mississippi. (T. Allen Platt)

Hubert with the Ford Drag Team's *Going Thing* Cobra Jet Mustang 1969. (T. Allen Platt)

According to Platt he only ran the car one time before being offered the driving chores on the former Dick Brannan Mustang.

Question: As I recall you set a national record with the Paul Harvey Ford-sponsored Mustang. Is that right?

Hubert: "I set the record about four or five times. I could set the record anytime I drove it. I think the last time I set it was about 8.20 something at 179-180 miles per hour."

The November 1966 issue of *Drag Racing* magazine announced, "Platt sweeps NASCAR Nationals with Brannan's Mustang at West Salem, Ohio. Hu Baby, one of the sport's great personalities, proved his driving talents in addition to furnishing the fans with much humor. Entry featuring Platt as pilot was a pleasant surprise for everyone concerned except competitors. Hubert has parlayed a magnetic personality into one of the biggest drawing cards in drag racing."

Hubert Platt also took the Paul Harvey Ford-sponsored, stretched Mustang to the A/XS win at the 1967 NHRA Winternationals, recording an 8.49 elapsed time at 171.42 mph. Platt continued to drive this car until mid-1967 and while doing so set and re-set the class record and claimed two other major event wins, the NASCAR Summer Champions at Dragway 42:—West Salem, OH, and the Atco Grand Finale in New Jersey.

Question: Arlen Vanke told me that 1967 would have been a pretty good year for Mopar had it not been for Hubert Platt and that "pesky Fairlane."

Hubert: "That's right. By that time Jere Stahl had the record and everything. I took it to Indianapolis and outran his ass, set the record, everything. I had a seminar over at the Ford place

Dressed sharp for the occasion, Hubert and Randy pose for a publicity photo with their Drag Team cars. (T. Allen Platt)

in Detroit and I told them people, 'You all don't know who I am, but I'm Hubert Platt. You know Jere Stahl from Chrysler was the (expletive deleted) until I got here and I put him on the (expletive deleted) trailer.' Do you know what the paper said the next day? The Detroit paper said "Hubert Platt, southern racist, comes to Detroit." I was called on the carpet and Ford almost fired me, and said, 'You got to quit using all those slang words.' I said 'Shoot, that's all I know.'"

On May 8 through May 12, 1967, Hubert Platt and Dick Brannan ran tests on a 1967 Fairlane with the 427 engine at Bristol Dragway in Bristol, TN. Brannan's report identifies Platt as the driver, with the vehicle weighing 3405 pounds with fiberglass ram air hood, 4.86 rear axle and four-speed manual transmission. The engine is described as a 427 Medium Riser with 13.2 to 1 compression, L-1 P-1 camshaft, and two-inch inside diameter exhaust headers. After two days of preparation a total of 18 test runs were made using both M&H and Goodyear slicks of varying sizes between 8.20 x 15 to 10.50 x 15, and diameters from 29" to 30.3. The quickest and fastest run produced an elapsed time of 11.42 at 123.79 mph. Dick Brannan's conclusion: "This vehicle is expected to be very competitive at the forthcoming NHRA Spring Nationals, June 10 & 11, 1967, since it consistently recorded times better than the national record."

Question: And after the Fairlane came the Cobra Jet Mustang?

Hubert: "That's right."

Question: And I understand that after your amazing performance at the '68 NHRA Winternationals you set and re-set the class record several times with that car?

Hubert: "That's exactly right."

Hubert held the NHRA SS/E record at 11.67 and 120.96 mph.

The East Coast Ford Drag Team transporter and race cars of Hubert Platt and Randy Payne sit in front of Ford World Headquarters in Dearborn, MI. (T. Allen Platt)

Question: What became of the Cobra Jet Mustang?

Hubert: "I had two. I wrecked the one and I don't remember what happened to the other one. I rolled it in Dallas, GA. I remember kicking the windshield out to get out of it."

Prior to wrecking the Paul Harvey Ford-sponsored Mustang, Hubert was in action with it at the NASCAR Winter Championship drag races in Deland, FL, where he found himself in the final runoff for Super Street Eliminator. Going off against Tom Crutchfield's SS/BA Dodge, Hubert got the handicap head start and was off into the night with the Mopar in pursuit. Arriving at the stripe well ahead of his opponent, Platt applied the brakes to avoid running out, but the track's timing devices, which had been acting up for the entire event, indicated that the Ford had run under with an 11.18 elapsed time. Hubert's take on this? "There ain't no way in the world this car'll

Hubert and Randy pose with the West Coast Ford Drag Team race cars of Ed Terry and Dick Wood. (T. Allen Platt)

go 11.18, not even if you dropped it off a stone mountain." Sadly the officials did not see Hubert's logic and awarded the win to Crutchfield.

The second Cobra Jet Mustang that Hubert spoke of was the Foulger Ford-sponsored car with its unique black, gold and white paint scheme. The

In 1969 and '70, lucky Ford fans could attend Ford Performance seminars given by drag racing legends Hubert Platt, Randy Payne, Ed Terry, and Dick Wood at their friendly local Ford dealers. (T. Allen Platt)

January 1969 issue of *Super Stock and Drag Illustrated* magazine provided in-depth coverage of a major Super Stock event run at Orange County International Raceway in Southern California, where fifty of the nation's top competitors were entered. Showing the anti-Ford bias so typical in the automotive press, the magazine's subheadline read, "The golden west recently got a real good taste of what real Super Stock racing is all about, with a special surprise ending: A Ford won." Further into its coverage *SS&DI* somewhat contradicted themselves by indicating in the caption under the photo of Platt's Mustang that he was considered, "The man to beat," perhaps based on the fact that he uncorked a sub SS/EA record 11.79 elapsed time during a timed run. Although Hubert did not ultimately go on to victory at this particular event, his Ford teammate Jerry Harvey, at the wheel of Geno Redd's SS/E *Crazy Horse* Mustang, carried the day for the Ford camp, apparently to the chagrin of *SS&DI*'s writer.

For some period of time in late 1968 and early 1969, Hubert found himself at the wheel of the former Bob Ford A/FX Mustang, which by this time had passed through the hands of Jerry Harvey and carried Paul Harvey Ford livery.

Question: In 1969 Ford gave you the East Coast Drag team and you and Mr. Big Stuff, Randy Payne, were tearing them up on the drag strip and doing performance seminars at Ford dealerships. I can still remember when you came to a dealership in my hometown. The traffic was backed up down the road waiting to get in and see you and the cars. That was a pretty big deal to a teenaged guy in my neighborhood at the time. Everybody knew who Hubert Platt was.

Hubert: "That's right, we had a lot of fun back then. If we were gonna be somewhere all they had to do was advertise that we were going to be there and they would pack the place. I really enjoyed all that."

Some of Hubert's 1969 Drag Team accomplishments include: setting the NHRA SS/IA class record at 12.41 and 112.92 MPH; taking home the SS/IA class win at the NHRA Spring Nationals; winning the Super Stock Eliminator title at the NHRA Winter Championships, where he faced and defeated teammate Randy Payne in an all-Ford Drag Team runoff; and taking the Top Stock title at the AHRA U.S. Open in Rockingham, NC, where he defeated Don Carlton at the wheel of the Sox and Martin Plymouth Road Runner in the final. Ford Drag Team members Platt and Payne were featured in the April 1969 issue of *Car Craft* magazine and Hubert with his Ford Drag Team SOHC 427-powered Mustang graced the cover of the January 1970 issue of *Super Stock and Drag Illustrated* magazine.

Question: And with the Drag Team you became involved in the early days of Pro-Stock racing with first the Mustang with the SOHC engine and later the Maverick correct?

Hubert: "That's right."

Hubert took his Ford Drag Team Cobra Jet Mustang to a runner-up finish at the 1970 Super

A Performance Seminar at your local Ford dealer provided an up-close look at the Ford Drag Team race cars and performance tips from the Drag Team members. (T. Allen Platt)

Hubert Platt and Randy Payne pose proudly with their 1969 Ford Drag Team cars. (T. Allen Platt)

Stock Nationals in York, PA, and on September 14, 1969 set the NHRA SS/HA class record at 11.79 and 118.26 MPH.

Question: After Ford pulled the plug on the racing program you carried on running in Pro-Stock with a series of Pintos right into the mid-seventies as I recall?"

Hubert: "Pinto was the car I had back then and I ran them into the late seventies and then retired from racing."

Question: How did you do with the Pintos?

Hubert: "I did fair. I remember one time I was at Indianapolis and I ran Jenkins in the first round. I put a gate job on the S.O.B. and outran him. I won't tell you what he said to me after that, but when I came up the return road the crowd gave me a standing ovation. I got outrun in the next round but that didn't matter cause I beat Jenkins. I can tell you, and this is the truth, there ain't nobody had more fun in drag racing than me."

Hubert in action in the Ford Drag Team SS/IA Cobra Jet Mustang (T. Allen Platt)

Hubertisms

Along with being known as the consummate showman and drag racing legend, Hubert Platt has coined some of the most colorful phrases in motorsports, many of which could hardly be considered "politically correct." Volumes could be written relating the sayings attributed to Hubert over the years, but when asked by his son T. Allen, at my request, to provide a few examples, Hubert replied that he couldn't really remember any funny sayings he ever used. He was just being Hubert and that is just the way he speaks. Allen remembered once, "I was at the track with him and he lost a race. So I asked him, 'Daddy why did you lose?' He said, 'I don't know, I had it W.A.O.'" This was a Hubertism for Wide Ass Open.

Dick Brannan tells of a time when he and Hubert were eating in a restaurant after a race. Some men at a nearby table kept looking over, appearing to recognize the two famous racers. Hubert informed Dick, "Hey Brannan, I think you got some fans over there." Brannan's retort was, "I think they're looking at you, Hubert." After finishing his meal Hubert approached the men, extended his hand and said "Hi, I'm Phil Bonner," to which one of the fans said to his friends "See, I told you it was Phil Bonner."

Hubert told me of a time when he was working at his restaurant after retiring from racing and a customer kept staring at him. Finally the man approached and asked, "Don't I know you from somewhere?" to which Hubert, being Hubert, replied, "I don't know, you ever been in jail?"

As of 2011 Hubert Platt remains in demand for personal appearances and continues to be praised for his contributions to drag racing through recognition by numerous organizations.

The Ford Drag Team cars attended local and NHRA national events when not putting on clinics. Hubert is seen at the NHRA Nationals in the Cobra Jet Mustang. (Tom Kasch)

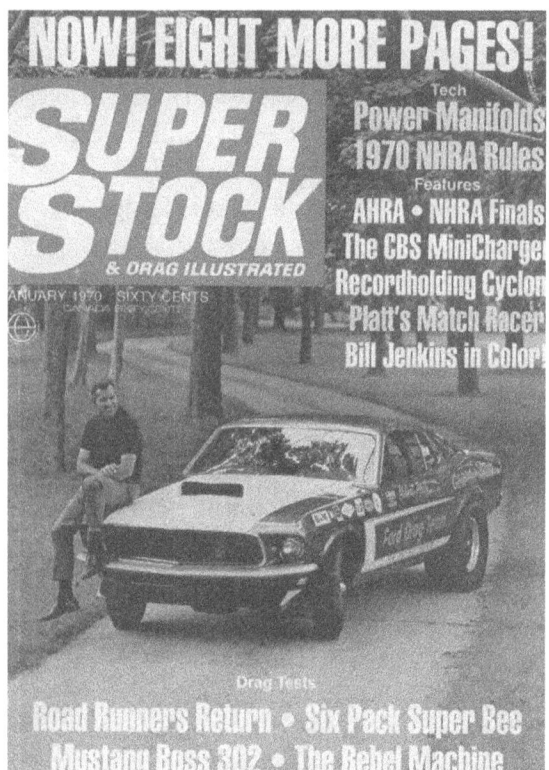

Hubert and his Pro/Stock Drag Team Mustang graced the cover of the January 1970 issue of *Super Stock and Drag Illustrated* magazine. (T. Allen Platt)

Hubert in a publicity shot with the 1970 Mustang Pro/Stock car. (T. Allen Platt)

RANDY PAYNE, "MR. BIG STUFF"

Looking back on the life experiences and background of George Randle Payne, Sr., it becomes abundantly clear how he was the perfect choice to complement fellow Georgian Hubert Platt as part of Ford's East Coast Drag Team. Just as Hubert was honing his driving skills hauling moonshine and drag racing, Randy was rubbing elbows with whiskey runners and tearing up the quarter mile himself.

Being involved in the automobile business with his father Tom, whom he affectionately called "Chief," Randy learned a great many things. One of these was to feature unique vehicles on the family car lot in order to attract customers. When Randy obtained two new 1966 Hemi-powered Dodges, it wasn't long before a pair of local bootleggers arrived. They offered to buy both cars and pay better than top dollar for them at $8,000 each.

When asked if he had a problem with taking a "little change" in payment for the cars, Randy glibly responded, "Money is money." Much to Payne's surprise the change his customers referred to turned out to be a 55-gallon drum filled with nickels, dimes, quarters, and half dollars. Leaving Randy with the formidable task of counting the coins, the moonshiners drove off with the cars, promising to make good on any shortfall in the coin count. After more than a day of counting the total amount came to more than $2,000 over the agreed sale price for the cars. Payne would later learn that the coins were the proceeds from a crime committed against a local Coca Cola bottling plant.

These would not be the only Hemi Dodges that passed through Randy Payne's hands under less than savory circumstances. Randy relates the story of how he came to be in possession of yet another Hemi-powered Dodge. This time it would come by virtue of a card game held at a friend's home where, after many hours of gambling, Payne and his friend had pretty much emptied the pockets of the other players. According to Randy the other players in this particular game consisted of a couple of pimps, three bootleggers, and a couple of car dealers. As the evening drew to a close one of the losers challenged Payne to roll the dice, putting up the title of his Hemi Dodge against the considerable amount of cash in Randy's pocket in a last-ditch effort to get back even.

On the first throw Randy rolled two fours. In order to make the point he would have to roll the

Power for Hubert's Pro/Stock Mustang came from this SOHC 427 engine. Elapsed times were in the low ten-second range. (T. Allen Platt)

The Mustang's SOHC 427 engine gulped air through an enlarged version of the Boss 429 Mustang hood scoop. (T. Allen Platt)

Hubert, at the wheel of the SS/IA Cobra Jet Mustang, gives some encouraging words to fans. (T. Allen Platt)

The Ford Drag Team not only visited Ford dealerships—they also took their performance clinics to vocational schools and prisons.

same again. With every eye in the room fixed on the dice, Randy let them fly and rolled two fours yet again! After collecting the keys to his new Dodge, Payne found himself faced with the dilemma of now having two vehicles, the new Ford pickup with which he had arrived at the game, and the Dodge. Fearing that a sore loser might be tempted to tear up one vehicle while he was off securing the other, Randy quickly formulated a plan. He parked his pickup what he thought was a safe distance away and then returned to claim the Dodge, which was delivered directly to his garage for race preparation. Upon returning for his truck, Payne discovered that his plan had not worked. The pickup had been rammed from both sides. The Dodge would go on to become a race car, bearing the phrase "Two block fours, a pair of squares" in honor of the two rolls of the dice that had won him the car.

That brings us to 1969, when Randy Payne's old buddy Hubert Platt came back into his life. Explaining to Randy that he had a deal in the works with Ford Motor Company, Hubert asked Randy to drive him up to Detroit. Randy's contemporary analysis of Hubert's offer is, "The reason he called me is he didn't have a damn driver's license and he wanted me along as a chaffeur and for protection."

The pair drove from Georgia to Michigan in Payne's Cadillac. Upon arrival they checked into a motel prior to attending a banquet hosted by Ford. Randy recalls meeting Ford CEO Lee Iacocca, who showed an interest in the Georgian's racing history. Iacocca described the concept of Ford forming specialized teams of drag racers who would, through their efforts on the track and company-sponsored performance seminars at dealerships, promote Ford's performance image. Apparently impressed with Payne's personality and racing credentials, Iacocca offered him the position as Hubert Platt's assistant on one of the proposed drag teams. The only problem that Randy could see with this arrangement was his knowledge that another racer had already been offered the job. With Iacocca's assurance that the other driver would be appropriately compensated, Randy Payne came on board as a member of Ford's East Coast Drag Team for 1969.

Ford's official biography of Randy Payne as included in their Drag Team press kit reads as follows:

"A veteran of twelve years of drag strip competition Randy Payne works with Hubert Platt as assistant captain of the Eastern Ford Drag Team. Payne, who looks like a football tackle at 245 pounds and, in fact played that position on his local high school team, had one of his finest years in 1968 as he campaigned a Cobra Jet Mustang throughout the Southeast. The Rome, GA, driver has handled a variety of machines since competing in his first drag meet in 1956. In addition to a number of stock cars Payne has campaigned a trio of sports cars plus a 1939 Willys, all fuel injected and supercharged. Payne made his move to Ford during the 1967 season, taking over the wheel of a Super Stock Mustang. He compiled enough points during the season to qualify for the NHRA World Championships at Tulsa, OK and also established NHRA class records for

Hubert's Cammer-powered Pro/Stock Mustang in the pits at the York Super Stock Nationals May 1970. Tommy Grove's Mustang Funny Car is in the background. (Mashie Mihalko)

When the Mustang proved too heavy for Pro/Stock competition, Hubert went with a Maverick body. An SOHC 427 provided the power at first but was later replaced with the Boss 429 power plant. (T. Allen Platt)

A classic Hubert Platt move is shown here as he does a burnout in his Pro/Stock Maverick while holding the door open. When asked years later why he did this, Hubert replied, "In case I had to jump out real quick." Always the showman. (Fred Simmons)

In this photo from 1971, the Ford Drag Team logo is gone from Platt's Maverick and a Boss 429 engine has replaced the Cammer. (Bob Bowman)

elapsed time and top speed. For the 1969 season Payne will again be relying on Ford's Cobra Jet 428 cubic inch engine for power. Introduced early in 1968 the Cobra Jet engine produces 335 horsepower at 5400 RPM and 440 lbs/ft of torque at 3400 RPM. As part of a two man team with Platt, Payne will conduct performance seminars at Ford dealerships and will help form drag racing clubs. He will continue to race weekends competing in all major events."

Back home in Georgia, Randy's father was less than thrilled with his son and right-hand man in the auto business taking what amounted to a pay cut (Ford was paying $12,000 plus expenses, race winnings kept by driver) to go off and drive race cars. Nonetheless the newly formed Ford Drag Team of Platt and Payne prepared to get down to the business at hand. And the first order of business was for the team members to report to the shop of Holman-Moody Stroppe in California to oversee the preparation of their respective race cars.

Platt later teamed with Jim Yates on the Platt and Yates Pro/Stock Maverick.

The arrangement was for Randy and Hubert to meet at the Atlanta airport for their flight to California. This sounds pretty simple until you consider the fact that not only had Randy Payne never flown before, he was also terrified at the prospect. To quote Randy, "I told my friends if you ever hear that Randy Payne died in an

Randy Payne, Hubert Platt, Ed Terry, and Dick Wood pose with Ford Drag Team transporters and race cars for an official Ford publicity photo. (T. Allen Platt)

airplane accident that means one fell out of the sky on him." On top of this you add Hubert being Hubert, and Randy's account of the trip becomes quite entertaining. In an effort to calm his nerves Payne downed an entire bottle of Crown Royal whiskey and ended up experiencing his first flight in an airplane "drunk as a race car-driving skunk."

After arriving safely in Los Angeles, the partners rented themselves a new Lincoln for transport. But upon discovering that the car's radio didn't work, Payne made a quick u-turn and brought the car back to the rental agency for another. While waiting for another car the duo heard a public address announcement for boarding on a Las Vegas-bound flight. In an it-seemed-like-the-right-thing-to-do-at-the-time moment, Platt nodded to Payne and said "Let's go." After landing in Las Vegas they hailed a taxi and were soon on their way to the Desert Inn. From here Randy relates one of the many stories that made Hubert Platt the legendary character that he is. "I was sitting out in the taxi waiting for Hubert to get us a room. I saw him running out the door and he stuck his head in the cab and asked if I had any money." (Randy had left Georgia with three thousand dollars on his person) "I handed him the whole wad of money less a few hundred."

A period of time passed, during which Payne believed Hubert must be waiting in line to check in—until Platt returned asking for more money.

"I realized that Hubert had gone straight to the gambling tables and lost my money when he walked inside that hotel."

Luckily (?) Payne remembered that a friend from back home, who was known to be a high roller, was in Las Vegas at the time. Having located and explained his plight to the aforementioned high roller, known as Pork Chop Pilgrim, Randy was able to secure a $5,000 loan. However, within a few hours he and Hubert had lost that money too, and Payne found himself asking Pork Chop for yet another advance. Lady luck finally smiled on the two boys from Georgia as Randy was able to win back the $5,000. "I never did get my $3,000 back, though," he lamented.

Some time after their Las Vegas adventure, the team of Platt and Payne found their way to California and the shop of Holman-Moody Stroppe, where the two cars, a 428 Cobra Jet Mustang for Platt and a 428 Cobra Jet-powered Torino for Payne, along with a state-of-the-art transport truck, painted in a scheme that matched the race cars, were made ready to go.

Randy described his official duties as a member of the Ford Drag Team: "We educated the public through seminars and demonstrations at Ford dealerships and competition races at major race tracks across America. The company's goal was to move drag racing from the streets to sanctioned tracks. Hubert Platt and I were the professional

Randy Payne seems to be very interested in what Miss Hurst Golden Shifter Linda Vaughn has to say as she reclines on the hood of the Ford Drag Team Mustang. (T. Allen Platt)

Hubert Platt (left) and Randy Payne pose with NHRA National event trophies, their transporter, and race cars, and with Ford World Headquarters in the background. (Randy Payne)

drivers who met with the public representing Ford Motor Company. I prepared the speeches for the seminars and demonstrations where Hubert and I discussed innovative techniques in engine performance."

Randy Payne's drag racing accomplishments from the time he began racing Ford products onward are impressive to say the least. In 1967, he was NHRA Division 2 Champion and earned enough points to be invited to participate at the

Hubert and Randy pose proudly with race cars and transporter. (Randy Payne)

Randy Payne charges off the starting line in his Ford Drag Team Cobra Jet Torino in this 1969 photo. (Randy Payne)

Teammates Platt and Payne would often end up facing one another for the Super Stock Eliminator title at races. Here Randy, in the Torino, goes off against Hubert's Mustang. (Randy Payne)

NHRA World Finals in Tulsa, OK. In 1969, he won the IHRA Nationals in Bristol, TN. He was a class winner all three nights at the NASCAR Winter Championships in Daytona Beach, FL, and has the distinction of being the only driver to face himself in the finals, as he won class driving both team cars on the third night of competition. He also won his class and set an NHRA record at Pomona, CA. Driving the Platt and Payne *Going Thing* Ford Drag Team Torino, Randy Payne won his class at every event entered and was nominated as Driver of the Year in the Super/Stock class by *Car Craft* magazine in 1969, 1970, and 1971.

Following the demise of the Ford Drag Teams in 1971, Randy Payne continued to carry the blue oval banner, handling driving chores for the Paul Harvey Ford Boss 429 Pro/Stock Maverick and later a Maverick of his own powered by a SOHC 427 engine. "Mr. Big Stuff" is still in the automobile business in his native Georgia and regularly attends drag races and nostalgia racing events with his old friend and teammate Hubert Platt.

CHAPTER 9

PHIL BONNER

"I got started racing back in the fifties. They had a dirt drag strip—that's right, we ran on dirt. They oiled up the first three or four hundred feet of it and you'd slide all over the place. The trick there was not to have too much power, but learn how to keep it going all the way and you'd win a lot of them."

Question: Do you credit this with ultimately making you a better driver?

Bonner: "It did, because it made you learn to drive on slick surfaces. It was like driving on ice. But of course the old cars didn't have that much power then either."

Question: What kind of car where you running back then?

Bonner: "The one I had that ran so good was a Flathead Mercury with a Merc-O-Matic in it. You could just stand on it and it didn't have the power to spin the tires. While the others were spinning and had to start over four or five times I'd be sailing right on down through there. And that's what we started with in '53."

Question: Where did you go from there?

Bonner: "We started racing a good deal in '54, '55, '56, and '57. I didn't do much in '58–'59, [but] then started back pretty heavy in 1960, then really heavy in '61."

Question: Is that when you had the two Starliners?

Bonner: "Yes, I had a '60 Starliner too, but I didn't run that too much, maybe eight to ten times. The '61 Starliners were extremely good. I had the red one to start with and a dark blue one after that. And they got notice from Ford. That, and we were selling a ton of cars. I sold 78 retail in one month myself. We got number one retail sales in the United States at that time."

At this time Bonner was a salesman at Al Means Ford and photos of his red Starliner show lettering done with white shoe polish that reads "Bonnerville" on the car's sides. It was also around this time that Phil's cars began to sport the acronym BBARC which stands for "Bonner's Bad Ass Race Car."

During the formation of the Drag Council in August, 1962, Phil Bonner was among those successful Ford drag racers chosen, thus making him a charter member of the company's first organized drag racing effort.

Question: Now in 1962 did you have both an all-steel and a lightweight Galaxie?

Bonner: "Yes I did. I had both. I had the original lightweight and it was doing real good and then a friend of mine was towing it and he lost

Phil Bonner shows off an assortment of trophies he collected with one of his two 1961 Starliners. Note the shoe polish lettering on the car. Bonner's success with this car would attract the attention of the people at Ford. (P. Bonner)

it. So I had to go get another body and I took all the parts off the wrecked car and that became the red one. I later sold it to Oscar Parker and he put the name *Bad News* on it. Then I had the one that Stark-Hickey Ford had. I needed it for parts and Ford told me to come get it. We needed another match race car so I just turned it into another match car and that was the white car."

While the all-steel '62 Galaxie was legal for NHRA Super/Stock class competition, the lightweight versions were forced into the A/Factory Experimental class because of their low production number. Once again the Fords found themselves in competition with much lighter vehicles fielded by the other manufacturers. Included among these were the Pontiac-backed Tempests fielded by Mickey Thompson, who would later become a member of the Ford Drag Council himself.

It is safe to say that the concept of matching two stock-bodied, contemporary, Detroit-built cars against one another on a drag strip was born in the South. These "match races" were not often run under the rules set down by the NHRA for Super Stock or Stock class competition. This gave rise to the descriptive phrase, "Run what ya brung,"

Bonner poses with his all-steel '62 Galaxie and trophies in front of Al Means Ford. Phil's success on the drag strip brought customers to the dealership. Win on Sunday, sell on Monday. (P. Bonner)

Big Ma Mau sits in front of Frank Vego Ford. By this time his Galaxie has taken on the look of a Southern-style Super/Stock match racer. (P. Bonner)

which was inevitably followed by, "And hope ya brung enough." So it was common for Southern racers like Bonner to field both a class-legal car and a considerably lighter and modified match racer.

Former Bonner crew member Linton Parker described the towing accident that claimed the first lightweight '62 Galaxie. He related that the young man entrusted with driving the tow vehicle "couldn't drive a lick," and did something contrary to how he had been instructed to drive while towing, which caused a jack knife. When the race car separated from the tow bar (yes, even factory-sponsored racers flat-towed their vehicles to and from the track in 1962), it rolled over at least twice and was totaled. Parker, who was asleep in the Galaxie's back seat, was ejected through the shattered back windshield, luckily suffering only minor injuries.

Match racing was very popular in the South, with track promoters offering appearance money to name drivers, a practice that until then had been unheard of. It was just this fact that brought "Dyno Don" Nicholson from California to the Atlanta area in late 1961. Operating the Nally-Nicholson Dyno shop out of Nally Chevrolet, Nicholson and his 409 Chevy were crowd favorites at tracks throughout the South. And

This '62 Galaxie two-door sedan was built to replace Bonner's factory '62 lightweight car, which was destroyed in a towing accident. (P. Bonner)

Bonner's 1963 1/2 lightweight Galaxie, with Al Means sponsorship, appears in Virginia for a match race with 9-inch tires and no front bumper: "Southern style" (Bubba Wright)

nothing would bring the fans out to the track better than the classic Ford vs. Chevy match race. Thus, ace Chevrolet driver Nicholson and Ford pilot Bonner were destined to meet on many a drag strip throughout the 1961 and 1962 seasons.

The late Don Nicholson once related to me how he would often have a little fun at Bonner's expense. After facing Bonner's Ford in a weekend match race, Nicholson would call the Al Means dealership on Monday morning and inquire as to the outcome of the race between their man and the Chevy driver. Don laughingly recalled that no matter what the actual outcome of the race had been, he would be cheerfully informed that Bonner's Ford was the victor—a classic application of the "Win on Sunday, sell on Monday" strategy.

Putting the claims of both camps aside, we are certain of at least one outcome in the Bonner vs. Nicholson match races, as the publication *Racing Roundup* reported that on January 11, 1963, Bonner, at the wheel of his '62 Ford, defeated Nicholson's 409 Chevy. Bonner would also claim the title of Georgia State Super Stock Champion in 1962.

Bonner: "After that the '63s came out and I took the frame out from under one of the '62 cars and put it under the *Big Ma Mau*, the car that ran so good. Then we had the second car, which was the Lafayette Ford car. I ran that car a lot; Fred Lorenzen drove it, Curtis Turner drove it, and Fireball Roberts drove it, and they all did well in it."

The 1963 1/2 lightweight Galaxie that wore the Lafayette Ford livery was primarily a match racer and the aforenamed NASCAR circle track stars were often enlisted to drive the car in match races. In one such match race a contemporary drag racing newspaper reported that Junior Johnston (sic), at the wheel of a '63 Z-11 Chevy, defeated Lorenzen, who was piloting Bonner's Ford. In another reported match-up between Johnson and Lorenzen, Fearless Freddie dropped Johnson, who was at the wheel of a '63 Dodge, recording an 11.55 at 129 mph in Bonner's match-race Galaxie. According to Bonner, Fireball Roberts was the best drag racer among the NASCAR drivers he worked with during this time.

Question: I understand that you had some problems with axles and pinion carriers back in '63. As a matter of fact some give you credit for Ford's development of better axles and pinion carriers. Is that right?

Bonner: "I would have broke 'em if they didn't do it. They (Ford) said they wanted to run fast, and

Two of Bonner's 1963 1/2 lightweight Galaxies. The car in the foreground was a match racer often driven by such noted NASCAR drivers as Fred Lorenzen. The other car was Bonner's regular mount for S/S events and match races. (P. Bonner)

I told them, 'You ain't got the equipment to run fast.' They said, 'You don't know what you're talking about.' So then they sent Dick Brannan down to see what was happening. We would either win or bust. That's just the way it was. I'd shoot the pinion out, wring the transmission off and everything else. That's the way that started. We went from one thing to another and I started shearing those axles off and they would break jagged and I'd pull the pinion out the front."

A perfect example of Phil's rear end problems with the '63 Galaxie was reported in the publication *Drag Speed Illustrated*, with their coverage of a Super Stock meet that took place on November 3, 1963, at Kinston Drag Strip. Reporting on the day's competition indicated that Bonner had warmed up his big Ford with a 12.00 elapsed time at 120.00 mph only to break a rear in the first round of competition. The publication went on to say that the intrepid Mr. Bonner got the car fixed in time to run for fourth-place money only to break a second rear end.

Question: Is the story true about you taking axles out of the new cars on the dealer's lot to carry with you to the track as spares?

Bonner: "Yeah it is. But I didn't hurt anyone. Let me tell you why. The axles that we took out of the cars on the lot we had to use because I couldn't get but two or three runs out of them and then they'd get a little twist in them. You could never break them in a regular car. I never caught any problem over that. I couldn't get enough axles. I needed a pickup truck full of them. I could only make two runs and then had to change axles or I'd tear everything up. So that's when Ford came out with the super rear end that they are still running to this day in NASCAR and everywhere else. Dick Brannan had a lot to do with getting it done and I had a lot to do with breaking everything they'd throw at me."

Phil poses proudly with his Drag Council Thunderbolt and this state-of-the-art transporter. Bonner raced this car successfully in the Super/Stock class, but Southern-style match racing was his real bread and butter. (P. Bonner)

On January 6, 1963, the Georgia State Super Stock races were held at the Yellow River Drag Strip, with a $600 purse up for grabs to the winner. Bonner was there along with some of the biggest names in southern Super Stock racing, including Don Nicholson and Hubert Platt. Despite an injured leg from a motorcycle accident, Bonner prevailed and took home the top prize.

On January 20 Bonner was back at Yellow River for the Race of Champions, and again he emerged victorious. In his writing on the history of the Yellow River Drag Strip, Dr. Marvin T. Smith reported that in 1962 and 1963 Bonner ruled at the track, winning more than 50 trophies. On September 15, 1963, Bonner's Ford faced off against 31 of the South's top Super Stocks for a $5,400 purse. At this point Bonner held the track elapsed time record for Super Stock cars at 11.74. After his September 15 victory Bonner came back to Yellow River on September 29, where pre-race publicity stated, "If Bonner wins first place again, his engine will be torn down and checked, bore, stroke, cam, heads, and valves. They must be strictly stock." Bonner remembers winning the event, and the subsequent tear-down proved his engine to be legal.

Bonner's Thunderbolt lies broken alongside a drag strip after being wrecked by a crew member who took the car without authorization while Phil was away. (P. Bonner)

The remains of Bonner's wrecked Thunderbolt sit on a trailer at his shop. The car would be restored to its former glory many years later, but at this point it was just another old—and unusable—race car. (P. Bonner)

Question: And then in 1964 you received one of the first 11 Thunderbolts?

Bonner: "That's right, and I did real good with it too until one of my crewmen took it out without my permission and wrecked it.

Question: How long did you have the T-Bolt before it was wrecked, and was the Falcon already under construction before that?

Bonner: "I had the Thunderbolt four or five months before it got wrecked and I had already built the Falcon during that time.

Phil Bonner participated at the NHRA Winternationals with his Thunderbolt and while he didn't prevail in the Super Stock class (won by Drag Council teammate Gas Ronda), Bonner did post the quickest elapsed time of any T-Bolt in competition with an 11.57. And on March 9, 1964, Ford's Frank Zimmerman sent a congratulatory letter to Bonner informing him that by virtue of his and Bill Lawton's elapsed times at the

THUNDERBOLT RUN-IN

Phil Bonner was slated to receive Thunderbolt #6 (VIN: 4F41K118358) and on October 22, 1963, Dan Jones of Ford's Performance and Economy Department performed a drag strip evaluation of this car. His report indicates the following:

Run #1: 12.17 @ 118.57 mph,
Run #2: 12.27 @ 119.52 mph.
Following these two runs the carburetor float levels were changed.
Run #3: 12.33 @120.00 mph,
Run #4: 12.16 @ 120.16 mph.
New carburetors were then installed.
Run #5: 12.16 @120.64 mph,
Run #6: 12.05 @121.13,
Run #7: 12.12 @121.13 mph.

Subsequent to the car's release to Bonner, weekly race reports were filed with Ford by each Drag Council member indicating the date, track raced, performance, and outcome of event. A summary of Bonner's reports is as follows:

11/10/63 Orangeburg, SC won S/S class with 11.89 @ 126 mph. Set new track record.

11/17/63 Latherton Mountain, Birmingham, AL. won S/S class with 11.26. (Taking into consideration the elapsed time, it is likely that Phil had by this time installed wider slicks on the car and was running in the A/FX class)

Ford pressured Bonner to run his Thunderbolt in legal Super/Stock trim, so in order to pursue his match-racing obligations in 1964, Bonner built this Falcon powered by a 427 High Riser engine and called it *The Warbucks*. (P. Bonner)

Here Bonner's Falcon, now wearing Al Means sponsorship, dispatches Huston Platt's Chevy in a match race. (P. Bonner)

aforementioned event, the East Coast contingent of the Drag Council had been declared the winners of an intra-team competition. Bonner was additionally presented with an all-expenses-paid vacation to Bermuda from the grateful company.

With the coming of Spring 1964, Bonner reported breaking two transmissions in competition over the weekend of May 11 at Golden Triangle and Tampa Dragway in FL. and included the notation, "Watched from the sidelines."

On May 31, 1964, things were much better as Bonner defeated the *Honker* Dodge of Bud Faubel in a match race at Mason-Dixon in MD and set a new track record at 11.31.

June 6, 1964, Nashville, TN: Bonner won the Super Stock Bonanza, defeating Tom Sturm's A/FX Comet in the final.

June 14, 1964, International Raceway Park, Anchorville, MI: Bonner defeated Arlen Vanke's Plymouth in a match race, recording an 11.34 E.T. in the process.

On the weekend of June 19-21 Bonner was entered in the A/FX class for the *Drag News* Invitational at International Raceway Park. Up for

Bonner unloads his Falcon at Bee Line Dragway in Arizona, early in 1965. His new A/FX Mustang sits on the trailer, where it would stay due to Ford's ban on its factory cars running against the "funny" Mopars. As it turned out, Bonner didn't need his Mustang. On this day he gave the Chrysler teams fits with his year-old Falcon. (Ron Bell)

WHERE THERE'S SMOKE.

Subsequent to the running of the NHRA Winter nationals at Pomona, CA, Mr. Charles E. Gray submitted a report to his managers at Ford outlining the performance of the Drag Council cars at the event."

"The only car faster in Stock Eliminator runoffs than the 11.5 of Bonner and the 11.6 of Brannan was the Ramchargers Dodge at 11.35. It is interesting to note that even though this Dodge was faster than any other vehicle, it lost both the S/SA and Stock Eliminator classes to slower Plymouths. This offers the thought that maybe the Ramcharger was not legal and if this is so the Ford Fairlanes were the fastest legal machines at the Winternationals."

My research has turned up numerous accounts of less-than-legal cars being fielded by factory teams with the express intent of eliminating the vehicles of another manufacturer from competition to increase the odds of a teammate winning. As stated in Mr. Gray's report, the illegal car would intentionally lose the class runoff in order to avoid the post-race teardown.

Bonner received permission from Ford to have a match-race Falcon built for the 1965 season. Here he oversees the building of his one-of-a-kind car at Holman-Moody. (P. Bonner)

Here's Phil, helmet in hand, with his new Falcon match racer in 1965. (P. Bonner)

grabs to the overall winner was a cash purse and a new Ford Mustang. After winning the A/FX class, Bonner was slated to face the S/S winner, Bill Shirey, driving *The Professor* Plymouth. Just prior to the run Bonner was notified that his car was under protest. Despite the fact that all protests were to be filed prior to eliminations, Bonner was told that his car would have to be weighed prior to making the final run. After being assured that the class runoff would be held until his return, Bonner took his car to the scales were it was declared to be legal (minimum weight was 3,200 pounds and

Bonner in action with his *Daddy Warbucks* Falcon. Note its radically altered wheelbase. (P.Bonner)

Bonner's car weighed in at 3,285). Believing he had dispensed with the protest and could return to competition, Bonner was informed that "track officials" wanted to check his car for "non-stock equipment." Once again the Ford was found to be legal. But by the time that Bonner returned to the staging lanes, he discovered that the final round had been run as a single and that Shirey had been declared the winner, awarding him the purse and new car.

June 30, 1964, Tampa, FL: Bonner defeated a local Mopar three straight in a match race, recording an 11.03 @ 125.60 mph.

As well as Phil Bonner did with his Thunderbolt, match racing was his bread and butter. Because Ford frowned on any radical modifications or deviations from legal Super/Stock competition with the Fairlanes, Bonner set out to build himself a proper match racer. A powder blue six cylinder-powered 1964 Falcon hardtop got the nod. Bonner

In this photo it appears that Phil is a little late off the line against Bud Faubel's Honker Dodge. This didn't happen often. (R. Ladley collection)

Bonner goes into a giant wheelstand against teammate Dick Brannan at the AHRA Championships. Brannan went on to win, but Bonner got all the publicity. (R. Ladley collection)

Crowds lined the fences for a closer look at Bonner's wild Falcon whereever he appeared. (P. Bonner)

and company went to work modifying the compact to receive a 427 High Riser engine and all the driveline trimmings required to make the little Ford a big winner. Word has it that Ford caught wind of Bonner's project and offered some parts support, but Bonner is quick to point out that the Falcon was his idea and purchased with his funds. During the same time frame Dearborn Steel Tubing Company was preparing a similar Falcon for Dick Brannan.

Bonner's Falcon, officially named *Georgia Peach* by him, but quickly dubbed *The Frog* by the automotive press as a result of its spectacular wheel-standing leaps off the starting line, took the match race world by storm with early race reports revealing back-to-back match-race victories over Huston Platt's Chevelle at Jackson, SC on August 1 and Yellow River in GA on the 4th. A visit to Greer, GA on August 25 found Bonner and the Falcon taking home Top Stock honors. On Sept. 12, 1964 he traveled north to York, PA, where he set the A/FX track record at 10.90 @ 125.70 mph. On September 22, Bonner defeated Gas Ronda's Thunderbolt in a match race at Mason-Dixon. On this day the flying Falcon posted a 10.88 @ 125.75 mph. Bonner picked up the pace on October 4 when he ran 10.75 @ 126.58, defeating Malcolm Durham's Chevy. While on the road match racing the Falcon, Bonner learned that his Thunderbolt had been wrecked in a racing accident at Paradise Drag Strip in Calhoun, GA by a crewman who did not have permission to take the car out.

The AHRA World Championships were held in Green Valley, AZ September 3-7, 1964,

By late in the season, Bonner had outfitted his Falcon with fuel injectors and was running exotic fuels. Here he prepares for a match race against Dick Landy's Dodge at Englishtown, NJ (Joel Naprstek)

and the subsequent headline for the event read "Phil Bonner Sweeps." Bonner's *Georgia Peach* Falcon started off the weekend by claiming the top qualifying spot for the sixteen-car field with an elapsed time of 11.34 seconds. Going into the semifinal round of eliminations for the title of Mr. Stock Eliminator, Bonner faced the *Friendly Charlie* Dodge of O.R. Mitchell while the Plymouths of Gene Snow and Roger Castor did battle. With Bonner eliminating Mitchell and Snow emerging victorious over Castor, the final was set: Ford vs. Plymouth; Bonner against Snow. Snow had no choice but to push his luck against the quicker Ford and in doing so fouled away his chances while Bonner eased through at 11.45 and 120.32 mph. Bonner's weekend was far from over, however, as he mowed down all eligible competition to also take home the Top Stock Eliminator title.

September 27 found Bonner and his flying Falcon at Dover Dragstrip in Wingdale, NY for

Bonner under the lights at Atco Dragway in New Jersey. He has his game face on in this photo. (Author's collection)

Phil strikes a promotional pose with his radical, stretched Mustang Funny Car. (P. Bonner)

a match race against Malcolm Durham's Chevy. Bonner took the match three rounds to one, posting a 10.59 at 128.9 mph.

Bonner's '64 Falcon was featured on the cover of the February 1965 issue of *Super Stock and Drag Illustrated* magazine, and writer John Raffa's interview of Phil appears on the pages within. In this interview Bonner relates being "awfully happy" about a victory over the legendary Don Nicholson's Chevy at Georgia's Yellow River drag strip in 1961. A victory over Nicholson was always hard to accomplish and certainly a benchmark in the career of any up-and-coming drag racer at the time. Bonner also related to his interviewer that the '61 Starliner had won 72 out of 75 races entered.

Question: When you stepped up to the SOHC 427-powered '65 Mustang the problems with axles started all over again. Isn't that right?

Phil: "Yes, well by that time they had come out with the 31-spline axles and after a while we went to Henry's Axles and that took care of it."

At the 1965 NHRA Winternationals, Bonner's A/FX Mustang broke a rear on his first timed run. During eliminations he fell victim to more drivetrain breakage in the second round, which ended his day early. Bonner related having been asked by a Ford representative what they could do to assist him, and his sarcastic answer was, "Park a pickup truck full of axles right here."

Question: At what point did you build the '65 Falcon? Was that going on at the same time that you had the A/FX Mustang?

Phil: "Well, I had the regular Mustang with the Cammer engine in it and knowing that I had to run in the South and run match races and run what ya brung, I had to make a living. You know you can't eat trophies. So the Falcon became a full-fledged run what ya brung car and as long as it was on gasoline it was very difficult for anyone to beat that car. That orange car, absolutely, it didn't break. After we got it I used a Borg-Warner (four speed transmission). I didn't like the Top Loader and I

Bonner's injected *Daddy Warbucks* stretched Mustang in action against Ronnie Sox's Barracuda Funny Car. (P. Bonner)

never broke one. The only time I broke one was if I tore up a rear and that took it out. And I never missed a gear with one."

On May 25, 1965, a memo was issued to Ford subcontractor Holman-Moody regarding specifications for the construction of Phil Bonner's newest Falcon drag car. The modifications to the Falcon ordered were as follows:

- The front suspension was to be converted to A/FX Mustang using Holman-Moody parts
- The front end was to be assembled with spindles and hubs only with no brakes.
- Motor support from Mustang (A/FX cars) was to be modified to fit Falcon sub frame and the upper fender wells were to be boxed as were those in the Mustang.
- The engine would utilize '65 motor supports and be located in the rear hole of the boxes.
- The front half of the rear fender wells was to be removed, and the springs located inside of the frame rails.
- The center of the front spring bolt was to be moved seven inches forward and two inches down while the rear shackle would be relocated seven inches forward and three inches down.
- Torque arms were to be constructed of .083" tubing and 31 inches in length. The torque arm cross member was to be constructed of .083" tubing with the torque arms mounted parallel to the ground.

Bonner personally oversaw the construction of what was to become the *Daddy Warbucks* Falcon at Holman-Moody, a fact that was covered in depth by an article that appeared *Super Stock and Drag Illustrated* magazine. Phil would run the Falcon exclusively after retiring his A/FX class-legal

Mustang and in doing so became one of the top match race winners in the nation. Phil fondly recalls the Falcon.

"I won 49 straight races with that orange car on gas and then when we went to nitro, at least 60 to 70 percent of those races. The car was good on fuel too, but you're good one day and don't know how to mix it the next. We were all learning and I wasn't used to all that. And we had to go to an automatic transmission because you couldn't shift a four speed on nitro. And I liked shifting gears."

Phil and his flying Falcon would again face Brannan's Mustang at an invitational multi-car match race held at Cecil County, MD dubbed the Factory Showdown. In attendance were; Paul Rossi with his '65 Comet, Cecil Yother's *Melrose Missile* Plymouth, Sox and Martin's Plymouth, Bud Faubel's Dodge, the Ramchargers Dodge, Bob Harrop's Dodge, Ed Schartman's Comet, Dyno Don Nicholson's Comet, Al Joniec's Mustang, Dick Brannan's Mustang, and Bonner's Falcon. Unfortunately the Comet of Nicholson and the Mustang of Joniec suffered mechanical woes during timed runs. To fill out the field, track promoters included a local racer's B/FX Comet. The event was to be run in two heats, or rounds. After losing to the Ramchargers in the first round on a hole shot, Bonner loaded the Falcon to leave the track

How Ford Promoted Phil Bonner

The following are quotes from a Ford Division News Bureau press release dated February 8, 1966, regarding Phil Bonner's '65 Falcon.

Phil Bonner is a blond, likeable Georgian who has enjoyed such success with his various match race cars that he has come to be called the King of Southern Style Racing. In Southern drag racing circles it is largely a case of "run what you brung," and a driver has to have the finest in equipment if he is to build a reputation for himself. That's why Bonner, who at one time devoted part of his time to a career as a salesman but now is exclusively a drag racer, was the first of the Ford drivers to switch into the ranks of the so-called "funny cars."

While Bonner's 1965 Mustang was one of the fastest A/FX cars around, he had work started on a lightweight Falcon at Holman and Moody Inc., in Charlotte, NC with the season fairly young. Bonner's instructions were to build a car that was both light and safe. Substituting fiberglass for the fenders, hood, doors, deck lid, and bumpers brought about most of the weight reduction,

The 427 cubic inch single overhead cam engine was moved back 3 1/2 inches while the wheelbase was reduced to 102.5 inches by moving the rear wheels forward nine inches and the front wheels two inches. This was done for better weight distribution.

The Falcon proved it was capable of running in the low ten seconds with a top speed in the neighborhood of 140 mph. This was accomplished on carburetion and gas. Now Bonner has taken the next logical step. He has outfitted his 427 SOHC engine with fuel injection. Late in the season Bonner nearly repeated as Mr. Stock Eliminator in the AHRA Nationals. He moved through competition to the final round, where he performed a spectacular wheelstand in losing to Dick Brannan in a Mustang.

Bonner started drag racing while still in his teens and in his 15 years in the sport has won more than 200 trophies. He resides in Atlanta, GA, although you won't find him there often because his race activity keeps him on the road much of the year.

and keep another booking, but was persuaded by the promoter to stay for the second stanza. In the second round Bonner dropped Bob Harrop's *Flying Carpet* Dodge 9.96 to 10.25 and next took revenge on the Ramchargers Dodge. The final round came down to Bonner facing first-round winner Dick Brannan's Mustang for the overall winner title. Once again Phil was bitten by the Falcon's superior traction off the starting line and launched into a giant wheel stand, again handing the win to Brannan.

Phil: "When they (Ford) snuck me and Brannan out West to that meet at Lions (The AHRA Nationals) and we won the whole thing, I went straight up in the air on the final run. All four wheels came off the ground and there was no recovering from that when it came down. I swear I got more publicity from that than I ever would if I had won, but I still hated it because I was so far out in front of him and I wanted to win that run."

Question: What about the '66 Fairlane that you built? Did you ever run that car?

Phil: I made one of those Fairlane's with right-hand drive. Everyone was putting the weight over the right side so I made one with the seat on the right and started running that. But everyone started running fuel and things were changing so fast by the time you got one done it was obsolete. So we went from there to the long-nose Mustang with the Cammer and that was good."

The *Daddy Warbucks* Mustang sits alongside the *Melrose Missile* in the pits at Atco Dragway in the summer of 1967.

Apparently Bonner's long-nose Mustang was good on January 22, 1967, as he took home top honors and the title Funny Car Champion at Miami Dragway, posting a 9.38 elapsed time at 157.34 mph in the process.

"Then I had a spill when an axle broke at the wheel. It was a real powerful run and it went around a bunch of times. The right wheel left the car and when you're under full power and that happens you're looking at the starting line immediately. I was running Shirl Greer. I had so much power that day that it spun three times in front of him and he never hit us. That's when I went through that 30-foot high pile of cow manure that they had in a field out there and got crap all over me. Stuck up under my helmet, and it was cow doo. I said that was the shittiest ride I ever had. And from there we kept going on and on.

Subsequent to his crash in Tennessee Bonner debuted his newly stretched Mustang at Raceway Park in Englishtown, NJ for a match race against Hayden Proffitt's Chevy Corvair. The local drag racing paper announced "*Daddy Warbucks* meets Old Pro." And on this day Bonner, in the still-unpainted, stretched Mustang, recorded an 8.76 @ 168.22 mph in the car's first pass down the track and went on to prevail over Proffitt.

Question: You got yourself one of the factory 1968 1/2 Cobra Jet Mustangs eventually, right?

Phil: "Yeah and I did well with it. Again, I did that because Ford wanted me to. Now that wasn't a car that I could make any money off of."

Question: Ford wanted you to run the car in NHRA Super Stock trim?

Phil: "Yeah and I wanted to go match racing. I had to make a living. Everyone thinks Ford paid me, everybody. They didn't pay anybody, they paid nobody. They gave us stuff, but they didn't give us trucks, they didn't give us a car to drive. They gave us race cars and parts, and that's all. And that was the factory team. Everybody thought they gave you a jillion dollars. No, that's not what it was, never was, never. Now, they did pay us to go to some special events."

Question: Your last car was the '69 Torino Funny Car?

Phil: "I had Logghe build me a chassis and Fiberglass Trends did the body. The car had the best of everything. But I had a break-in at my shop and a bunch of stuff was stolen, and when the factory got out of it I decided to quit and do something else in life. And that's what I did."

Phil's '69 Funny Car was indeed a showpiece and was one of the few cars to ever use a Torino body. While he downplays his experience with this car I did find a reference to his making a 7.78 second pass at 202.06 mph before he retired from racing and sold the car.

Phil Bonner went on to run several successful businesses and now divides his time between homes in Georgia and Costa Rica.

CHAPTER 10

TOMMY GROVE

"FORD CHARGER"

Possessed of an engineer's mind and great driving skills, Tommy Grove was successful in every type of vehicle he chose to drag race. His successes running the SOHC 427 Ford engine with a supercharger and nitromethane are legendary, much admired, and unrivaled.

Question: Where did you grow up?

Tommy: "I was born in Walnut Creek, CA, and grew up in Alameda. My dad had a repair shop there and he did a good business working on cars for the guys from the nearby Naval Air Station. I went to Alameda High School and worked for my dad."

Question: What was your first car?

Tommy: "I had a '31 Model A that I put a flathead V-8 in. That was before I was old enough to drive, so my dad suggested I let my brother drive it. When I installed the engine one of the head bolts contacted the steering gear right where the column connected to the steering box, and while it didn't seem to be a problem at first, after a while it rubbed through when my brother was making a turn. He lost the steering and went through a hedge and ended up on someone's lawn. Luckily no one was hurt that time, but later on my brother rolled the car over. After that I had a '32 Plymouth that I put a Cadillac flathead V-8 in, and I used to race that around parking lots. My dad had circle-track cars, first a Ford and then a Plymouth. I helped him and that's where I started to learn how to do internal modifications to engines.

"We put a Chrysler six in the Plymouth. [The engines] looked exactly the same but the Chrysler engine was bigger. You weren't allowed to do any obvious modifications to the engine, but I cut the intake manifold apart, ported it internally, and then welded it back together.

"My next car was a '48 Oldsmobile convertible. I was at a junkyard and I saw this Cadillac engine with twin two-barrel carburetors on it and a Hydramatic transmission. It was war surplus and had come out of a WWII tank. I bought it and put it in the Olds. I found out that for use in a tank, the transmission had bronze clutch plates. In my car it shifted so hard that it would squawk the tires every time it shifted no matter how slow you were going. I learned how to fix Hydros from that. I drag raced that car and did well.

"I had been helping a friend with a '56 Chevy and going to the drags with him and then I built a '41 Plymouth powered by a small-block Chevy and six two-barrels for street racing. I built headers for it but ran them through a stock exhaust

Tommy Grove at speed in his first Ford factory ride, the *Charlie Horse* 1965 Mustang. Powered by a 427 High Riser with lots of Grove innovation included, the wedge Mustang proved very successful for the young Californian that season. Grove had previously run both Chevrolet and Chrysler products successfully. (R. Ladley collection)

system so the car was real quiet. That was a big advantage if the cops came to where we had been racing, since this green Plymouth didn't look like anything someone would run."

Question: Didn't you have a car called the *Weiner*?

Tommy: "Yes I did. That was a customized '55 Chevy. The previous owner had painted this standing hot dog character on the front fenders. I had a small block with four carburetors and a Herbert roller cam in it. It didn't do much up to 4,000 RPM but from there to 8,500 it came alive. I was tearing the facing off of clutches and that taught me to use bonded clutch discs. I set the D/Gas record with that car and later sold it to a guy from North Dakota. After that I had a '55 Chevy that I put a 348 and three deuces in. That was a street and strip car. A guy offered to trade me a beautiful '57 Chevy hardtop for it so I did. By that time I was tuning cars for a lot of guys and Dick Hubbard invited me to use his shop. He had a cam grinder and I learned to use it."

Question: Did you have any Ford products before 1965?

Tommy: "In 1960 I bought a T-Bird. My wife had said that if I would stop racing she would stop bitching. She didn't stop bitching. There was a guy in town who had a '60 Ford sedan with one of the new high-performance 352 engines and he was having a hard time keeping it running right. So I traded him the engine from my T-Bird for his."

Question: You put a high-performance 352 in your new T-Bird? With the automatic transmission?

Tommy: "Yes I did. And I ran the automatic transmission."

Question: Did you drag race the T-Bird?

Tommy: "Yes, I ran it in New/Stock Automatic for a while and then they figured out it had the high-performance engine and made me run Super/Stock Automatic. But I still won with it."

Question: What came next?

Tommy: "I had a '62 Chevy with a 409 that I was racing and one weekend I ran this Plymouth for class and I only beat him by a fender. I had exhaust cutouts on the Chevy at the time. Well, I wasn't going to let any Plymouth beat me so I went home and built headers for the Chevy. The next week the Plymouth was back and we ran again, and even though I ran much better than before I barely beat him again. Around this time Ford had a good high-performance cam, so I made a master off a Ford cam and then ground one for the 409 that had more lift and would give it more power. The following weekend I ran the Plymouth again and even though I went 111 MPH I still only beat him by a fender.

After the race we all would go to this restaurant, so I was sitting there and this guy comes over and asks if we can talk. He explains to me that he was one of the guys with the Plymouth, that they were Chrysler engineers and that after each race the car had been flown back to Detroit so their engineers could make changes. He told me they were called The Ramchargers and that they were on a nationwide tour to develop parts for Chrysler's racing program. He asked me if I would be interested in racing one of their cars and how fast I thought I could make a car like that go. I told him what I thought the car should do and they got me a car. It came through Melrose Motors because the factory didn't want to reveal its involvement. The first time out at with the car at Vacaville, CA I ran right at what I told them the car would run. They were always after me to tell them what I knew, but I never would."

At the wheel of a series of *Melrose Missile* Plymouths, Tommy Grove quickly established a reputation as one of the top Super/Stock racers in the nation.

Question: Did you receive any formal training as an engineer?

Tommy: "No, I learned by the seat of my pants as I went along. I knew to listen to what oth-

At the end of the 1965 season, Grove sold his A/FX Mustang to Bill McDuell, who renamed the car *She Devil* and ran it on the East Coast in the NASCAR drag racing series. This photo shows what remained of the Mustang after a crash caused by a flywheel explosion. (R.F. Bissell)

ers were doing and learn from it. It was never my way or the highway for me. Back in the '60s I was working on a distributor when a guy who raced outboard boats asked me if I paid any attention to flame patterns on pistons in my engines. He explained to me how he had improved the performance in his outboard engine and from that time on I started to read flame patterns on pistons. I did that on the 409 and saw what it needed. I matched the heads to the block and really woke it up."

Question: When we spoke before you told me how your concerns over the acid-dipped '65 car that Plymouth gave you caused you to switch to Ford. Was it all about safety?

Tommy: "The '65 A/FX car had the wheelbase altered two percent, which was legal. I didn't like the look of cars with the wheels moved way up that came later. I had to add 800 pounds of ballast to that car to get it to 3,200 pounds. When I took it out to test, the first time I let out the clutch it ripped the seat right out of the floor. It buckled the quarter panels and the trunk lid caved in. That car was unit construction, so I had to weld in all kinds of bracing to strengthen it. And they wanted me to run Valiant spindles and hubs, which were lighter and allowed the front end to come up further. They never took into consideration how this would affect the front end alignment, and when it came down the car wanted to make a left hand turn. They were asking us to alter the wheelbases, put on injectors, run fuel, and match-race the Fords without agreeing to any rules. They wanted to beat the Fords real bad. I didn't like all that and thought the car was unsafe. Charlie Gray had been after me for a while to come and drive for Ford so that's when I contacted him."

Question: What kind of deal did Ford offer you?

Tommy: "Charlie told me that they had already built their cars for the year, but he wanted me to come on board real bad so he told me if I got a car he would see to it that I got all the parts I needed to run it."

Question: Did you have to buy the Mustang?

Tommy: "Yes, I got it through Ed Terry at Broadway Motors. Ed had a close relationship with the owner and got a good deal. They gave me a truck and I had to buy a trailer."

Question: Was the car prepared at Broadway Motors?

Tommy: "Yes it was. There was a two-bay building back by their body shop that I got to use and that's where it was built."

Question: Did you get all the Holman-Moody A/FX parts, including the torsion-leaf front suspension?

Tommy: "I got all the parts from Holman-Moody but Charlie told me they didn't have any SOHC 427 engines available. He suggested I call Butch Leal because he had a 427 High Riser for sale. I called Butch and bought his engine for $750. I changed the cam timing and with that engine the car ran 132 MPH the first time out, which was faster than "Dyno Don" had set the record at with his Comet that had the SOHC

This 1966 Ford Drag Council promotional photo shows Grove at speed in his Ford *Charger* 1966 stretched Mustang Funny Car. Power came from a fuel injected SOHC 427.

engine. In match-race trim at 3,000 pounds with Weber carburetors the car later ran 145 MPH."

Question: What became of that car?

Tommy: "I sold it to Bill McDuell for $6,000 dollars and he crashed it. I think he had a flywheel explosion that cut the steering and that caused the crash."

Question: Did you get a stretched Mustang from Holman-Moody in '66?

Tommy: "Holman-Moody built me a '66 car. It had a frame built from two by two tubing. The body was all fiberglass, but it still had doors that opened. It had a solid front axle with coils, SOHC 427 with an automatic transmission. I had Algon build me a fuel injection setup for it. Everybody else was using Hilborn injectors and I didn't want them to know what I was doing so I went with Algon."

Ford's official press release biography on Tom Grove for 1966 reads as follows:

Tom Grove of Oakland, CA is the complete professional drag racer, a man who not only drives against the competition available but also builds up his own cars. A veteran of ten seasons, Grove has concentrated in the Factory Experimental and altered wheelbase areas of drag racing. He finished the 1965 season in a Mustang powered by a 427 cubic inch wedge engine. Grove turned in some remarkable times with the wedge Mustang, a tribute to his ability to prepare a car. His top speed was 134.96 MPH and his low elapsed time 10.21 seconds. Running a single overhead cam engine Grove turned, on gas, 139.86 MPH and 9.89 seconds. His car for 1966 is a lightweight Mustang with a 427 wedge power plant (Author's note: Grove's '66 car was powered by an SOHC 427) which will

Tommy tunes the supercharged SOHC 427 that powers his *Going Thing* 1969 Mustang Funny Car. (Bob Bowman)

Grove boils the hides on his *Going Thing* Mustang Funny Car. Tommy had unprecedented success in keeping the SOHC 427 Ford engine together when running a supercharger and nitromethane. He campaigned Cammer-powered cars until all his parts ran out and he couldn't find more. (H. Hagen)

run in the Factory Production category in AHRA competition and in NASCAR Ultra Stock competition. Grove has won many of drag racing's biggest titles during his career, including the Mr. Stock Eliminator title in the 1964 NHRA Winternationals. That same year he had the best speed and elapsed time in the AHRA Winter Nationals. In his Mustang last year he was second eliminator and second low qualifier in the AHRA Nationals. Grove has been building cars for both the street and the drag strip since 1949 when he built up a Model A Ford. His early Ford cars for the strip included a 1955 Thunderbird and a 1960 Thunderbird that he equipped with a 360 horsepower engine.

Question: Did you go to a new car and a supercharger for 1967?

Tommy: "In the '67 car I ran a supercharged Cammer on fuel."

Question: There are many who say that Tommy Grove was the only guy who could keep a Cammer together successfully when supercharged on fuel. What was your secret?

Tommy: "It was in the fuel system. When everyone else ran a pump that delivered 14-16 gallons per minute I had one built that delivered 50 gallons per minute. Then I dropped the compression to 5 to 1 and slowed down the blower. I ran the supercharged engine for six months without ever having the heads off."

Question: What happened to the '67 car?

Tommy: "I crashed it at Virginia Beach as a result of a parachute failure. So I put the supercharged engine in the '66 car and a week later I had a torque converter explosion at Orange County, CA. I rolled out of the car like I was climbing out the window and then when I turned and looked back I saw that the roof was gone. I could have just stood up and stepped out of it."

Question: What did you do then?

Tommy: "The Mercury team was going over to the Cougar body from the Comet because they felt they could run faster with the Cougar. So Al Turner told me that Schartman's Comet was available if I wanted it. Mercury debuted the new Cougars at U.S. 30 and I rolled in late and almost didn't make the show. When I took the Comet and ran 111 MPH, which was faster than they were going with the Cougar body, it shook a lot of people up. They had spent a lot of money and their jobs were on the line."

Question: You eventually went back to a Ford body right?

Tommy: "After the Comet I had a Logghe chassis car and then my last car was a Linblad chassis (both with Ford bodies)."

Question: Did Ford pressure you to run the Boss 429 engine?

Tommy: "Ford wanted me to run the Boss 429 so I did. The first time out at Aquasco, MD I bent all the pushrods. The 429 had a problem with the head castings being too thin. Ford finally cast four sets with thicker castings and I got one of them. I was on my way north, to Epping, NH I think, when the car and truck burned because the guy who was helping me had left the battery switch on."

Question: Did you continue with the Boss 429?

Tommy: "No, I went back to the Cammer and ran that all the way into the '70s. I ran Chrysler engines also and would switch back and forth between the Mustang body and the Vega. At Cayuga, Canada with the Setzer Vega I qualified the car with the Chrysler engine but I hurt it so I put the Cammer in it. In the first round I beat Tom McEwen and the announcer made a real big deal about the Chevy being powered by a Ford engine. He got the crowd all fired up."

Question: Did you finally give up on the Cammer because you ran out of parts?

Tommy: "I ran out of high nickel blocks."

Question: What made you decide to quit racing? Did you finally get tired of it?

Tommy: "I never got tired of it. I realized that I needed to devote all of my time to the textile business in order for it to work. I found that being successful in that business was just like winning a race; it gave me the same satisfaction."

After having left racing behind for other ventures Tommy was called upon to assist the Top Fuel Dragster teams of Chet Herbert and Joe Amato in the 1990's. Working with Sid Waterman on a fuel delivery system of his own design, Grove helped both teams achieve heretofore unheard-of performances, with Amato posting a 296 MPH run the first time out with the new technology.

Tommy Grove's talent for engineering also revolutionized the textile manufacturing process. He has since retired from business and now lives near Atlanta.

CHAPTER 11

MICKEY THOMPSON & BUTCH LEAL, "THE CALIFORNIA FLASH"

MICKEY THOMPSON

Marion Lee (Mickey) Thompson was born December 7, 1928 in Alhambra, CA. By the 1950's he had become deeply immersed in California's car culture and the growing sport of organized drag racing. Mickey Thompson would prove himself to be a motorsports pioneer—not just as a driver but as the architect of an aftermarket performance parts empire that grew out of his insatiable need for more power.

Mickey began his affiliation with major U.S. auto manufacturers in 1960 when he took his home-built Challenger I race car, powered by four Pontiac engines, to the Bonneville salt flats and set a new land speed record. It wasn't very long before Thompson became one of the nation's best-known producers of performance parts for Pontiac engines. Some of his pieces were so effective that GM began affixing corporate Pontiac part numbers to M/T parts, admitting that the hot rodder from California knew best when it came to wringing the most horsepower out of its engines. The Pontiac-Thompson partnership would result in numerous speed records at Bonneville and many of the top-performing Super Stock and Factory Experimental drag cars of the early 1960's.

But by early 1963 an edict from the top brass at General Motors ended all overt factory involvement in motorsports. This left the California speed merchant looking for more fertile ground in Detroit. Ford wisely added Thompson to its fold in 1963 and it wasn't long before he was churning out some very innovative aftermarket parts on behalf of the blue oval bunch. Thompson built a dragster powered by an FE engine stuffed with his parts, called the car the *Harvey Aluminum Special*, and took it on a tour of England to help introduce the popular American sport of drag racing to the British. Thompson would also develop cylinder heads with hemispherical combustion chambers for the big Ford V-8 just as he had for Pontiac. A 1963 M/T catalog shows the Ford hemi head conversion available for sale to the public, but all indications are that no more than a few sets were actually ever built.

Thompson was the recipient of two 1963 1/2 lightweight Galaxies and his driver, Butch Leal, showed the same skills that he had earlier when at the wheel of Chevrolets. Leal gained notice in *National Dragster* after an early outing in the new Ford produced a 12.25 second elapsed time. At one point the second lightweight Galaxie was fitted with the Hemi head conversion, but it is unknown if the car was ever raced in this form. One

West Coast driver, world land speed record holder, and speed parts manufacturer Mickey Thompson came on board with Ford Motor Company in 1963 after Pontiac dropped official support of its racing program. Thompson received this 1963 1/2 lightweight Galaxie, which was handled by his talented young driver Larry "Butch" Leal. *National Dragster* reported that the M/T Ford with Leal driving showed promise with early runs in the low 12-second range. Leal took the car to the NHRA Nationals but lost out in the first round to another Ford. (Mark Ascher)

of two Thunderbolt Fairlanes that M/T Enterprises fielded in 1964 featured a 427 engine fitted with the radical heads. According to contemporary reports, when equipped with the Hemi heads the 427 Ford engine made so much power that the standard drivetrain was not up to the task. Thus driver Jess Tyree had no success with the car due to breakage. Thompson's Ford efforts would fare much better with ace driver Leal at the helm of his Thunderbolt. Butch would take home many class wins, score a runner-up finish to fellow Ford driver Gas Ronda at two major events, and finally find himself in the winner's circle at the prestigious NHRA Nationals at the end of the 1964 season.

Thompson's membership in the Ford Drag Council quietly ended as Butch Leal took over a factory-backed Chrysler ride for 1965.

But in 1969, after hiring Thompson's old friend from his Pontiac days, Bunkie Knudson, Ford came knocking again and so did Butch. Thompson was tasked with assisting Ford in the development of high-performance parts for the new Boss 429 engine. On March 19, 1969 he took delivery of a 1969 Boss 429 Mustang (VIN 9F02R117319) for the sum of one dollar. Ford's agreement with Thompson regarding this car was that it be used for "drag strip racing."

The car was prepared for competition by the shops of Holman-Moody Stroppe, and M/T Enterprises again requested the services of Butch Leal to drive the car. Butch, along with Fritz Vogt, built the engine and got the car ready for competition in the Heads Up Super Stock class that would soon become Pro/Stock.

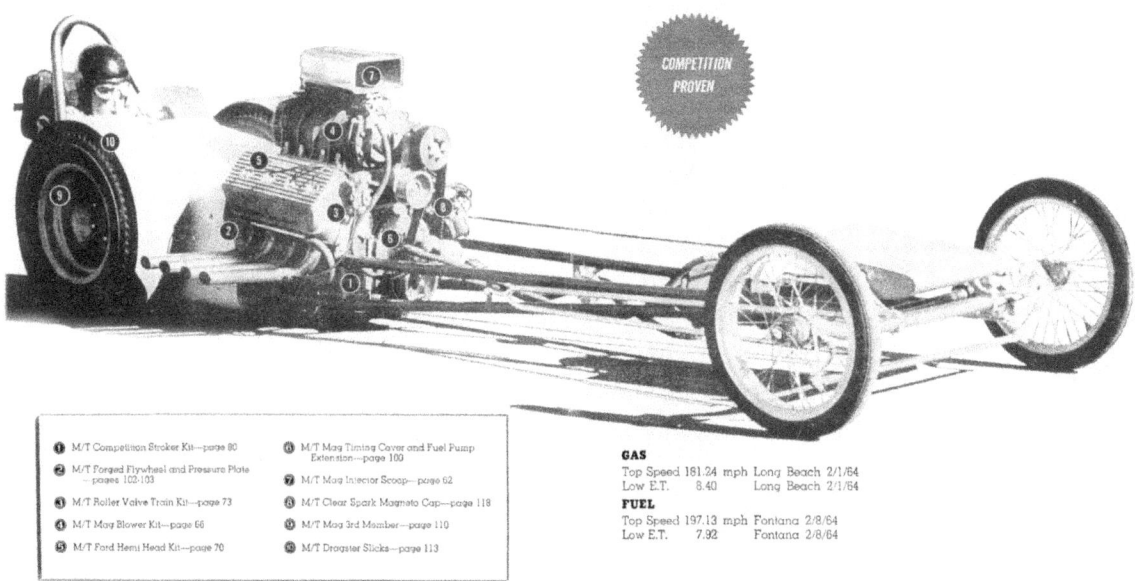

Mickey Thompson developed cylinder heads with hemispherical combustion chambers for the Ford FE series engines that were similar to those he developed for Pontiacs. This ad from the M/T catalog boasts of the performance achieved from Thompson's Ford-powered dragster. (Author's collection)

This close-up shows one of the rare M/T hemi-head conversion engines installed in one of Thompson's lightweight Galaxies. The engraving on the valve cover reads "dyno room." This was obviously a test engine not intended for racing duty in this car.

Mickey Thompson's renewed relationship with Ford would also result in his fielding two Mustang-bodied Funny Cars, one driven by Danny Ongais and the other in the capable hands of Pat Foster. Ongais would go virtually undefeated during the 1969 season.

As 1970 dawned Butch Leal had once again gone his own way. M/T enterprises was under pressure from Ford to drop the SOHC 427 power plant from its Funny Car line up and concentrate on the Boss 429. Thompson debuted a Maverick-bodied, Boss 429 fuel burner for 1970. As successful as his 1969 season had been, that's how bad 1970 would be for M/T—the Maverick won only once during the season. Also in 1970, Thompson once again showed his flair for innovation and thinking outside the box. Thompson tried what *Hot Rod* magazine described as a "revolutionary" Funny Car concept when it featured M/T's latest venture on the cover of its April 1970 issue. Thompson had applied the monocoque style of construction used in Formula One racers to a Mustang-bodied Funny Car. The unique body was a clamshell design where the nose remained fixed while the portion covering the engine and driver's compartment could be raised. Power would come from a supercharged, fuel-burning Boss 429 Ford engine.

Aside from the coverage provided by *Hot Rod*, I have not been able to find any mention of this car being entered in competition. Perhaps Mickey Thompson was unaware of an internal Ford Motor Company memo authored by Emil Loeffler titled, "Drag Program Withdrawal Proposal," dated February 13, 1970. In this memo Mr. Loeffler recommends dropping support of M/T and canceling his existing contract while allowing him to retain

The former M/T lightweight Galaxie, fitted with the hemi head conversion engine, is shown at the 2003 Lightweight Galaxie reunion in Carlisle, PA. The car is lettered as it would have been for racing, but this particular car was not raced to the best of my knowledge.

The class designation painted on the M/T Hemi lightweight's quarter panel indicates Super Stock / Limited Production.

parts and cars in his possession. An accounting of Ford's costs relating to the Mickey Thompson race team, consisting of the two Funny Cars and the "Heads-Up" Mustang of Leal, came to $180,000 as of January 9, 1970.

Soldiering on with the parts left in his possession when Ford pulled its support, Thompson continued his Funny Car program into the early 1970's. His last Boss 429 engine found itself in a Pinto bodied car before the inevitable switch to Chrysler-based power plants took place.

Sadly Mickey Thompson and his wife lost their lives to assassins' bullets on March 16, 1988. After a protracted investigation, authorities eventually arrested and convicted a former Thompson business partner with contracting the murder.

BUTCH LEAL

Larry "Butch" Leal was born in Tulare, CA and grew up around the nearby towns of Tipton and Pixley. By age 14 Butch had developed a love of cars and at 16 he took a summer job working at his dad's trucking business with the promise of a new car as payment for his labors.

The new car in question turned out to be a 1960 Chevy El Camino with the top-line 348 engine, three deuces, and a four speed transmission. It wasn't long before Butch took his El Camino to the local drag strip and won his first trophy. He was hooked.

Thompson received two Thunderbolts as a member of the Ford Drag Council in 1964. The more successful of the two was driven by Butch Leal, "The California Flash." Leal was runner-up to Gas Ronda's Thunderbolt at the NHRA Winternationals and won the Super/Stock class at the NHRA Nationals in 1964, along with numerous other titles and match races. (J. Demmitt, Jr.)

Young Butch Leal leans on the Thunderbolt of Ford Drag Council teammate Phil Bonner in the staging lanes. His car and the Thunderbolt of team captain Dick Brannan are in line behind Bonner. (L. Wolfe)

His friendship with famed tuner and engine builder H.L. Shahan helped Butch keep his car in the winner's circle and fuel his desire for faster cars. Butch's next ride would be a '62 409 Chevy and with help from H.L. and tips from "Dyno Don" Nicholson, this car was also a winner. At a very early age Leal, while not yet nationally known, had gained a regional reputation as a talented driver.

His success with the 409 led Butch to Bill Thomas, a man with factory connections that led to Leal becoming the recipient of one of the limited-production Z-11 factory lightweight Chevys. When GM pulled its support of racing part way through the 1963 season, Thomas set Butch up with Mickey Thompson. Thompson had recently forged a deal with Ford, and Butch came on board as driver for Mickey's 1963 1/2 lightweight Ford Galaxie.

According to Butch the car's performance was sub-par until Les Ritchey performed some of his magic on the carburetors and additional set up tips were received from fellow Drag Council members Dick Brannan and Phil Bonner. At this point the M/T Ford caught the attention of a writer for *National Dragster* who reported that times in the low 12-second range, reachable with Leal's driving abilities, would surely make the car a factor in Super/Stock competition that year. At the 1963 Nationals Leal was eliminated from competition by a similar lightweight Galaxie, but his racing career was about to take a big leap forward as his affiliation with Thompson afforded Butch the opportunity to work on the cars he drove and begin building his own engines.

On October 20, 1963 Butch Leal was on hand with Mickey Thompson at the Ford proving grounds to take delivery of their new Fairlane Thunderbolt (VIN 4F41K118360, one of two such cars that Thompson would receive). The Drag Council members had drawn numbers to see which vehicle they would receive. When Leal drew the number seven car, his apparent disappointment was noticed by Thompson, who figured a 19-year-old kid getting the opportunity to drive the latest and greatest factory race car available should be a little more enthusiastic. When questioned by his boss, Butch revealed that he and team member Gas Ronda had gotten a peek at the cars the night before and noted that while the majority of the cars had an unusual clover leaf-style hood scoop the number six car had the more appealing bubble hood that the Thunderbolts would later come to be known for. The next day as the cars were presented, Leal was delighted to find that Mickey had worked some behind-the-scenes magic and the number seven car was now sporting the more desirable hood.

Ford's pre-delivery performance report on the M/T Thunderbolt indicates that Dan Jones recorded times of: 12.23 @ 119.36 MPH, 12.21 @ 120.32 MPH, 12.14 @ 120.96 MPH and 12.14 @ 120.80 MPH.

After a hiatus from Ford, Mickey Thompson was back in 1969 with several successful Mustang Funny Cars powered by supercharged SOHC 427 engines. Thompson's white Mach I funny car says Boss 429 on the side but actually used the tried-and-proven SOHC 427 while M/T continued to develop the Shotgun engine for racing. Mickey Thompson's blue Mach I Funny Car, with Danny Ongais driving, went virtually undefeated in 1969. (Hank Richards)

By December 7, 1963, with the help of Les Ritchey's Performance Associates, Butch had the Thunderbolt running well as he clocked a 12.02 @ 122.95 while winning his class at Fontana, CA.

On December 15, 1963, Leal had the Thunderbolt at Long Beach, CA, where he copped the Number 3 Eliminator title and had low E.T. and high MPH for the meet at 12.01 and 120.16 MPH.

Butch was runner up to teammate Gas Ronda in the Super Stock Class at the 1964 NHRA Winternationals in Pomona, CA in February.

On March 6-8, 1964, at the U.S. Fuel and Gas Championships held in Bakersfield, CA, Butch had the Thunderbolt flying, winning the Super/Stock class with a phenomenal 11.49 @ 123.95 MPH.

On May 24, 1964, Leal won Top Stock Eliminator at the NHRA Regional held in Inyokern, CA with an 11.89 @ 123.00 MPH.

On June 13-14, 1964, at the NHRA Championship race held in Riverside, CA, Butch was once again runner up to teammate Ronda's Thunderbolt in the Super Stock class run off.

On the weekend of June 26-28, 1964, Butch Leal traveled to Green Valley Raceway in Smith, Texas, where he defeated Dick Harrell's 427 Chevelle in a match race.

On August 2, 1964, at Vineland, NJ, Leal defeated teammate Bill Lawton in the semifinal round of a well-attended Super Stock meet, only to lose in the final because of a red light start. Butch recorded a best E.T. of 11.33 @ 126 MPH.

Mickey Thompson drew from his Indy car experience when he built this Mustang Funny Car with a clamshell-style body and monocoque construction. The car used a supercharged Boss 429 for power, but aside from being featured on the cover of *Hot Rod* magazine, it made no mark in drag racing. (J. Demmitt, Jr.)

On August 23, 1964, Butch ran against Malcolm Durham's Chevy in a much-publicized match race at Pocono Drag Lodge in Pennsylvania. Apparently tired of Fords winning races at his track the promoter offered a cash incentive to any racer who could defeat a Ford in a match race. On this date Malcolm Durham intended to collect at Leal's expense. He might have done so too, had it not been for a young man who had driven his dad's new '64 Fairlane to the track that

Thompson's Boss 429-powered, Maverick-bodied Funny Car was another short-lived project with just one notable win to claim. (Hank Richards)

Mickey Thompson was another racer who soldiered on with Ford power into the early 1970's after the factory withdrew its support of racing. Thompson's Boss 429 Pinto funny car, with sponsorship from Peter Paul Candies, is shown here. (Bob Bowman)

day. It seems that Leal, being unfamiliar with the layout of the track, drove off the end on a practice run and damaged some front suspension parts on the M/T Thunderbolt. A call went out for help and this anonymous young Ford man allowed Leal to remove the required parts from his dad's daily transport. After fixing the T-Bolt and dispatching Durham in three straight runs, Leal thanked his benefactor and replaced the parts he borrowed. On that date Butch ran a best of 11.21 @ 124.95 MPH.

On Labor Day weekend 1964, Butch Leal had his biggest win of the year as he took home Super Stock class honors at the NHRA Nationals. Lady Luck certainly smiled down on Butch and the M/T team on that day. Facing Dave Strickler's Dodge in the first round of competition the transmission broke. Fortunately for Leal, Strickler had red-lighted and with minutes to spare the team was able to replace the transmission in time to compete in the next round.

On October 3, 1964, Leal ran his Thunderbolt at Oroville, CA winning his class with a 11.65 @ 124 MPH and on the following day at Vaca Valley, CA he won again, recording an 11.20 @ 124.95 MPH.

At the end of the 1964 season Butch accepted an offer of a ride in a factory-backed Plymouth. He would go on to many victories for the Chrysler camp before once again returning to M/T and Ford in 1969. A brand new engine series was being introduced by Ford, in a new class of drag racing that would eventually become what we know as Pro/Stock today. Butch and Fritz Vogt built the Boss 429 engine that would power M/T's new H-M Stroppe-built Mustang in the "Heads up Super/Stock" class. Butch and Mickey shared the cover of *Car Craft* magazine with the new Mustang upon its completion, but it was apparently much ado about nothing. Although Butch eventually got the car down into the high nine-second range at 135 MPH it was plagued by breakage that left a man so used to winning very frustrated. By late 1969 Butch had again moved on, to continue a career as a Pro/Stock driver that lasted into the late 1980s. Butch is now retired and divides his time between playing golf and attending nostalgia racing events as an honored guest.

CHAPTER 12

EARLY DRAG COUNCIL MEMBERS, REGIONAL RACERS, AND DRAGSTER DRIVERS

Several individuals and dealers were members of the Drag Council early on but for various reasons did not continue in the program past 1964. There were also a number of Drag Council members who raced more on a regional basis. In spite of their successes, they are less widely known than those who traveled from coast to coast and attended all the National events. There were also Fuel Dragster drivers who were supported by Ford and considered members of the Drag Council who, while widely recognized, may not be known as actual Ford team members. Some of these racers were not long-time members of the Drag Council and others have sadly left us, but their contributions certainly deserve mention.

CLESTER ANDREWS / WICKERSHAM FORD

Clester Andrews of Orange, Texas passed away in 2003 but not before leaving a regional racing history that goes unrivaled.

Clester became a Ford man in 1963 when he was offered the opportunity to drive a 1963 1/2 lightweight Super Stock Galaxie for Charles Wickersham, owner of Wickersham Ford in Andrews's home town of Orange. It soon became apparent that the young Texan would be very successful in Ford products as he started claiming Super Stock class titles and Top Stock Eliminator crowns on a regular basis.

During 1963 a number of the Ford dealers in Texas got together for a little inter-brand rivalry for the honor of claiming the title "Fastest Ford in Texas." When the smoke had cleared from this quarter-mile gun fight it was Clester Andrews's Wickersham Ford lightweight with that title proudly lettered on its fiberglass deck lid.

The Wickersham Ford team's 1963 successes apparently did not go un-noticed in Dearborn, as when the 1964 Fairlane Thunderbolt was announced, Wickersham was high on the list to receive one of these beasts. Thunderbolt number 10, VIN 4F41K118362, was delivered on November 4, 1963 to Wickersham Ford, listing Clester Andrews as driver. Clester's friend Brent Hajek related the account of how the new Wickersham Ford Thunderbolt made its way to Texas. It seems that Charles Wickersham had also made a deal to buy Lee Iacoca's personally customized Thunderbird when the Thunderbolt deal was struck, so Clester and his crew chief Cecil Spears flew to Dearborn to retrieve both cars. Their trip back to Texas had to be one-of-a-kind; they flat-towed the race car home behind the Thunderbird of none other than Ford's CEO.

Clester Andrews' Wickersham Ford lightweight Galaxie won many Super/Stock events in 1963 and claimed the title "Texas's Fastest Ford." (B. Hajek)

Clester Andrews picked up with the Thunderbolt exactly where he had left off with the lightweight Galaxie the previous year, winning class and Top Stock Eliminator honors throughout the region, including the Louisiana State Super Stock title. But the 1964 season was not without certain small setbacks for the Wickersham Ford team. Hajek says that Clester had sought the advice of one of the nation's most successful Super Stock drag racers, Dyno Don Nicholson, regarding legal modifications for the car that might give him that edge over the competition. Being the gracious man that he was, Nicholson informed Andrews that he could reduce his car's rolling resistance, and thus increase performance, by removing the grease from the front wheel bearings and replacing it with the popular engine additive STP, which was less restrictive. While this trick worked well for Dyno Don, he apparently overlooked the fact that while he carried his race car to and from the track on a ramp truck or trailer. Clester, as was most common for drag racers of the time, flat towed the Thunderbolt. This oversight resulted in the failure of the Wickersham Ford racer's wheel bearings in short order.

Ford race reports from the 1964 season reveal:

On June 28, 1964, at Houston Dragway, Andrews won Super Stock and took Top Stock Eliminator. He then filled in for Butch Leal in a match race against Dan Dean's 427 Chevelle, winning in two straight runs.

On July 21, 1964, in Beaumont, Texas, Andrews took a match race with Bob Harrop's Dodge in three straight and also took home Top Stock Eliminator.

Back in Beaumont on August 2, 1964, the Dodge of Ray Trevathon fell to the Wickersham Ford T-Bolt in three straight.

On August 15, 1964, at Biloxi, MS, Andrews took home top honors at the Stock Car Money Meet over a field containing two A/FX Comets and several Hemi Mopars.

On October 4, 1964, at Beaumont, Texas, Clester won the Super Stock class and set a class record of 11.97 @ 120.96 on 7" tires, and took Top Stock Eliminator and Little Eliminator as well, setting yet another record of 11.41 @ 121.78 on 10" tires.

Wickersham Ford took delivery of this Thunderbolt in 1964 and with it Clester Andrews won the Louisiana State Super Stock Championship along with numerous match races. (Sol Stewart)

As the 1965 racing season dawned, Ford was once again sufficiently impressed by the performance of the Wickersham Ford team to offer one of ten Ford Mustangs being specially prepared for racing in the A/Factory Experimental class by Holman-Moody. On January 31, 1965, Clester Andrews took delivery of a Mustang drag car, VIN 5F09K380234, from Holman-Moody in Charlotte, NC. The Wickersham Ford A/FX Mustang was one of those delivered with a 427 High Riser engine because of the shortage of SOHC 427s at the time of delivery. The lack of what was considered the top-of-the-line racing power plant did little to curb the success that Clester had with the car during the 1965 season as he rolled up an enviable record of 40 wins out of 42 match races run, and a class win at the AHRA Nationals. By virtue of their 1965 performance the Wickersham Ford team was chosen to represent Ford in the south-central United States during 1966. Ford's official press release on Andrews reads as follows:

Wickersham Ford and Clester Andrews were invited to join the Ford Drag Council in 1965 by virtue of their previous performances with Ford race cars. This A/FX Mustang was one of ten built for Drag Council members by Holman-Moody. The Wickersham car was one of those powered by a 427 High Riser engine because the SOHC 427 was in such short supply. Clester did well with this car and continued to run it for several years. (Ron Bell)

The Wickersham Ford A/FX Mustang gets a tire change in the pits. Clester Andrews enjoyed regional success in 1965 as he had in the previous two years since switching to Ford products. (B. Hajek)

Clester Andrews was one of a number of talented drivers who dominated A/FX factory experimental racing in 1965 in a specially prepared Mustang. In 1966 the Orange, TX driver again will be at the wheel of a Mustang powered by Ford's dependable 427 cubic inch wedge engine. His 1965 Mustang was a consistent winner in A/FX competition. Andrews' Mustang will run in the factory production category in AHRA competition and in NASCAR's Ultra/Stock division. This is Andrews' fourth straight year in Ford equipment. In 1963 he drove a Super Stock Galaxie and won the Louisiana State Championship. He was twice regional Stock Eliminator in NHRA competition in 1964 in a Super Stock Fairlane. He had his best year to date in 1965. In the AHRA Nationals Andrews drove his Mustang to a class victory and was the No. 2 Mr. Stock Eliminator. He also maintained an excellent record in match racing, competing largely in the Southwest.

And as was usually the case with race cars at the time, the Wickersham Ford Mustang continued to evolve during the 1966 racing season. The 427 High Riser engine was fitted with fuel injectors and eventually the car took

For the 1966 season Clester altered the wheelbase and added fuel injection to the Wickersham Mustang. He is shown here in a match race against Doug Thorley's Chevy. (Sol Stewart)

By late 1966, The Wickersham Ford Mustang had been more extensively modified for match racing. The 427 High Riser engine was radically set back in the chassis and fuel injection had been added. (B. Hajek)

on an early funny car appearance through radical body modifications, including an engine setback. Clester continued to compete with the car through the 1968 season and in 1969 he purchased the former Dick Brannan/Hubert Platt stretched Mustang from Sidney Foster. This car eventually received a new body, was renamed the *Bardahl 555*, and was run for a number of years until Clester retired from racing.

JIM PRICE / POPE FORD / MARV TONKIN FORD

At the wheel of his Pope Ford-sponsored 1961 Ford Fairlane, powered by the 401 horsepower 390 cubic inch engine, Jim Price put Ford on the map both in his native northwest as well as nationally in 1961. Jim won the NHRA Northwest Division championship and more than likely would have finished better than his fifth place overall nationally had he traveled more extensively. By virtue of his stellar year in 1961, Jim was one of the lucky few chosen to receive a lightweight Galaxie in 1962 and had a new sponsor in Marv Tonkin Ford. At the 1962 NHRA Nationals

The former Clester Andrews Wickersham Ford Mustang has now been restored to it's original A/FX configuration by noted collector Brent Hajek.

BILL IRELAND / NORTHWEST FORD DEALERS

The late Bill Ireland would become Ford's man to beat in the Pacific Northwest as his lightweight Galaxie scored numerous victories during the 1963 season. This put him in line to receive a Thunderbolt through Damerow Ford in Beaverton, OR for 1964. While it is indicated that Ireland's Thunderbolt was delivered with an automatic transmission, it apparently wasn't long before a four speed conversion was done, like most of its automatic-equipped contemporaries. Ireland continued his winning ways in 1964, becoming Ford's top performer regionally. Bill also found the time to give the Corvettes fits in 1964 behind the wheel of an A/SP Cobra.

Ford's plans for the 1966 season included Bill Ireland, and early on it was indicated that a car would be built for him to represent the Drag Council in the Northwest. As it turned out Bill received one of the '65 A/FX Mustangs. There is some confusion over exactly which car Ireland received, as Phil Bonner remembers his mount, sans the SOHC engine, going to Bill, while records indicate the car he took delivery of (for the sum of one dollar) was the former Gas Ronda car.

Ford's official biography for Ireland in 1966 reads as follows

> Bill Ireland of Portland, OR is as familiar a figure at drag strips in the north west section of the country as Smokey the Bear. At 38 Ireland is an 11 year veteran who has collected more than 100 trophies for his drag racing achievements. He has driven off with an NHRA Divisional Championship in four of the last five years, missing only in 1963. In 1965 he had great success in a Mustang fastback with a 289 cubic inch engine, setting a national record and accumulating 40 class victories. For 1966 Ireland has stepped up a notch and is driving a Mustang equipped with a 427 cubic inch wedge engine. In his long drag racing career Ireland has driven in

Bill Ireland strikes a classic pose next to his Oregon Ford Dealers A/FX Mustang in 1966. Ireland also ran in the NASCAR series that year, earning a top-ten points finish. (L. Wolfe)

Price's Ford suffered from mechanical woes related to incorrect valve spring retainers and was not a factor in competition. Rick Kirk, noted Ford historian and current owner of the Jim Price '62 lightweight Galaxie, indicates that the car was also driven at one point by Bill Ireland and spent its entire life in the Pacific Northwest.

My research was unable to uncover any information concerning Jim Price's racing activities during the 1963 season but it is known that by 1964 he was campaigning the Marv Tonkin Ford Thunderbolt in Super Stock competition and recorded a Top Stock Eliminator Win at Pocatello ID.

While Phil Bonner believes his 1965 A/FX mount went to Bill Ireland for the 1966 season, official records seem to dispute this. Either way the car was one of the original Drag Council cars built by Holman-Moody. Ireland ran the car with a 427 High Riser engine. (J. Demitt, Jr.)

various classes including B/Gas, Super/Stock and A/Sports Production. He had a highly successful season in 1964 in a Cobra in which he set a national record. Ireland owns and operates an auto electrical shop and does a little fire fighting on the side. He is one of drag racing's biggest boosters and conducts youth group programs in the Northwest.

Ireland would take his poppy red Mustang, which he dubbed *Trojan Horse*, to class victories at the 1966 AHRA Winter Nationals and the NASCAR Super Stock Championships. Along the way he also set an NHRA record in the C/XS class at 10.81 seconds. Bill Ireland also made a foray into the NASCAR drag racing series during the 1966 season, finishing ninth in series points. The Mustang would go on to receive an outlandish paint scheme and a new name, *The Klein Bird*, with which Ireland competed in the A/Modified Production class.

Bill was also the recipient of one of the very few factory 427 Fairlanes produced in 1966, with which he once again carried Ford's banner very successfully in the Pacific Northwest. This car would later be sold to Jim Van Cleve, who converted the car to '67 trim and took it to many class wins and NHRA National records.

The 1968 season found Bill Ireland at the wheel of one of the 50 factory lightweight Cobra Jet Mustangs under the banner of Oregon Ford Dealers, along with a 428 Cobra Jet-powered Torino. During my research I was unable to uncover any indications of Ireland's racing activities past the 1968 season, and there are no indications that he received support from Ford in 1969.

HOLMAN-MOODY / PAUL NORRIS

Up until 1965, Ford high performance subcontractor Holman-Moody had concentrated mostly on other forms of motorsports, particularly NASCAR and boat racing, where it had established a reputation for preparing winning Ford

Always a strong competitor in Ford products, Bill received one of the rare 427 Fairlanes for competition in NHRA SS/B. He did well with this car, which later continued its career in the hands of another Ford racer from the Pacific Northwest, Jim Van Cleve. Van Cleve converted the car to 1967 trim and went on to hold multiple national records with it.

products. Upon receiving the contract to build 10 Ford Mustangs for drag race competition in the A/FX class in 1965, H-M not only got to work, it got on board by building a Mustang drag car of its own. Holman-Moody built and then paid Ford the princely sum of one dollar for its '65 A/FX Mustang (VIN 5F09K380236), and with driver Paul Norris on board, the company began its first foray into the world of drag racing.

In the beginning the H-M Mustang, dubbed *Big John*, was very much like the other Drag Council Mustangs but along the way H-M applied some of its own tricks to the mix. Modifications to the lower control arms, consisting of reinforcing plates welded to the torsion spring attachment points, along with a relocation of the front spring eye for more caster, reduced wear and aided tracking. The SOHC 427 engine's oil sump was modified for additional capacity, and the traction bars were lengthened to plant the Goodyear slicks more effectively.

Subtle use of lighter weight components, including an H-M-designed aluminum water pump, got additional weight off the car's front end. While it appears that Norris' activities with the H-M Mustang were geared toward match racing, he did have the car at the AHRA Nationals, where he defeated Bud Faubel's Dodge in the first round of competition with a 10.78 @ 129.49 MPH to a quicker 10.75 @ 128.38 MPH. In the second round Norris blistered Bill Rieck's *Quarter Bender* Dodge with a 10.58 @ 131.57 MPH, but a foul start put him out of competition.

For the 1966 season the H-M Mustang continued in competition without major alterations other than the addition of fuel injection to keep pace with the increased level of competition, and a name change to *The Fugitive*. Norris finished 14th in the NASCAR drag racing series in 1966. In an ad for a match race at Sportsman Park Drag Strip in Farmington, NC, where Norris was to face Shirl

While building A/FX Mustangs for Ford in 1965, Holman-Moody built one for itself and became a member of the Ford Drag Council. The H-M Mustang was used for both testing and evaluation as well as racing, with Paul Norris doing the driving. The car apparently went through a number of changes during its short career as a factory-backed racer. In this photo the name on the Mustang as been changed from *Big John* to *The Fugitive*, and the U/S-2 on the quarter panel shows that it was competing in the NASCAR drag racing series. (Rodell Cranford collection)

Greer's Dodge, the promoter advertised the H-M Mustang as "Runner up for world champion." My research failed to locate which racing series was being referred to. Nineteen sixty-six would mark the end of Holman-Moody's active participation in drag racing, although it would continue to develop drag racing components for Ford up until the company's withdrawal from racing in 1971.

DARRELL DROKE / AUTODYNAMICS / DOWNEY FORD

"Ford wins Pike's Peak Hill Climb," read the headline for an ad for Darrell and Larry's Autodynamics of Downey, CA. The Darrell in question was none other than Darrell Droke who, along with brother Larry, prepared Curtis Turner's Pike's Peak-winning 1962 Ford. Turner outran the second-place Chevy by five seconds and set a new record in the process. The ad reads:

> The job of preparing and tuning this '62 Ford Galaxie for the highest, steepest, and toughest race in the world was given to Darrell and Larry's Autodynamics shop in Downey, CA. The work was well done indeed; bringing home a winner your first time at Pike's Peak is not just luck but the result of an excellent car, driver talent, plus superb tuning and preparation. This same thorough service is now available to you. Autodynamics clean and modern shop is fully equipped with the latest and finest tune-up equipment, chassis dynamometer and custom engine building facilities.

Preparing stock cars for Pike's Peak was not Darrell Droke's sole effort during 1962; he was in the thick of drag race competition in the Super/Stock and A/FX classes with a 1962 Ford. Darrell's devotion to and success with the products of Ford would lead to an invitation to join the Drag Council in 1965 with one of the most unique of all Ford drag cars produced during the era.

It was quite obvious that Ford's intention was to put the lion's share of its performance emphasis for 1965 on the newly introduced Mustang. The

Fairlane, which had carried Ford's banner onto America's drag strips in 1964, would be relegated to passenger car status. However, someone at Ford decided to build two 1965 Fairlanes in the manner of the famous Thunderbolts of the previous year. Of the two '65 cars, modified by Dearborn Steel Tubing Co. one would go to Les Ritchey's Performance Associates, where it would receive a small-block engine for stock class competition, and the other went to Darrell Droke to be run as the only 1965 Fairlane Thunderbolt.

Originally delivered with a 427 High Riser engine, Droke soon replaced the wedge with an SOHC 427 and added weight to bring the car up to a hefty 3800 pounds, making it legal for competition in NHRA's B/Factory Experimental class. Darrell had the Fairlane running fine as he claimed the Mr Sportsman Eliminator title at the 1965 AHRA Nationals. He followed this up with

Darrell Droke received one of just two Fairlane Thunderbolts built by Dearborn Steel Tubing in 1965. Originally delivered with a 427 High Riser engine, it was soon converted to SOHC 427 power. With added weight the car ran in the B/FX class and gave an added dimension to Ford's dominance. Note the cam cover for the SOHC engine is off and sitting on the car's roof in this photo. (Rodell Cranford collection)

Darrell Droke charges off the starting line in his unique '65 Fairlane B/FX car. Returned to Ford at the end of the season for destruction, the car found new life in the hands of Jerry Harvey, who also had great success with it. (L. Wolfe)

Another one-of-a-kind car for Droke was this 1966 stretched Mustang with a fuel-burning, supercharged SOHC 427 for power. Here it sits in the pits at Atco Dragway in New Jersey during the summer of 1966. Jack Chrisman's unique topless Mercury Comet-bodied Funny Car is in the background.

a B/FX class win at the 1965 NHRA Nationals.

Anytime Droke brought the Fairlane out he was assured of stiff competition in his class, which often included small block-powered factory Comets and the SOHC-powered Galaxies of Jerry Harvey and Mike Schmitt. Elapsed times in the high tens and speeds approaching 130 MPH ensured that Darrell's car was always a threat to win.

Darrell Droke began the 1966 season with the Fairlane. He narrowly lost the Mr. Stock Handicap title at the AHRA Western Super Stock Nationals to Butch Leal, when the car got loose and crossed the center line of the track.

Ford's official 1966 biography material for Darrell Droke reads as follows:

> Whether the situation calls for the heavy foot or the ultra-light touch Darrell Droke has proven repeatedly he can fill the bill. In early spring you usually can find Droke feather footing his way across the country in the Mobil Economy Run. He's one of the best in this area, taking class honors in the 1965 event in a Fairlane. The Fairlane that Droke drove last year on the drag strips and the one he'll handle in 1966 is another breed altogether. Droke's drag Fairlane comes equipped with a 427 cubic inch single overhead cam engine and is one of the most powerful stock cars in competition. In addition, Droke will be at the wheel of a new lightweight Mustang, which will feature a supercharged version of the 427 SOHC engine. This is a similar

Droke charges off the starting line in Biloxi, MS during a 1966 match race. Primer paint indicates recent bodywork to the car's rear quarters. (Sol Stewart)

setup to that used by Connie Kalitta and Pete Robinson in their rail dragsters and should put more than 1,000 horsepower at Droke's disposal. Droke has been active in drag racing circles for only four years, but already numbers his trophies in the hundreds. He had one of the fastest B/FX cars in the country last year and was a constant threat for stock honors in the nation's big meets. In the NASCAR Nationals last year he was Top Stock Eliminator, he took a divisional points title in Junior Stock in NHRA, and was the Sportsman Eliminator in the AHRA. Droke has tried a little bit of everything in racing.

With a new Holman-Moody-stretched '66 Mustang on the way, Droke returned the Fairlane to Ford for what he was told would be its destruction (a common practice used by manufacturers to keep race cars from ever being street-driven), only to see it resurrected with Paul Harvey Ford livery and Jerry Harvey at the wheel, as a result of some internal politics at Ford.

Nonetheless Droke received his stretched Mustang, which would differ from those delivered to other Drag Council members in that it would be run with a supercharged, fuel burning SOHC 427 engine. Darrell describes the car as ill-handling, and in fact it was so bad when run on nitromethane that he took to using only alcohol to reduce power. After a season that featured many successful match race appearances and performances in the high eight-second range at 157 MPH but no national titles, Droke returned the Mustang to Ford and this time the car was destroyed as agreed.

While he was no longer counted as a member of the Drag Council after the 1966 season, Darrell Droke continued to have success with Ford products, including the O'Connor Mercury-sponsored *Top Cat* Cougar, which used a Gurney-Weslake-equipped, Indy-style, small-block Ford engine, and later an SOHC 427-powered Maverick Pro/Stock car known as *Mr. Roll Bar*.

ED MARTIN FORD / DON TURNER

"Home of the Fast Fords," was the sales slogan for Ed Martin Ford of Indianapolis, IN during the

The Ed Martin Ford team ran this 1961 Starliner, powered by a 401-horsepower 390, in Super/Stock competition. The car is seen here in action at the 1960 NHRA Nationals. (Alan Wood)

Ed Martin Ford Sales had two Galaxie lightweights in competition at the NHRA Nationals in 1962. This particular car was retrofitted with steel parts in order to run in the SS/S class, where it was believed to have a better chance of winning. Les Ritchey handled the driving chores on this day. (Rick Kirk)

Total Performance years of the sixties. Ed Martin was in the thick of the, "Win on Sunday, sell on Monday," theory that inspired many dealers in the 1960's. A successful dealer-sponsored 1961 Super/Stock class Starliner led to an invitation from Ford to become a member of the newly formed Drag Council in 1962.

As a member of the Council, Ed Martin Ford received two 1962 Ford Galaxies (VINs 2W516G156039 and 039), the latter of which was equipped with steel body parts in order to compete in the SS/S class at the 1962 NHRA Nationals (it was believed that the car would have a better chance of winning in SS/S than A/FX). Top Ford preparation ace and Drag Council member Les Ritchey handled the driving chores for the Ed Martin team at the Nationals, but lack of testing and prep time equaled poor results. Prior to the 1963 season this car would become one of five Drag Council 1962 Galaxie lightweights to be re-bodied as 1963 1/2 cars. A pre-production, non serial-numbered body was procured from the Wayne Assembly plant and the car was set up to run in the Super/Stock class with a 427 Low Riser engine. With Don Turner at the wheel, the Ed Martin Ford entry had a very successful year, which culminated in a runner-up finish in the S/S class at the 1963 NHRA Nationals. The car that defeated Turner was subsequently declared illegal, but as per NHRA rules the win was merely nullified and the Ed Martin entry was not awarded its place in history. For the 1964 season the car received an automatic transmission and competed successfully in the A/Stock Automatic class, with Ford employee Ben Smith doing the driving.

Ed Martin Ford received Thunderbolt #3 (VIN 4F41K118363) and during pre-delivery testing by Dan Jones the car recorded elapsed times of 12.34 and 12.38 @ 119.68 and 119.84 MPH respectively.

Ford's official performance reports for the Don Turner-driven Ed Martin Ford Thunderbolt are as follows:

On November 17, 1963, Bowling Green, KY, Super/Stock class win with an 11.72 elapsed time.

On May 25, 1964, Don Martin faced off against Stanley Bird's SS/A Plymouth in a match race at Tri-State Dragway in Hamilton, OH, winning three straight rounds with a best time of 11.57 @ 121.08 MPH.

The Ed Martin Ford 1963 1/2 lightweight Galaxie in action at the 1963 NHRA Nationals. The team made it to the final round in the Super/Stock class before losing to a car that was later found to be illegal. In keeping with NHRA rules, the class win was simply nullified, robbing the Ford of a well-deserved win. (D. Kolodziej)

Ed Martin's Super Stock 1963 1/2 lightweight Galaxie goes off against a 426 Dodge. Note the long, rearward-facing traction bars developed by tuning ace Les Ritchey. (D. Kolodziej)

The Ed Martin Ford team received a Thunderbolt for Super/Stock competition in 1964. The car, and one of the trophies it won, is proudly displayed at the dealership. (D. Kolodziej)

On June 6, 1964, Don Turner took the Ed Martin Thunderbolt to a Super/Stock class win in Muncie, IN with a 12.25 @ 121 MPH.

On the weekend of June 26-28, 1964, at Muncie Don was runner-up in the Super Stock class final against the Jerry Alderman Ford Thunderbolt because of a broken transmission. Turner had recorded 11.9 second elapsed times prior to the mechanical failure.

On August 2, 1964, Don Martin won the Super/Stock class at Capitol Raceway, defeating the Bob Banning Hemi Dodge in the final with an 11.60 @ 121 MPH.

On August 22, 1964, at Muncie, IN, Turner won the Super Stock class with a 12.46 @ 117.0 MPH but suffered transmission woes in the eliminator runoff.

On the weekend of August 28-30, 1964, Turner again took the Ed Martin Ford entry to victory in the Super/Stock class at Muncie, IN with an 11.99 @ 121.00 MPH.

Turner had a banner day on September 13, 1964, at Bunker Hill, IN where, before 3,000 cheering fans, he won both the Super/Stock class and Top Stock Eliminator along with claiming the "King of the Hill" title by defeating the Dodge Boys Hemi two out of three rounds in a match race. Turner recorded a best elapsed time of 11.29 @ 126 MPH on that date.

On October 11, 1964, Don Martin and the Ed Martin Ford team were declared NHRA Division 3 Champions for 1964.

I have no specific information as to why after the 1964 season there is no further mention of Don Turner or Ed Martin Ford in the record books. It is known that the dealer did not receive factory support in 1965, which could have led to a cessation of their drag racing program.

Bob Martin drove the Jerry Alderman Ford Starliner in Super Stock competition during the 1961 season. Paul Harvey, who would go on to work at Bob Ford and later his own dealership, was Alderman's general manager and a force in performance efforts. (Alan Wood)

JERRY ALDERMAN FORD / BOB MARTIN / JERRY HARVEY

The Jerry Alderman Ford team fielded a Tucson yellow 390/401 Starliner during the 1961 season, with Bob Martin handling the driving chores. Alderman Ford was chosen as a member of the Drag Council for 1962 and as a result received a 1962 lightweight Galaxie (VIN 2W51G56036). It was picked up at Dearborn Steel Tubing Co. and prepared by Bill Rider and Bob Meyers for competition at the NHRA Nationals on Labor Day weekend.

With a lack of preparation and testing time, Bob Martin suffered from lack of traction and top-end horsepower at the event. The Alderman car did not take advantage of the set-up modifications recommended by Les Ritchey prior to the nationals according to an official Ford report on the outcome. Subsequent to the Nationals the Galaxie was repainted from it's original white to the Tucson yellow color preferred by Mr. Paul Harvey, who was the general manager of Alderman Ford at that time. Bob Martin continued in competition with the Galaxie through the 1963

The Alderman Ford *Sudden Service* 1962 lightweight Galaxie was barely ready by the time the NHRA Nationals were held. Being unprepared, and forced into the A/FX class because of the car's limited production numbers, doomed the team's efforts here. Nineteen sixty-three proved a better year as Bob Martin scored a number of victories with the year-old car. (Rick Kirk)

The Alderman Ford team ran this Thunderbolt, named *Little Emmett*, in the Super/Stock class during the 1964 season. Alderman Ford-sponsored cars seem not to have existed after 1964. (Nick Smith)

Young Jerry Harvey's first factory ride with this unique 1965 Galaxie. Powered by a SOHC 427 engine, the car competed in the B/Factory Experimental class and won its first major event at the 1965 NHRA Winternationals. *The Quiet One* was neither quite nor light, as it came in at 3855 pounds. (Fermier Brothers)

The B/FX class featured big cars with big engines, like Harvey's Bob Ford ride and ones like the small block-powered Mustang in the opposite lane. Both combinations worked well, and victory was often decided by driver skill. (Fermier Brothers)

Paul Harvey's B/FX Galaxie waits in the staging lanes. Note the Performance Associates logo on the rear quarter. Most top-running Fords of the era depended on Les Ritchey for tuning and product development. (Martino Family)

After the 1965 Spring Nationals, when Len Richter took his leave, Jerry Harvey became the driver of the Bob Ford A/FX Mustang. For the 1966 season the car was repainted with Paul Harvey Ford livery after Jerry's dad opened his own dealership. Young Harvey had great success with the Mustang and it later passed into the hands of both Hubert Platt and Don Nicholson. (L. Wolfe)

season, and while I found no information regarding specific event wins for the car that year, I found a photo of it going off against Ed Schartman's Jackshaw Z-11 Chevy. *National Dragster* reported that Bob Martin took the car, renamed *Little Emmett*, to a match-race win over the Z-11 Chevy of Bud Gates at Muncie, IL during the season. Martin still had the '62 car in action as late as November 20, 1963, as an official Ford race report indicates he took a win over the Ed Martin Ford Thunderbolt at Bunker Hill Dragstrip in IN, with elapsed times in the high 11-second range.

Jerry Alderman Ford took delivery of a 1964 Fairlane Thunderbolt (VIN 4F41K167201), which was subsequently painted Tuscon yellow and named *Little Emmett* as its predecessor had been. The car would also be driven by Bob Martin, but Alderman Ford, while no doubt receiving some factory support, was no longer a Drag Council member. I can only speculate that with the departure of Paul Harvey for the Bob Ford agency, the Drag Council membership must have followed.

Now repainted with Paul Harvey Ford sponsorship, Jerry charges off the starting line in this 1966 photo. (Fermier Brothers)

Mike Schmitt's Desert Motors AA/SA High Riser Galaxie undergoes maintenance in the pits early in the 1964 season. (Mark Ascher)

MIKE SCHMITT / DESERT MOTORS

Mike Schmitt got his start as a Ford drag racer with a 1963 Galaxie powered by the 330-horsepower Police Interceptor 390 engine. In 1964 he was selected to receive one of 25 lightweight Galaxies built to compete in the AA/SA class. With his Desert Motors-sponsored Ford, Mike would win the NHRA Little Stock Eliminator World Championship. Schmitt and Gas Ronda, who won the Top Stock Championship would bring Ford its first NHRA manufacturer's titles.

Schmitt received a 1965 Galaxie with conventional 427 wedge power for the 1965 season, but what Mike described as sub-par performance from the car caused him to revert to his old reliable '64 lightweight for most of the '65 season. Things would get better for Schmitt in 1966, as he

Schmitt's Galaxie, adorned with World Champion lettering as a result of his 1964 NHRA Jr. Stock Eliminator title, is now restored and housed in the collection of Don Snyder, Jr.

Mike Schmitt held the NHRA AA/SA automatic national record in 1964 with his 427 High Risher-powered lightweight Galaxie and won the NHRA Championship that year. Mike would continue to race factory-supported Galaxies through the 1966 season.

was the recipient of a SOHC 427-powered Galaxie for competition in the B/FX class.

Ford's official 1966 press biography on Schmitt reads as follows:

> Mike Schmitt is a fast man with cars, whether it's racing them or selling them. Schmitt is a salesman for Desert Motors Inc. in Ridgecrest, CA and a former NHRA World Champion. He has proved his selling ability by earning membership in Ford Division's 300-500 club for top salesmen. Schmitt currently drives a B/FX Galaxie powered by a 427 cubic inch single overhead cam engine. For the past couple of seasons he has been at the wheel of a 1964 Galaxie with a 427 Wedge engine. Schmitt holds the AA/SA speed and elapsed time records, both set

Nineteen sixty-four lightweight Galaxies featured this unique means of ducting cool air from the grille to the two huge Holley four-barrel carburetors that fed the 427 High Riser.

in 1965. At 10-year veteran of drag racing at 28 years of age, Schmitt has been a dominant factor in stock car competition. He was the NHRA Junior Stock World Champion Eliminator in 1964, when he won the AA/SA class championship in the Nationals. Last year, in his 1964 Galaxie, he was Top Stock Eliminator in the NHRA Spring Nationals at Bristol, TN. Just to prove he is equally at home in a car with a stick shift, Schmitt won the AA/Stock class in the NHRA Winter Nationals last year at Pomona, CA.

At the 1966 NHRA Winternationals, Schmitt was runner-up to Ford teammate Jerry Harvey's Mustang in the Street Eliminator final. Mike's factory support would end after the 1966 season, but up until then he and his big honkin' Desert Motors Galaxies gave Ford fans from coast to coast much to cheer about. His World Championship-winning '64 has been restored to its former glory and is currently in the possession of noted collector Don Snyder of Springfield, OH.

FORD'S TOP FUEL EFFORTS

CONRAD "CONNIE" KALITTA / BOUNTY HUNTER

Ford Motor Company scheduled a District Manager's Display of Drag Cars for January 26, 1965 in Riverside, CA. Included on the list of vehicles to be displayed was the following description of the company's first-ever factory-supported Top Fuel Dragster:

AA/FD, Gold, Supercharged Hemi SOHC 427, Kalitta. This vehicle has a 145" wheelbase and has a race-ready weight of 1375 pounds. The supercharged, 90% Nitro burning, SOHC 427 produces over 1,000 horsepower and pushes the car to one quarter-mile elapsed times and speeds of less than 8

A young fan gets a closer-up look at Connie Kalitta's office and blown SOHC Ford engine. Kalitta was the first Top Fuel Dragster competitor to receive factory support from Ford when he was added to the Drag Council in 1965. (Martino Family)

seonds and greater than 200 MPH respectively. Power is transmitted to the ground through two 11" wide rear tires. Braking is accomplished by parachute and rear-wheel brakes.

Kalitta gave the Ford fans plenty to cheer about in 1965. He served notice on the other Top Fuel entries as he debuted the new SOHC Ford engine in his latest *Bounty Hunter* dragster at the NHRA Winternationals. Kalitta came off the trailer with a 7.82 @ 199.54 qualifying pass and backed it up with a first-round 7.78 win over the Chrysler-backed Ramchargers Top Fuel team. Kalitta scored another victory over Art Malone in the second round, only to lose in the semifinal round on a red light. It wasn't long however before Kalitta had the big Ford engine clicking off consistent 200-plus MPH passes.

Ford's press biography of Kalitta for the 1966 season reads as follows:

A sure crowd-getter for any drag strip promoter is the combination of Connie Kalitta, his *Bounty Hunter* rail, and the supercharged Ford 427 cubic inch single overhead cam engine. Kalitta started his drag racing career while still in

A later version of Kalitta's Ford-powered *Bounty Hunter* Top Fuel Dragster sits in the pits. Note Doug Nash's unique fuel-burning small-block *Bronco Buster* Funny Car in the background. (Bob Bowman)

his teens and today at the age of 28 is a 10-year veteran of the sport. Connie not only has a reputation for driving, but his engineering knowledge makes him one of the foremost driver-mechanic combinations in the country. When Ford Division of Ford Motor Company decided to place one of its new single overhead cam engines in fuel dragster competition, Kalitta was chosen to drive and maintain the car since he had exhibited the skill in this area in five successful rail cars in seven years. This was late 1964. For the 1965 season Kalitta had the Logghe Stamping company, old hands at constructing rails, build him a new car specially designed to handle the big 427 Ford engine. It didn't take Connie long to make his presence felt in the fuel dragster ranks. Early in the season he turned a run of 206.42 MPH at Bakersfield, CA. In June at Bristol, TN, Connie turned a speed in excess of 209 MPH. The car consistently turned in elapsed times in the 7.70 second bracket. "That car I ran in 1965 was pretty and it was one of a kind" Kalitta said, "but it was too heavy and too short." So between seasons Kalitta went back to the Logghe Stamping Company and had a new car built. The new chassis is lighter than its predecessor and, with a 173-inch wheelbase, is considerably longer. The greater length is for better stability at high speed. The new car also provides Kalitta with much greater visibility since he sits higher and the car has a lower silhouette. The streamlining effect of the previous *Bounty Hunter* has been eliminated since little body sheet metal is used, but Kalitta feels the lighter weight will make up for this.

Pete Robinson gets to push-start his NHRA title-winning SOHC 427 Ford-powered dragster. (H. Hagen)

The 427 SOHC engine in the new rail is similar to the one Kalitta used last year. With the boost from the supercharger, the engine turns out well over 1,000 horsepower. "I know one thing," Kalitta remarked, 'since I've had the Ford SOHC engine I haven't been to a meet where I thought anyone had more horsepower than my car."

Connie doggedly continued to develop and run the Ford engine. After several close-but-no-cigar national event appearances and many match race wins, Lady Luck finally smiled upon him in 1967. After blistering the competition to win the NHRA Winternationals, Kalitta went on to take home the Top Fuel titles at both the AHRA and the NASCAR Winternationals, capping a great season for the long-time racer and Ford.

With the advent of the Boss 429 engine in 1969, Kalitta got to work developing the new combination for drag racing's top echelon with both a Top Fuel Dragster and later a Funny Car effort. Problems with the Boss engine, lack of development time, and waning support from Ford often resulted in Kalitta reverting back to his successful 427 SOHC engine for competition.

SNEAKY PETE ROBINSON / TINKER TOY

Pete Robinson was perhaps one of the most innovative and forward-thinking drag racers of

Robinson's *Tinker Toy* Ford-powered Top Fuel Dragster at full song, smoking the tires. (H. Hagen)

his time. "Sneaky Pete," as he was affectionately known, successfully raced Chevrolet-powered dragsters in the Gas ranks for years until he learned that the newly-released 289 cubic inch small block V-8 from Ford was fifty pounds lighter than a comparable Chevrolet engine. In true drag racer form Robinson sought to gain any advantage he could over the competition, and he saw the performance potential of the light new Ford engine.

In very short order Robinson proved his theory of Ford's superiority over the time-honored Chevy small block by winning the prestigious 1964 Top Gas Championships at Bakersfield, CA. Robinson's experience and success with Ford power caught the attention of the folks in Dearborn. When the company decided to make its first foray into the Top Fuel dragster ranks Robinson was a natural choice to receive one of the new SOHC 427 engines.

It didn't take the veteran racer long to prove himself and the new Ford powerplant as he took his latest *Tinker Toy* to a runner-up finish at the 1965 NHRA Spring Nationals. Robinson went on a tear during the 1966 season, winning the Top Fuel crown at the NHRA World Championships with a 7.17 @ 189.86. At the 1967 NHRA Spring Nationals Robinson was again runner-up, this time to fellow Ford driver Don Prudhomme. Also during 1967, Pete tied the existing NHRA Top Fuel class record with a 6.92.

Along the way Robinson continued to develop innovative features on his dragster, including a ground effects package that had the appearance of a vacuum cleaner, and a gear drive for the SOHC Ford engine that replaced the six-foot timing chain.

The 1970 NHRA Summer Nationals found Pete Robinson and Ford power in the winner's circle once again. By early 1971, when almost all others had abandoned the Ford engine, he had recorded elapsed times as quick as 6.50 seconds. Sadly Pete Robinson lost his life due to an accident suffered during a qualifying run for the 1971 NHRA Winternationals when a front tire came off the rim, causing him to lose control of the car at speed. Pete Robinson was just 37 years old when he died, but in his short life time he had given much to the sport of drag racing.

Robinson's dragster, with unique ground effects in place under its bodywork, sits in the pits at Pomona prior to the 1971 Winternationals. Tragically, Pete would lose his life on this day when his car crashed during a time run. Drag racing lost a true innovator. (Bob Bowman)

Ford developed the Super Mustang dragster, powered by a fuel-injected SOHC 427 engine and tapped Tom "The Mongoose" McEwen to be its driver. The car ended up becoming mostly a show car for the Ford Performance Program. (Dick Brannan)

TOM "THE MONGOOSE" McEWEN

Perhaps seeing his supercharged fuel-burning, Chrysler Hemi-powered Barracuda outperformed by Gas Ronda's SOHC-powered Mustang was the impetus for Tom McEwen to get on board when Ford came knocking, offering him the opportunity to participate in the development of a car that would be called The Super Mustang. The innovative machine was essentially a dragster chassis fitted with a bubble-canopied streamliner body, which was powered by a fuel injected version of Ford's SOHC 427 engine. And while the car never met its expected performance potential, it proved to be good marketing for Ford as a show car and brought yet another experienced Top Fuel dragster driver into the Dearborn fold. When Top Fuel team owner Lou Baney opened a Ford dealership called Brand Ford, he decided to switch from Chrysler power to SOHC Ford and he hired McEwen to be his driver. Mongoose's tenure in the Brand Ford car was to be short-lived as he was replaced by his racing rival—and arch enemy of the mongoose in the wild—the "Snake."

DON "THE SNAKE" PRUDHOMME

When Lou Baney combined forces with Don Prudhomme and Ed Pink the folks at Ford got a big bang for their buck in several ways. First, Baney, now a Ford dealer, had chosen the SOHC 427 Ford engine for his new Don Long dragster.

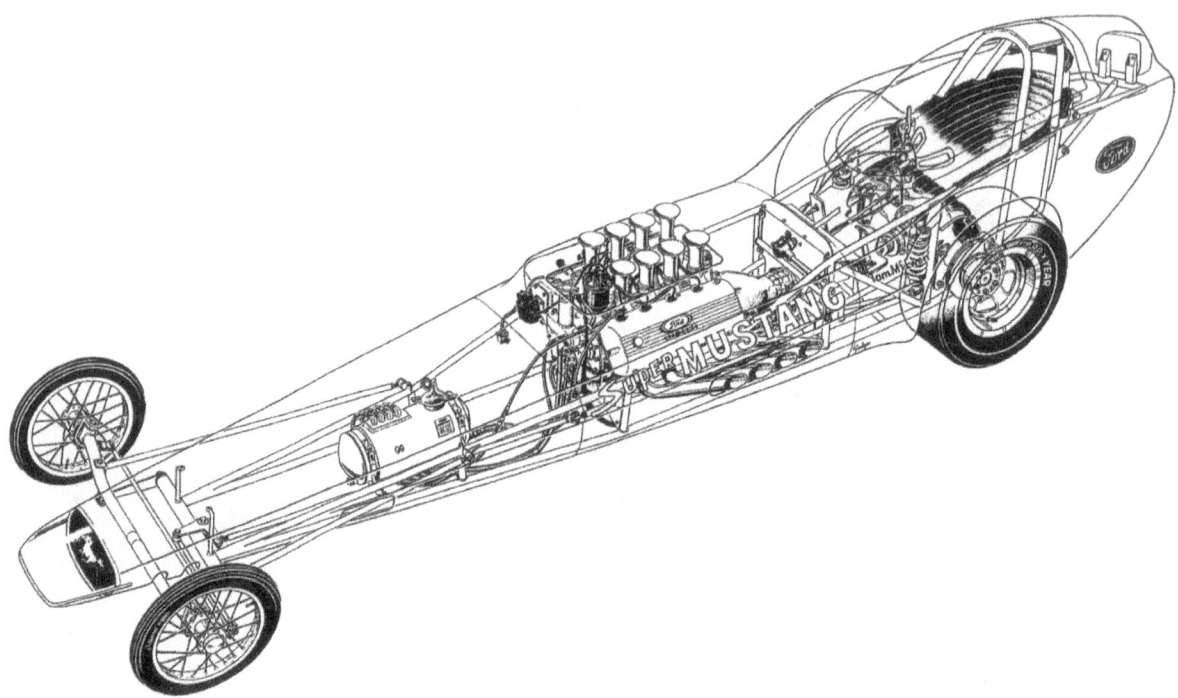

A line-art cutaway rendering of the Ford Super Mustang dragster. (Ford)

Tom McEwen did finally get a Ford-powered ride with which to do battle in the Top Fuel dragster wars of the 1960s when Lou Baney received corporate backing for his *Brand Ford Special* supercharged SOHC 427 dragster. McEwen was later replaced as the driver by his rival Don "The Snake" Prudhomme. (L. Wolfe)

Second, Prudhomme was one of the top dragster drivers in the country. And third, Ed Pink was a highly successful and respected engine builder. The combination would result in the first National event win for the newly formed team with

The Shelby Super Snake Top Fuel Dragster gets rolled out for another six-second pass down the quarter mile with Ford power. (Bob Bowman)

a six-second elapsed time when Prudhomme took home all the marbles at the 1967 NHRA Spring Nationals in Bristol, TN. At that particular event no other Top Fuel competitor ran in the six-second range. Pruhomme only recorded one run outside of the sixes when he shut off early against Jimmy Nix, who had fouled. Pruhomme saved his best performance for the final round, when he unleashed a 6.92 @ 222.76 MPH to defeat fellow Ford driver Pete Robinson.

For 1968 Baney obtained new sponsorship from racing legend Carroll Shelby and the car was repainted, quite appropriately, as Shelby's Super Snake. While on tour with the car in 1968, without the assistance of Pink, who had stayed in California due to other obligations, Prudhomme and Baney suffered a number of mechanical woes, which led to the team coming home early and Snake leaving the partnership to form his own team.

Don "The Snake" Prudhomme came on board with Ford power when he took over driving chores on the Lou Baney-owned *Brand Ford Special* Top Fuel Dragster from Tom McEwen. The following year Baney got support from both Ford and Shelby American for his Prudhomme-driven, Ed Pink Cammer-powered Shelby Super Snake dragster. (Bob Bowman)

CHAPTER 13

BILL HOLBROOK

A VIEWPOINT FROM BEHIND THE SCENES

While not a member of the Drag Council or Drag Teams per se, Bill Holbrook acted in the capacity of supervisor at the Experimental Vehicles Garage, where many of Ford's one-off and prototype drag cars were built. Bill's experiences and insights have proved extremely helpful to me, and over the years he has provided both his recollections and copies of documents that have been invaluable to myself and others doing research on Ford's racing programs.

Born on April 28, 1927, in Detroit, MI, World War Two Navy veteran Bill can claim membership in America's Greatest Generation along with his many other accomplishments. The son of a career Ford mechanic and dealership shop manager, Holbrook followed in his father's footsteps, taking a job as a tune-up specialist in various Detroit-area Ford dealerships over a ten year period after his wartime service on a Navy submarine chaser with the rating of Motor Machinist Mate.

In 1955 Bill accepted a position at Ford Motor Company as an Experimental Mechanic in the Scientific Research Garage, earning a monthly salary of $370. It was during this time that Bill established a long-time friendship with Al Turner, who would later become Holbrook's counterpart at Lincoln-Mercury during the drag car development program.

"Let me tell you about this young tech we had working at the Scientific Research Garage back in 1955," Bill says, going on to describe how a section of the garage was designated as the On/Off Crib, where test engines were stored. The young tech in question was tasked with removing the spark plugs from stored engines and "fogging" the cylinders with protective lubricant prior to storage, but he was often difficult to locate when needed. "I soon learned I could usually find the young fellow hiding in the On/Off crib. That young man's name was Al Turner."

Over the course of our friendship Bill has often responded to my numerous questions relating to his involvement in Ford's racing programs with the admonishment, "You know I'm not as young as I used to be and my memory isn't what it once was." This is unfailingly followed by an astonishingly accurate account of the times in question.

During his time at Scientific Research, Bill had a hand in such projects as the development of wiring harnesses for Ford's 1956 tilt-cab trucks, the push button automatic transmission controls for the new Edsel car line, a prototype mechanical fuel injection system, and a variable engine valvetrain timing system that was controlled by engine oil pressure (remember, this was in the days before build his famous Batmobile for the Batman T.V. series in the mid 1960's.

Question: What did the Lincoln use for power?

Bill: "Initially it had a Lincoln 368 cubic inch engine and then later, when Barris had it, a 390 with a B&M Hydro behind it."

In 1957 Holbrook assumed the duties of senior mechanic at the Experimental Garage. There he had a hand in numerous aspects of Ford's performance vehicle development including the supercharged 312 cubic inch Y-Block engine that Ford used to dominate stock car racing, prior to signing an agreement brokered by the Automobile Manufacturer's Association (AMA) to end development of high-performance engines for highway safety reasons.

After a short layoff from Ford in 1958, Bill came back to work for the company as a Hardware and Accessories Division electrical mechanic at the Experimental Vehicles garage, where he worked under John Cowley, Dave Evans, and Bill Patterson. Holbrook was later promoted, and he supervised six mechanics who worked on vehicles that participated in the Mobil Gas Economy Run and the 1960 high-performance 352 cubic inch engine program. With Ernie MacEwan building engines and Bob Hyde handling drivetrains, the Experimental Vehicles garage team began racing cars at local drag strips with limited success.

"We were learning as we went since Ford had not yet decided to become officially involved in drag racing.

"Then in 1962 at Detroit Dragway I met Dick Brannan. He brought his '62 Galaxie to the track and whipped everyone. He ran three or four tenths quicker than everybody, as I recall."

Subsequent to being told of Brannan's performance with Ford products, Dave Evans hired the young man from South Bend, Indiana as Ford's Drag Race Coordinator. The Drag Council began to take shape as the company realized the potential parts development and dealer sales to the youth market that might come from such a pro-

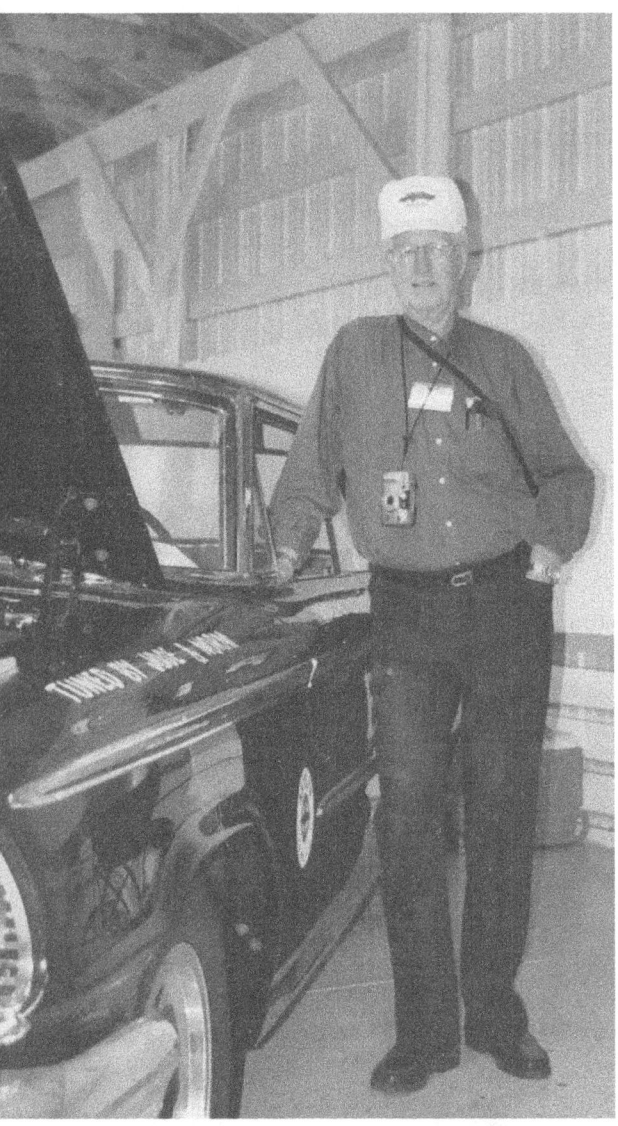

Bill Holbrook, former supervisor at Ford's Experimental Vehicles Garage, poses with the now-restored Bob Ford 1963 1/2 lightweight Galaxie formerly driven by Len Richter. This car was one of the re-bodied 1962 lightweight Galaxies that allowed Ford to come out swinging against the competition at the beginning of the 1963 racing season.

computer engine controls of any type). One particularly interesting vehicle that Bill got to work on was the Lincoln prototype vehicle that had been used in the movie, "It Started With a Kiss," starring Glenn Ford and Debbie Reynolds. This car was later sold to George Barris, who used it to gram. In late 1962 Charles E. Gray came on board to replace Dave Evans at the Experimental Vehicles Garage and when he asked who the "little guy" over in the corner was (referring to Brannan) he was told, "That's our drag racing guy. Just leave him alone."

Question: What do you recall about the 1962 lightweight Galaxies?

Bill: " I worked on the '62 Mule car with Dick Brannan at the Experimental Vehicles garage. When the drag racing program really started to take off we borrowed additional mechanics."

Question: That brings us to the 1963 1/2 lightweight cars, and I know you have an interesting story to relate regarding the Drag Council members' 1962 cars that were re-bodied as 1963 1/2's.

Bill: "Brannan's car, the one that would become his number 823, was re-bodied at the X-vehicles garage. The cars of Les Ritchey and Gas Ronda are another story, since they were located on the West Coast. I ordered two bodies-in-white on an inter company buying authority, after a phone conversation with the Los Angeles assembly plant resident body engineer on what type of paperwork and instructions he required. I was told that, being it was a unique request, we would have to physically follow the bodies through the build to accomplish the desired assembly and/or deletions. I flew to California and met with the LA assembly plant resident engineer. I believe to save time he had two empty bodies ready to put on the line. He and I followed the bodies down the assembly line to keep the workers from the jobs that we wished to delete. We were working from assembly process sheets that I had to mark up as we went along so that later when we ordered the production run we could generate a somewhat proper DSO assembly procedure. No dum dum, no sealers, no jute, no sound deadeners, etc. The bodies had, as I recall, upholstery, doors fenders, dash windows, and so on, because we needed all the attaching hardware when we installed the lightweight components. No radios, no heaters, glove compartment box, spare tire, jack, trunk lid torsion bar, one horn, etc.

"I remember that the bodies were not assembled on frames but were rolling on platforms and held at shipping until Bill Stroppe picked them up. I don't recall how we achieved the fiberglass, aluminum bumpers and arms or other lightweight components, but I'm sure I would have shipped them to Stroppe to install them when we assembled the vehicles. I'm assuming that the two drag cars (1962 lightweight Galaxies) were brought to Stroppe's after the bodies and lightweight components had been delivered and after they were through racing on the weekend.

"I do remember Gas and Les coming to Stroppe's on Signal Hill and asking me to see how far back I could put the bodies on the frames. I know I almost lost my mind. Just think a moment on what happens when you move a body rearward perhaps approximately an inch. I will tell you that anything that isn't already attached is either too long, or too short. Think about it. The clutch apparatus, shift linkage, accelerator linkage, wires, steering column, and so on. I vaguely remember cutting the handbrake cables off and shoving them into a hole in the frame. That is about all I remember. I think I wanted to forget, except someone later told me I switched the bodies and got them on the wrong cars. When I think about it, how can you switch two bodies that are both all white? Maybe I switched VIN plates. I can only assume that they were painted wrong after I left. I know that I was there a week doing a job that should have taken maybe three days. I'm sure I had help from the Stroppe crew. And yes Les and Gas were in and out. Probably more Gas than Les."

Question: Is there anything else you remember about the 63 1/2 lightweight Galaxie program?

Bill: "Bob Ford had three of them. The white car that Dave Lyall drove, an automatic transmission car that didn't run, and the black car, which Len Richter drove. The black car was one of the mule cars, or '62 re-bodies."

Question: Did you have anything to do with the Thunderbolts in 1964?

Bill: "No, that was entirely Dearborn Steel Tubing. Danny Jones and Dick Brannan were involved with the project also. The very first Thunderbolt went to Dick Brannan and the second car to Bob Ford. Vern Tinsler worked with Plaza Fiberglass on the lightweight parts. The first hood came in and the scoop was on it backwards."

Question: I'm assuming that it was the very rare cloverleaf style hood and having the scoop on backwards would make it even more rare. Do you know what happened to it?

Bill: "It was destroyed. I do remember that when the Drag Council cars were being given out to the team members that the hoods from the number six and number seven cars were switched so Leal could have the hood he wanted. (see the Mickey Thompson/Butch Leal chapter for more on this story.)

Question: Tell us about the '64 Galaxie with the fiberglass body.

Bill: "As part of the weight reduction program, Vern Tinsler had a 1964 Galaxie shipped over to the Experimental Vehicles Garage from the Wayne Assembly plant (VIN: 4W66R100023). The car was then sent to Plaza Fiberglass, where the body was replicated in fiberglass right down to the floor pan. The duplication process took six months, they had a lot of problems, and when the car came back it was heavier than the steel-bodied lightweight Galaxie. We used that car to go for coffee and run errands until we were ordered to destroy it as part of an inventory reduction in 1965. We removed the VIN tag, door and ignition locks, and turned them in but kept the car. One day Jacques Passino walked in and spotted the car on a lift and told me either the car would be gone by the end of the day or I would. I got rid of the car, but not by destroying it as ordered. I turned it over to Bob Snider, who was an engineer at Ford, and he hid the car somewhere. I don't know what happened to it after that."

Question: You were involved in the building of what was arguably the very first 1965 A/FX Mustang isn't that right?

Bill: "Yes, it was the twenty third Mustang off the assembly line at the Dearborn assembly plant. It was a white coupe. After Dearborn Steel Tubing did the engine compartment modifications it came to the Experimental Vehicles Garage, where we completed it. Len Richter drove the car at first and then it went to Kenny Salter, who had worked with Bonner. I understand he later wrecked the car."

Question: Since the first A/FX Mustang utilized basically a stock front suspension why did the later cars use the so called twisted leaf, or torsion leaf axle?

Bill: They did that to accommodate the SOHC 427 engine in the Mustang. We disagreed with that style of front axle as it was heavy and not really necessary. The Mercury guys building the Comets learned from our mistakes. If you notice, the 1965 A/FX Comets used a relocated stock suspension in the front and it worked better than the torsion leaf set-up. They also benefited from some of the very early wind tunnel tests done on the Thunderbolts. Al Turner repositioned the scoops on the Comets to the leading edge of the hoods, where they worked better. The A/FX Mustangs continued to use the Thunderbolt-style hood scoop."

Question: I saw a photograph of the Bob Ford A/FX Mustang where it lists W. Halfbrook as the crew chief on the front fender. How did that come about?

Bill: "Paul Harvey and Len Richter, who was his driver, wanted to put my name on the car since I had helped on it, but either Mr. Beebe or Mr. Passino didn't want it on there.

Question: Why didn't your bosses at Ford want your name on a car that was factory-supported?

Bill: "I suppose it was because they didn't want to show any direct connection to the factory. The same reason that the names of dealerships appeared on the cars. It gave Ford some deniability."

Question: So what happened ultimately regarding the name?

Bill: "Well, Paul Harvey wanted my name on

there so they settled for W. Halfbrook instead of W. Holbrook, crew chief."

Question: What are your recollections of the Bob Ford A/FX Mustang?

Bill: "I remember we had a lot a lot of problems with the Mallory Roto Faze ignition burning out the photo cell, and doing a lot of work to get the weight off the car for match races. We had to try a lot of tricks like lighter spindles and removing the front brakes in order to out-cheat certain Chrysler teams. Another problem we had was that the Mercury teams running the SOHC 427 were allowed to use Crane cams, while Ford insisted we use factory cams. That was a problem for a while too."

Question: I know you have a story about the 1965 Galaxie that Jerry Harvey drove. Could you relate that?

Bill: "As you know there was a big article printed in a magazine at the time how that car was built. Well, I'm here to tell you that the article is all wrong. We built that car entirely at the Experimental Vehicles Garage. Also, that car was initially built with a 427 High Riser engine and a Dana rear. It got the SOHC 427 installed later."

Question: What about the 1966 427 Fairlane project?

Bill: We built the prototype cars at the X-Vehicles Garage and if you remember one of the major magazines came in and did an article on how the cars were being built."

Question: And what about the Cobra Jet Mustangs?

Bill: "Bob Tasca brought his Mustang that was the Cobra Jet prototype to Dearborn and told everyone it would beat anything Ford had and bet a lunch on it. We built a '67 Mustang at the X-Garage to run against Tasca. It had a 427 with a 428 crank, hydraulic lifters, adjustable rocker arms, and an automatic transmission. That engine would turn better than 7,000 RPM, but we detuned it so it wouldn't smoke the street tires. "Jumpy" Snider drove it against the "Bopper" and he beat him."

Question: Did you have any other interesting projects around that time?

Bill: "We built a gray '68 T-Bird with suicide doors that had a 480 cubic inch Cammer in it. A real sleeper. The only outward indication that the car was anything unusual was that we had to louver the hood because the engine ran hot. It had power steering, power brakes, and air conditioning too."

Question: I understand you had some involvement in a program that brought about about one of Ford's very successful NASCAR race cars as well?

Bill: "We received a 1968 Torino from the Atlanta assembly plant with 14 miles on it. From that car we hand-made all the aero parts and built the car that was the prototype for the Talladega in 1969."

Question: "What became of that car?

Bill: "When we were done with it a Ford engineer bought the car and it disappeared."

Question: Did you have any other involvement in Ford's NASCAR program?

Bill: "The program ended in 1970, but I can remember in December 1969 Ford had rented the track at Daytona and they brought out five 1970 Torinos that had been prepared by Holman-Moody for testing. Those cars couldn't run within four or five miles per hour of a 1969 car that was there as a tire test vehicle."

Question: What happened to you when Ford pulled the plug on racing?

Bill: "I went to Engine Engineering after the racing program shut down. I was the last one to leave the department. My last assignment at racing was to close down the warehouse at Holman-Moody, which had a $13 million-dollar inventory."

Question: What happened to all those parts?

Bill: "A lot of it was divided up between Holman-Moody and Bud Moore Engineering. I remember Gratiot Auto Parts bid on the remaining inventory but Ford turned them down. I think they bid $150,000. At that time there were probably two- to three-hundred SOHC 427 engines left. You could buy one with a single four barrel for $300.00 and two fours for $400.00. All the two four barrel engines sold."

Question: Weren't there also cars at Holman-Moody that belonged to Ford?

Bill: "I remember they had the "J-Car" [prototype] racer that Ken Miles had been killed in, and Les Ritchey's Mustang. I don't know what happened to them."

Question: What did you do next at Ford?

Bill: "In 1974-75 I worked doing emissions re-certifications for fleet vehicles that had at least 50,000 miles on them. Then over the next few years I got two promotions and ended up as Senior Product Engineer on the Carb Czar prototype engines and worked on the high-performance engines when they started to come back until 1985, when I retired from Ford with 30 years of service."

EPILOGUE

DICK LOEHR / JOHN SKIBA AND THE END OF FACTORY SUPPORT

The February 1970, issue of the Ford Drag Club newsletter proudly proclaimed, "It's official! Dick Loehr joins Ford Drag Teams."

Loehr, of Portage, MI, began his drag racing career in stock-class Ford vehicles in 1957 and by 1961 had entered the Super Stock ranks, successfully running 406 and 427 Galaxies. Dick purchased the 427 High Riser-powered '65 Mustang coupe that had been built by Ron Pellegrini. With sponsorship from Rod Tyler Ford he took to the match race trail, establishing a reputation that led to a series of Funny Cars, each carrying the name *Stampede*, that derived their power from John Skiba-prepared SOHC 427 engines. In 1968 Loehr won the AHRA Grand National and numerous match race victories. For the 1969 season a fiberglass Mach I body encased the Skiba-built Cammer, which took Loehr to a best elapsed time of 7.31 @ 211 MPH.

The Central Ford Drag Team would be known as "The Gold Team," due to the transporter and race car paint schemes of gold, white, and Ford blue. The team consisted of Loehr and Skiba fielding a 1970 Maverick in the Pro/Stock class, which at the time was still referred to as Heads Up Super/Stock. The car was based on a production-line Maverick that was prepared at M&S Welding in Azusa, CA. To take advantage of NHRA's seven pound per cubic inch rule, Loehr had Skiba built a SOHC 427 engine de-stroked to 390 ci, which would allow them to run the car at 2730 pounds. The engine made a reported 700 horsepower on the dyno and produced low 10-second elapsed times at 137 MPH during testing.

But according to Ed Terry, the destroked engine did not perform as expected, and Loehr's car had even received one of his John Healey-prepared SOHC 427 engines on one occasion in an effort to make the car competitive. As things turned out, the wheels had already been set in motion to discontinue support of racing at Ford corporate headquarters. Almost before Loehr and Skiba had a chance to develop a winning combination of car and engine, the rug was pulled from under them. Loehr was allowed to keep his equipment, and during the 1971 season he ran the Maverick in the C/Gas class using a fuel injected Cleveland-based engine for power.

The axe had begun it's inexorable fall toward the necks of those who had faithfully raced the products of Ford and enjoyed the factory's support with a memo from Emil Loeffler dated February 13, 1970 titled, "Drag Program Withdrawal Proposal." The proposal memo read:

Dick Loehr was given the Midwest Ford Drag Team in 1970, not too long before factory support of the program ended. Loehr's Pro/Stock *Stampede* Maverick used a de-stroked SOHC 427 engine for power in an effort to take advantage of the NHRA weight break. (Ed Terry)

AA/FD: Drop support of Robinson, Baney and Hoover. Keep all parts now in their possession. Cancel all commitments with Kalitta as well as parts support. Keep all pieces now in his possession.

AA/FC: Drop support of Mickey Thompson, Ron Leslie and Gas Ronda. Keep all pieces now in their possession. Cancel contract with Mickey Thompson.

Super Stock: Clinic cars of Platt and Terry turned over to Car Merchandising.

McLellan, Coble, Caster and Foulger Ford. Turn vehicles over to them to campaign or sell. Dick Wood clinic Fairlane at Stroppe's. Sell vehicle and credit program.

Heads Up Pro/Stock: Paul Harvey Maverick still belongs to Performance Events Department. Continue development work with this vehicle. (Author's note: This indicates a reprieve for Dick Brannan)

Miscellaneous: George Montgomery. Give parts now in his possession to him. Drop further support.

Trucks: Tasca, Chrisman and Schartman turn in vehicles for resale. Kalitta, Harvey, Nicholson and Mickey Thompson continue usage until they stop campaigning Ford vehicles. Pete Robinson. Station wagon return for resale.

Expenses not received: C. Kalitta 429 development. D. Loehr Pro/Stock Maverick, pay for build, approximately $8,000.00.

On March 4, 1970, a document titled, "Estimated costs for continuation of drag clinic program," was submitted, although it appeared that

Loehr had little time for development or success with his Pro/Stock program before the end came for the Ford Drag Teams. (J. Demmitt, Jr.)

a decision had been made to discontinue the program. This estimate included:

> Engine build at H-M / Stroppe $119,485.00
>
> Engines given to drag teams with build & blueprint costs accomplished at sources of their choice: 10- 427 SOHC engines @ $2,000. Each. Blueprint costs: $10,000. Parts necessary for repair: $6,000. 10- used 429 Boss engines @ $3,000. Each. Blueprint costs: $10,000. Parts necessary for repair: $6,000.

Apparently someone at Ford either had not gotten the message, or was hopeful that the Drag Team program would be saved at the 11th hour, as the memo also included a second page which listed estimated costs for a two-car Tasca program of one Pro/Stock car and one match race car with a total cost of $50,831.00.

The folks at Lincoln-Mercury had folded their racing tents even sooner than Ford, and by the end of 1969 one of the all-time great drag racers, "Dyno Don" Nicholson found himself on the outside looking in. Luckily for Don and his legion of fans, he was able to garner some support from Ford in the form of a Maverick Pro/Stock car and 427 SOHC engines. With ever-diminishing assistance from Ford, "Dyno" soldiered on with two more Mavericks, winning the last NHRA title for an SOHC 427-powered Ford when he copped the Pro/Stock class crown at the 1971 Summer Nationals. Once all factory support was gone, Nicholson continued in Ford products and in 1977 he won the NHRA Pro/Stock World Championship with a Mustang powered by a 351 Cleveland engine.

Loehr was allowed to keep his equipment when Ford ended its support. In 1971 he ran his former Pro/Stock Maverick in the C/Gas class using a fuel-injected, Cleveland-based engine for power. (Bob Bowman)

Ford succumbed to government meddling into the auto industry in the name of safety and emissions, price gouging by the oil industry, and profiteering by insurance companies—all of which would lead to a decade of poorly designed, -constructed and -performing automobiles being produced by a manufacturer whose reputation had been built on the exact opposite. The fans of Ford performance would not see any bright spots on the horizon until the early 1980's.

As the old saying goes, "You can't go home again." The Total Performance years at Ford, along with the cars and stars they fostered, were gone forever. Thankfully, many of the historic cars from the greatest era of Ford performance have been located, restored, and saved for future generations, and many of my personal heroes have been properly recognized for their contributions not only to drag racing, but also to a great part of American culture.

March 18, 1964

To: Mr. A. J. Scussel

cc: Mr. N. Faustyn

Subject: Drag Race Engines

Please make available at the earliest possible date two 427 C.I.D. drag engines with the latest components including the lightened valves. One of these engines should be equipped for an automatic transmission and the other for a manual.

Please advise as to the maximum safe engine speeds for shifting and high gear operation.

Dave P. Evans, Manager
Performance and Economy
Special Vehicles

DPE:CEkk

FORD DIVISION

PERFORMANCE AND ECONOMY DEPARTMENT

Ford Motor Company
20000 ROTUNDA DRIVE
P. O. BOX 2053
DEARBORN, MICHIGAN 48121

May 5, 1964

Mr. Jack Hart, Executive Director
National Hot Rod Association
1171 N. Vermont Avenue
Los Angeles 29, California

Dear Jack:

    As you no doubt have heard, Ford has released lightweight, hollow stem intake and exhaust valves for the 427 CID engine. These valves have been run on the circle tracks in conjunction with heavier connecting rods and a steel crankshaft that provides better "lower end" lubrication. I'm sure you are not interested in the rods and crankshaft since this pertains to durability only. Parts numbers for the intake and exhaust valves are C4AE-6507-J and C4AE-6505-E respectively.

    These valves will appear in Factory Experimental vehicles immediately and will be run in Stock classes as soon as you render your approval.

Charles E. Gray, Jr.
Performance and Economy
Special Vehicles

cc: J. H. Cowley
    D. P. Evans
    J. H. Passino

CEG:jh

Ruby

May 12, 1964

To: Dave Evans

cc: John Cowley

Subject: Lightweight Valve Train Components

After trying to obtain light valves through various channels, a quanity was ordered through Engineering Procurement. The buyer has informed me that delivery cannot be expected before the third week in June. This means that it will be July 1, before even the Drag Council Members will be running high RPM equipment. It also probably means that other owners of 427 Fairlane Drag cars will not have this equipment available to them this year.

Rumors have it that several Comets are now running the lightweight components. This, of course, is depressing for the Fairlane Drag Council Members to think that another Division of Ford Motor Company can provide parts quicker for their drag cars. Even if these rumors are not true, it would definitely be a morale booster to provide each drag council member with these valves.

If 128 exhaust and 128 intake valves can be diverted from another program into the Drag Strip activity, this would provide each member with two sets. Besides the morale aspect, we would obtain definite answers concerning performance increase in the quarter mile.

Charles E. Gray, Jr.

CEG:ga

Intra-Company Communication

May 26, 1964

To: J. H. Passino

Subject: Lightweight Valve Components for 427 CID 8-V Drag Engines

Tests have confirmed that lightweight valves increase drag strip performance of the Super Stock Fairlane by approximately .2 second.

With this in mind, it would seem advisable to make available the intake valve, Part No. C4AE-6507-J, and exhaust valve, Part No. C4AE-6505-E, to drag racing enthusiasts. It would also seem advisable to inform Fairlane 427 owners of the availability of these valves.

John H. Cowley
Performance and Economy
Special Vehicles

JHC/CEG/s

Ford Motor Company

Intra-Company Communication

May 27, 1964

To: John H. Cowley

Subject: Drag Program Status Report - May 27, 1964

Revised Automatic Transmission:

o Durability - One vehicle is running durability cycles now at Livonia.

o Converter - The new converter failed before an evaluation could be run. Another has been completed and will be run shortly.

o Release - Must be released this week.

Weight Redistribution - 427 Fairlane:

Weight Savings
Number

26	Doors	Fiberglass doors are being released at this time.
11	Aluminum Radiators	One has been received and evaluated. Four more arrived today.
8	Magnesium Water Pump Housing	R. C. Industries should provide samples in four weeks.
12	Magnesium Bell Housing	R. C. Industries should provide samples this week.
9	Magnesium Intake Manifold	Buddy Barr and/or R. C. Industries could handle the job. Presently awaiting direction.
8	Induction Can	Aluminum induction cans will be omitted if okayed by NHRA.
12	Ultra-lightweight Sheet Metal	Ultra-lightweight fenders and hood available if approved by Management.
86 Total		

Page 2
Drag Program Status Report
May 27, 1964

<u>Weight Redistribution - 427 Fairlane</u>: (continued)

The fiberglass doors and omitted induction cans would pertain to all Fairlanes. The aluminum radiators, magnesium water pump housings, magnesium bell housings, magnesium intake manifolds, and light fiberglass would pertain to certain Drag Council members only.

<u>Mustang</u>:

o The engine has been built and installed.

o The drag suspension has been installed.

o Most other minor items have been completed.

o Fiberglass sheet metal has not arrived but should be here Friday, May 29.

o The front end has to be aligned.

Charles E. Gray

June 18, 1964

Mr. Jack Hart
National Hot Rod Association
1171 N. Vermont Avenue
Los Angeles 29, California

Dear Jack:

This will confirm our conversation on June 18 concerning the lightweight valve to be used in Super Stock competition by the Ford Fairlanes.

As you suggested, we will eliminate the swirl polish feature from the port side of both valves by some process, probably by shot peening. This should completely eliminate all manufacture marks on the intake valve; however, due to a harder material being used, some marks may still be identifiable on the exhaust valve.

Sincerely,

Charles E. Gray
Performance and Economy
Special Vehicles

cc J. E. Cowley
    W. Parks
    J. H. Passino

July 3, 1964

Mr. Jack Hart
National Hot Rod Association
1171 N. Vermont Avenue
Los Angeles 29, California

Dear Jack:

    This is to confirm our conversation concerning legality of the lightweight Ford valves for Super Stock competition. I understand that these valves will be legal within the immediate future. Please confirm the earliest date at which the valves can be used.

    Regarding the new automatic transmission which we have discussed, the first cars to receive these revised transmissions will be Bob Ford, Inc. of Dearborn, Michigan and Les Ritchey of Performance Associates, Covina, California. Additional automatic transmissions will be sent into the field shortly, and you will be so notified at that time.

    Also, will you please forward several sets of the revised stock car breakdown and additional copies of the revised 1965 NHRA rules.

Sincerely,

Charles E. Gray
Performance and Economy
Special Vehicles

cc Mr. John Cowley
     Mr. Wally Parks
     Mr. Jacque Passino

Ford Motor Company

FORD DIVISION

Intra-Company Communication

GENERAL OFFICE

August 6, 1964

To: C. M. Derda

cc: R. A. Geddes

Subject: <u>Replacement Parts for Drag Council Members</u>

Please ship by air freight 8 Exhaust Valves (C4AE 6505 E) and 8 Intake Valves (C4AE 6507 S) to each Drag Council member listed below:

Dick Brannan
2255 Inglewood Place
South Bend, Indiana

Phil Bonner
138 W. Ponce DeLeon Ave.
Decatur, Georgia

Bob Ford
14585 Michigan Ave.
Dearborn, Michigan
Attn. Paul Harvey

Ed Martin Ford Sales
8600 E. Washington
Indianapolis, Indiana
Attn. Ed Martin or Don Turner

Performance Associates
1647 W. San Bernardino Rd.
Covina, California
Attn. Les Ritchey

Russ Davis Ford
116 W. San Bernardino Rd.
Covina, California
Attn. Gas Ronda

Tasca Ford Sales
777 Taunton Drive
E. Providence, Rhode Island
Attn. Bob Tasca

Wickersham Ford, Inc.
Orange, Texas
Attn. Charles Wickersham

Special Promotions Expense No. 25AF 61463 should be used to cover these expenses.

Charles E. Gray
Performance and Economy
Special Vehicles

File

August 11, 1964

Mr. Jack Hart
National Hot Rod Association
1171 N. Vermont Avenue
Los Angeles 29, California

Dear Jack:

In reference to your letter concerning the large carburetor and fiberglass doors for our Fairlane, we do not intend for these components to be included in the super stock vehicles at the Summer Nationals due to the limited distribution in the field. Their use will be restricted to the FX type vehicle.

Sincerely yours,

Charles E. Gray
Performance and Economy
Special Vehicles

cc: J. H. Cowley
    W. Parks
    J. H. Passino
    W. Dismuke
bc: L. C. Beebe

www.ingramcontent.com/pod-product-compliance
Lightning Source LLC
Chambersburg PA
CBHW080502110426
42742CB00017B/2970